PRAISE FOR *Humanity at Work*

"A clear, compassionate, and thorough exploration of leadership that gets to the heart of being human."
Andrew Lee, Chief Curiosity Officer, Curiousmind

"Reading *Humanity at Work* is like sitting down with a truly knowledgeable friend to discuss real-life workplace problems and how to resolve them with humanity."
John Tivendell, PhD, L.Psych., FCPA, full professor, Industrial and Organizational Psychology, Université de Moncton

"*Humanity at Work* illustrates proven leadership principles with case studies told in a friendly voice that makes them both meaningful and memorable."
Paul Johnson, P.Eng., chairman and CEO, Quantum5X Systems Inc.

"The leadership lessons in *Humanity at Work* are invaluable at every level of an organization."
Thérèse LeBlanc, retired Regional Deputy Commissioner, Atlantic Region, Correctional Service of Canada

"Pierre Battah speaks to the valuable human side of organizational or business success by using vivid storytelling. A must-read for any leader!"
Andrée Savoie, president and CEO, Adelin Properties

"Pierre identifies the questions we need to ask ourselves to be more effective leaders for our teams and our communities."
David Savoie, president and CEO, Acadian Construction

"To lead with humanity, you have to do the work and ask yourself the tough questions. Pierre Battah's book will prompt you to deepen your understanding and shape how you will show up for your team."
Jennifer Meffert, vice president, People and Culture, MetroStar Systems

Humanity at Work

Leading for Better Relationships and Results

PIERRE BATTAH

LifeTree
MEDIA

Copyright © 2020 by Pierre Battah
20 21 22 23 24   5 4 3 2 1

All rights reserved. No part of this book may be reproduced, stored in a retrieval system or transmitted, in any form or by any means, without the prior written consent of the publisher or a license from The Canadian Copyright Licensing Agency (Access Copyright). For a copyright license, visit www.accesscopyright.ca or call toll free to 1-800-893-5777.

Cataloguing data available from Library and Archives Canada
ISBN 978-1-928055-74-7 (hardcover)
ISBN 978-1-928055-75-4 (EPUB)
ISBN 978-1-928055-76-1 (PDF)

Editor: Don Loney
Cover and interior design: Naomi MacDougall
Cover image: iStock.com / Irina Karpinchik
Author photo: Denis Duquette

Published by LifeTree Media Ltd.
LifeTreeMedia.com

Distributed in the US by Publishers Group West and in Canada by Publishers Group Canada

Printed and bound in Canada

Gabrielle: This book, and so much more, is only possible thanks to you. *Je t'aime.*

Alex, you inspire me each and every day.

Contents

1 Introduction

PART ONE / AWAKENING THE LEADER WITHIN

9 **(1) How Do I Lead Every Day?**
11   Employee Turnover Challenges: What They Can Tell Us
12   Maura McKinnon's People Solution
15   Taking Stock of Your Humanity at Work

16 **(2) How Do I Balance People and Results?**
19   The Impact of Change: Are Results Everything?
21   Situational Leadership
22   Situational Leadership Exemplified
24   Taking Stock of Your Humanity at Work

25 **(3) What Are the Values that Shape Me as a Leader?**
28   Values Are Your Personal Bottom Line
30   Keeping Your Word
32   Can Ethical Conduct Be Compromised by Loyalty?
34   Teachable Moments for Values and Ethics
38   What Did Kathleen Do?
39   Taking Stock of Your Humanity at Work

40 **(4) Am I a Positive Force?**
43   What the Leaders Chose to Do as Conductors
44   The Science of Positivity
46   The Keys to Positive Leadership
47   The Role of Self-Awareness
51   The Role of Self-Control
53   Positive Energy and Motivation
56   Taking Stock of Your Humanity at Work

58 **(5) How Do I Want to Be Heard?**
    60 Who Gave the Winning Speech?
    61 The Sound of Your Leadership Voice
    67 Taking Stock of Your Humanity at Work

PART TWO / KNOW THE COURSE. STAY THE COURSE.

71 **(6) How Can I Create More Meaningful Work for My Team?**
    73 The Kid from Away
    74 Connecting Meaningful Work and Self-Motivation
    76 The Continuing Saga of the Kid from Away
    79 Meaning in Work
    81 Taking Stock of Your Humanity at Work

83 **(7) How Do I Assess My Ability to Prioritize and Delegate?**
    84 Separate the Urgent from the Important
    87 Manage Distraction
    88 The Art of Delegation
    94 Taking Stock of Your Humanity at Work

95 **(8) What Are My Leadership Habits?**
    98 Multitasking: The Blight of the Contemporary Workplace
    101 Daily Success Habits for You and Your Team
    104 Leadership Habits to Nurture Well-Being
    106 Daily Rituals
    108 Taking Stock of Your Humanity at Work

PART THREE / AWAKENING THE LEADER WITHIN YOUR PEOPLE

- 113 **(9) Do I Set the Right Expectations for Myself and the Team?**
  - 116 Goals, Alignment, and Outcomes
  - 124 How We Work Together Is the Most Powerful Tool
  - 127 Taking Stock of Your Humanity at Work

- 129 **(10) How Can Receiving Feedback Well Make Me a Better Leader?**
  - 131 The Clash of Feedback, Assumptions, and Expectations
  - 132 The Power of Unsolicited Feedback
  - 134 The Positive Rewards of Feedback
  - 134 Active Listening: Feedback's Enabler
  - 137 Mentors: Find Many, Be One
  - 139 Taking Stock of Your Humanity at Work

- 141 **(11) How Well Do I Provide Feedback, Especially the Difficult Stuff?**
  - 144 Why Are We So Reluctant to Give Feedback?
  - 145 Weekly Feedback and Other Real-Life Suggestions
  - 149 The Praise-to-Criticism Ratio
  - 150 Not-So-Difficult Conversations
  - 152 Negative Feedback and Motivation
  - 153 After Giving Feedback—Then What?
  - 154 The Role of Candor
  - 157 Taking Stock of Your Humanity at Work

PART FOUR / GETTING INTERVENTION RIGHT

161 (12) Do I Practice Psychological Safety?
- 163 The Importance of Psychological Safety
- 167 Alongside: An Example of a Culture of Psychological Safety
- 168 Making a Commitment to Psychological Safety
- 172 Taking Stock of Your Humanity at Work

174 (13) Do I Find the Right Balance between Situation, Judgment, and Action?
- 175 When We Don't Intervene
- 180 Do Not Limit Your Choices
- 182 Tension and Conflict
- 187 Taking Stock of Your Humanity at Work

189 (14) How Do I Know If I Am Making the Right Call?
- 190 Four Ways to Get Involved
- 195 The Turnaround Interview
- 196 Knowing When to Lower the Heat
- 199 Taking Stock of Your Humanity at Work

PART FIVE / RECOGNIZING AND REWARDING

203 (15) Do I Reward and Recognize People Appropriately?
- 204 Extrinsic and Intrinsic Rewards
- 211 Recognition as Integral to a Learning Culture
- 215 Taking Stock of Your Humanity at Work

216 (16) How Do I Engage HR to Benefit People, Culture, and Leadership?
- 221 The Evolution of Human Resources
- 228 Embedded HR
- 236 Taking Stock of Your Humanity at Work

PART SIX / BUILD THE RIGHT CULTURE

241 (17) How Do I Align Culture with Team?
    245 Culture or Climate?
    247 The Expression of Values
    249 Microcosm: Culture and Team
    250 Macrocosm: Culture and Organization
    252 Taking Stock of Your Humanity at Work

254 (18) How Do I Build a Learning Culture?
    258 Learning and Leadership Practice
    261 Leading for Gender Equality and the Advancement of Women
    265 Leading so Leaders Learn Continuously
    266 Leading for Innovation and Change
    269 Taking Stock of Your Humanity at Work

273 Afterword
276 Acknowledgments
279 Endnotes
295 Recommended Reading
297 Index
307 About the Author

Introduction

"LET ME CLOSE my door..."

I can't tell you how often I've heard those words. They usually foretell a conversation about a challenging workplace- and people-related problem that you or a colleague may be struggling with. Or perhaps we may be talking specifically about you and your leadership practice, whether you're struggling as an emerging leader or are thriving as a seasoned one but are perplexed by change.

The closed door signifies the privacy these matters warrant, but it also signals your intent to make work life better for you and your team. Let's think of this book as one of those closed-door conversations.

In that room, we'd likely get down to talking about a scenario, an example, or a story that illustrates a people-related problem that is troubling you or someone else at work. It could be a person or a team that is not living up to their potential or a more systemic employee turnover or recruitment problem reflective of an unhealthy workplace; or perhaps you are wrestling with leading a departmental restructure or company-wide major change initiative. Or, the meeting could simply involve chatting about how you can help others learn and improve.

We would likely talk about other similar situations to give yours some context and then we might draw from our shared knowledge of the research and the best evidence-based practices used by other notable employers. After that, we would compare our experience-based "takes" and explore practical implications. That is what this book sets out to do. Think of it as a pocket mentor, your personal guide to developing a leadership style that puts humanity front and center.

What do I mean by "humanity," and why is it so important for effective leadership? Great question! (As you'll see in this book, I'm a big fan of using questions as a tool to bring insights to the surface.) The way I define it, leading from a place of humanity means recognizing the human nature of your employees—understanding who they are and what matters to them. It also means being realistic about their strengths and weaknesses—the personal qualities that drive them to succeed in their roles as well as the habits and blind spots that might be getting in their way. It means viewing your people with empathy and an open mind, rather than imposing arbitrary expectations and rigid demands on them. Humans are messy and complex animals, and the more you can accept that and seek to understand what makes them tick, the more engaged they will be and the better equipped to contribute to the success of your organization. In this book, I refer to this approach as "people leadership," which I believe is the key to unlocking the true potential of an organization.

Of course the bottom line matters, but how you make the numbers is through your people. Employees who are engaged at work have lower absentee rates, treat customers better, stay in their jobs longer, and cheerfully go the extra mile. Put simply, people leadership is good business leadership. Through the stories in this book, you'll have the opportunity to learn at the side of leaders who successfully balance people and results to drive the growth of their organizations.

But wait, there's more! It's not just about your employees' humanity; it's about yours, too. Your own attitudes, motivations, assumptions, and emotions strongly affect the way you show up at work, and your influence on the people you lead is profound. Cultivating self-awareness is key to setting a positive tone and fostering a productive workplace culture.

Okay, so hopefully I've got you on board with the concept. But how do you do it? What does it look like in real life?

Glad you asked. My experience as a trainer, consultant, and mentor has taught me that leading from a place of humanity isn't something you can learn from a checklist. It's organic. It's personal. It's about who you are and how you show up in all your interactions. It can be hard to describe, but you know it when you see it, which is why these values and habits tend to be learned at the knee of our own wise leaders and mentors.

That's why in this book I use storytelling as a tool to educate. Each chapter features intimate illustrations of real leaders facing real challenges. It's not just about being friendly and showing your employees that you care about them, although that's hugely important—it's also about tackling the tough stuff well. How do you give corrective feedback in a way that inspires people to perform better? How do you handle a branch closure or merger without destroying morale? These are the tests that make a great leader, who in turn makes a great company. Through these stories, you'll have the opportunity to look over the shoulders of managers and executives who embody this humanity-focused approach so that you can learn from their example.

These are the sorts of situations and solutions we would be exploring in that closed-door conversation I talked about earlier, or even in a very open yet intimate training workshop conversation. But if I were coaching you in person, we wouldn't stop there. Because this work is experiential and personal, I've also included a set of questions in each chapter to prompt reflection and build self-awareness, or at the very least to help guide your thinking.

As you work through the sections and chapters in this book, you'll notice that certain themes weave in and out of the text. When your brain says, "Hey, I've seen this earlier," that means the idea is important and you'll want to pay close attention to it.

You'll notice that some of the characters in the book are identified by their first name only. They represent composite characters and composite situations drawn from the thousands of people I have had the pleasure of interacting with in my work as an HR professional within organizations and later as a trainer, speaker, and management consultant.

The illustrations, stories, and anecdotes you'll encounter serve to illuminate, educate, and explain. Most are representative of ideas that have been rigorously examined and that align with the findings of credible researchers.

People remind me that in the human resources and leadership realms there will always be challenges at work—that we're never done. I agree. Humans are flawed and we bring those flaws to work. The most gifted and well intentioned among us are not perfect, and thus we lead and manage in less-than-perfect ways and our organizations reflect those limitations. The people and organizations in this book illustrate this fact. Like you and me, they are well intentioned, and some are struggling to find the know-how, tools, time, and courage to tackle our most intractable workplace challenges, often ones related to people. We can learn from their mistakes, flaws, and imperfections while being inspired by their thinking, efforts, notable accomplishments, laudable intentions, and determination to improve things.

By the time you reach the end of the book, my intention is to leave you more hopeful, encouraged, and far better equipped to lead your people and organization to success. Let's make work a rewarding and decidedly human experience. Let's make it about outcomes and delighting clients—a place where learning rules the day and we solve difficult problems together. Let's discover the difference it makes to our companies and communities when we bring our humanity to work.

How do leaders create positive, engaged, and productive workplaces? Simply put, balancing relationships and results is the key to leading with humanity. Employees who are engaged at work have lower absenteeism and stay in their jobs longer. But your attitudes, motivations, assumptions, and emotions strongly affect the way you show up at work and the influence you have on people. In this section, I explore how leaders can shape their leadership practices by using a team focus, expressing values clearly, and emphasizing the positive.

PART ONE

Awakening the Leader Within

(1)
How Do I Lead Every Day?

WHEN MAURA MCKINNON decided to leave a senior role with a high-profile insurance company to join a local sheet metal manufacturer as director of human resources, her career move raised a few eyebrows. No one doubted that she would have a huge impact wherever she went, but her colleagues worried she would be leaving her present position for a rough-and-tumble setting that would chew up and spit out the polished HR executive. Make no mistake—McKinnon hails from the Miramichi region of New Brunswick, and as we'll discover later in the book, the community surrounding its iconic eponymous river produces people who are spirited and fun, and also fierce and fearless. McKinnon was true to her roots on the river, very much a leader who brings her humanity to work.

But this was no ordinary sheet metal manufacturing facility. Imperial Manufacturing Group (IMG) was owned by Norm Caissie, a slight man with boundless energy who had grown his father's plumbing supply business into a notable North American player, supplying the likes of Walmart and Canadian Tire. There is a very good chance the air vents in your home are an IMG product. Caissie was renowned for sniffing out unlikely business opportunities in his highly specialized sector as he expanded IMG into the United States and central Canada.

The owner was at once a genius and a challenging man to work for—and with. Regarded with the highest esteem as an award-winning entrepreneur locally and nationally, he had secured his legacy by insisting on keeping a significant amount of the company's domestic production in his local community of twelve hundred. The plant employed six hundred people. While of huge benefit to the community, needless to say, the decision to invest locally created numerous recruitment headaches for the company—and those were only some of the ills that McKinnon inherited.

Added to the challenge of recruiting for specialized positions in a rural area was the company's reputation for burning through management talent, not necessarily holding safety in the highest of regards, and having a workplace culture that reflected the growing pains of a successful wholesaler and manufacturer. In an industry where productivity was everything, issues of low productivity and absenteeism reflected a worrisome state of affairs from an employee morale and engagement perspective.

McKinnon, an unapologetically optimistic keener, knew full well that if she were to adopt the same persona and approach that had garnered her promotions and praise in the highly professional insurance and gaming sectors, she risked being ostracized by the all-important production staff. Though her management colleagues might well appreciate her vision, strategy, and tactics, were she not able to establish her street cred on the plant floor, the many things she had in mind would fail miserably. McKinnon knew she had only one shot at making a first impression with the employees.

She wanted to position the HR shop as a center of excellence that would coach, nudge, and support front-line supervisors, managers, and executives, but especially the supervisors, as she felt her focus would have the greatest impact at that level. Supervisors were face-to-face with hundreds of workers every day. How they led their folks was key to engagement and productivity.

McKinnon was confident in her ability to get buy-in from her management colleagues. They quickly realized that her perspective on people and leadership was different. The company's culture had always been a hard and demanding one, focused on production above all else, but productivity was slipping. Concerns were raised: Would the forward-looking view of the HR function have a detrimental effect by softening the culture to the point where the company would lose its edge in the market? McKinnon's managerial colleagues soon came to trust her, but convincing highly skeptical workers on the shop floor would be another story. She had the smarts, relatability, and humility for the task, but could she pull it off?

McKinnon knew she had to make a compelling, evidence-based case that tied employee engagement to productivity and profitability. To this end, she would have to secure the support of the owner and senior management teams. She knew the front-line supervisors were the lynchpin in her plan. Without their support and ability to re-engage the workforce (many of them long-term employees), she was sunk.

Employee Turnover Challenges: What They Can Tell Us

How does McKinnon's challenge of finding the right people resonate with you as a leader? This challenge raises an important question of differentiation: Is it a recruitment challenge (i.e., getting a reasonable number of qualified applicants to choose from) or is it a selection challenge (i.e., where those suitable applicants who were hired are not working out)?

As for the issue of finding skilled people in rural areas, let's face it—skilled trades positions and many other specialties are tough to recruit for in the most ideal of conditions. Rural and more remote locations present a challenge often best met through partnering with other like employers, ideally noncompeting, to draw people to a region. Local economic development agencies are also a company recruiter's best friend, as are similar community agencies and partners.

Regarding turnover challenges, you may be able to relate to the problems unique to an employment market now characterized by workers who value mobility as opposed to those seeking a job for the long term. The rapidity with which some people are able to grow their careers by moving every two to five years creates a number of challenges for employers. Companies that have shaped their employment strategies for what is referred to as the "gig economy" are discovering new ways of working. Fast-service restaurants are offering signing bonuses, the promise to work with your friends (an employee engagement coup!), and flexibility in shift scheduling to meet the needs of their target employee market.

A deeper examination of turnover is always informative and raises important questions. If you've looked at employee turnover, you may have come to the same conclusion that I have. People decamp one workplace for another for career advancement; or they have a chance to take a job that is more conducive to where they live and their quest for work-life balance; or they simply receive an offer they cannot refuse. My observation is that something leads people to scratch the itch to leave, to look elsewhere. But turnover is much more informative in the aggregate, meaning that as we see a number of departures, patterns sometimes emerge. Those patterns include people leaving a particular department or supervisor, or people leaving for a better wage, benefits, and security.

Perhaps, like McKinnon, you have immediate challenges to face and are wondering where to begin, given the many factors that need attention. And perhaps how McKinnon tackled her new role is instructive for all of us.

Maura McKinnon's People Solution

As we have noted, McKinnon knew the front-line supervisors were the lynchpin in her plan. As she invested in leadership training, rather than following the usual approach of cascading from the top downward, she targeted front-line supervision, the role that has more impact on more people in how they lead every day. Understanding the flow of influence within the group, McKinnon knew that as she began measuring engagement, her core team of

HOW DO I LEAD EVERY DAY? 13

supervisors were going to either lead the way or resist and send her plan awry. As it turned out, they stepped up. By now, McKinnon had brought in an HR staffer, a dynamo named Teena Robichaud who would carry on the work with that critical supervisory group, work closely with the director of production and external trainers, and over a three-year period completely reinvent supervision at IMG.

McKinnon then expanded her leadership training program outward from the front line to the entire organization, implementing formal and informal recognition programs and moving people leadership training to the many shift leads, cell leads, and beyond. She was helping redefine a culture by bringing people leadership to the fore, all the while focusing hard with her management team colleagues on how such a transformation contributed to productivity increases, reductions in absenteeism, and most notably a discernable difference in morale, as documented by their engagement surveys and the uptake of their plant-wide recognition initiatives. She won the hearts and minds of the supervisors, and word was spreading in the plant about the "new HR woman and her boots!" The owner and McKinnon's C-suite colleagues backed her bold move to redefine the culture.

McKinnon's accomplishments at IMG were rewarded with an appointment to vice president, and her efforts helped the company garner a coveted Best Places to Work award. She was recruited by an employer ten times the size of IMG (a public-sector health authority) that essentially asked her to replicate the culture transformation she had facilitated in manufacturing.

If you had asked McKinnon what led to her making remarkable progress at IMG—how she overcame daunting obstacles of employee disengagement and skepticism and, most notably, given her background, how she gained widespread credibility in the plant (especially considering that she is a bottom-line HR executive who drives for results and makes tough and often unpopular decisions yet remains credible, liked, and respected)—she would point to a corner of her office where she keeps her personal protective equipment used on the plant floor. Nothing unusual to see here—neon safety vest, bright banana-yellow helmet, and cat's-eye wraparound safety goggles—until your eye falls on the well-scuffed pink steel-toed construction boots.

When McKinnon was introduced to hundreds of people on the plant floor over her initial weeks and months, and especially to those all-important supervisors, her pink boots were the ice-breaker, the bond builder, and the butt of many good-natured jokes and teasing. Given McKinnon's relatability and sincerity—not to mention her impressive ability to approach her work with earnestness but not take herself too seriously—the boots became a way in, a way to be known for the right things (in this case, safety), and mostly a signal that change was ahead and that things were going to be different. They were a tangible token of McKinnon's own humanity.

A great number of onlookers would say that McKinnon's moving the company towards important investments in people leaders by way of coaching and training, along with her design of HR systems such as timely and rigorous performance management and widespread recognition initiatives, galvanized IMG to make great progress on their culture, reigniting their safety culture and contributing to their continued success in the marketplace.

McKinnon would tell you it's all because of her pink boots.

IN CHAPTER 2, we explore another foundational challenge for leaders, which is finding the balance between focusing on the results an organization needs to see to be successful and on the well-being of people, giving them guidance and room to grow. Much depends on the situation at hand, as we will see.

Taking Stock of Your Humanity at Work

As you answer the following questions about your people leadership practice, reflect on Maura McKinnon's story and how her strategies reset the culture at IMG.

1. Do you have a "pink boots" memory or story?

2. Who is a people leader you've experienced that remains memorable for you—someone whose influence on you propelled you forward?

3. What is it that made that person stand out? How did they lead with humanity?

4. Which part of their people leadership practice have you experimented with or would you teach to others?

(2)
How Do I Balance People and Results?

Caisse populaire acadienne ltée (Les Caisses or Caisse) is a historical and cultural icon, a banking federation that for nearly a century functioned as the commercial hub of many New Brunswick towns and villages, with branches in virtually all francophone Acadian communities. The model was representative of a bygone time, with local boards directing the operations of their local Caisse, accessing system-wide services like IT and other back-office functions from the federation's central office. By 2013, federation CEO Camille Thériault, a former premier of New Brunswick, along with many other progressive thinkers on the board of directors, knew the model was anachronistic. The need for progress had been discussed, but effecting change would be challenging.

To begin with, for decades Les Caisses was the bank of the people when francophone Acadians could not get personal or commercial credit from larger and (in the earlier years) mostly English banks that ignored rural markets. Les Caisses was owned by one's neighbors and often meant economic survival for communities.

Francophone Acadians joined their local Caisse as children with school-assisted savings accounts. Those who lived in larger communities where major banks were present often remained loyal to the bank of their youth, with its patriotic tug that compelled francophone Acadians to bank with "their" financial institution. Les Caisses worked hard to be that go-to institution by trumpeting the healthy sums it returned to its members as dividends. In addition, its support of local causes and events has consistently been widespread and impressive. For many years, loyalty ran largely along linguistic lines: francophones at Les Caisses—and eventually at La Banque Nationale, headquartered in Montreal—targeted francophone Acadians. A modern unified Caisse needed to attract New Brunswick's majority English-speaking populace. This represented a new initiative and a new challenge.

In spite of Les Caisses' long-standing partnership with the Quebec-based cooperative financial monolith Desjardins Group for a number of services such as Interac, mobile banking, and other infrastructure requirements, Les Caisses' offerings were perceived as not keeping up with what a younger generation of urban francophone Acadians wanted from their bank. Les Caisses' survival was in jeopardy, and Thériault was tasked with leading the institution into the future. At the same time, Thériault recognized that the long-term viability of Les Caisses was inseparable from the history of the Acadian people and the need to create a community-owned local financial entity to enable the survival of small communities.

Thériault's preparation for this tricky puzzle was long standing, as evidenced by his many years in public office that culminated in his election as premier of New Brunswick. In his role as the chair of the National Transportation Safety Board, Thériault, a gifted communicator, led the investigation into the September 1998 crash of Swissair 111 off St. Margarets Bay, Nova Scotia, which killed all on board. The way in which Thériault carried out the assignment, meeting with families, politicians, and experts, says a lot about his humanity. It was a situation where he needed to balance the delicate relationships such tragedy engenders with a quest for answers, and to ultimately deliver results that could not, no matter how well executed, "resolve" the situation. At best, as Thériault shared with me, it might bring a bit of closure for families and establish the facts and offer corrective measures. His skill at balancing expectations within the reality of a difficult situation would continue to serve him well.

Les Caisses' transformation would also need to be a delicate maneuver given the tough requirements: the dissolution of fifteen boards of directors, the creation of one big Caisse with one board, and the ability of these combined bodies to act as one coordinated entity in order to compete without sacrificing the bank's historical roots. But the battle would be fought one community at a time, by informing members of this difficult transition and explaining the implications of moving to one larger financial entity. As rural communities had emptied into nearby cities and towns, branches had already been closing, and with a centralized operation, more branches would close. For the bank's employees, the disappearance of branches meant losing their jobs, and for long-time members, the branches' community and parish, it meant a direct threat to their survival.

Thériault knew the commercial viability of Les Caisses was at stake, as well as the longevity of some of the small communities that were the backbone of the system. He knew this only too well as his family hailed from a tiny village where the heart of the community was the church, the "Caisse Pop," and the wharf, and where economic activity was driven by fishing, subsistence farming, and a peat moss plant.

Could a man whose very identity was wrapped up in the fabric of rural New Brunswick divorce himself from his past, his people, and his relationships in order to deliver a result that would give Les Caisses a fighting chance to compete? Thériault faced many hurdles in transforming the multi-board, multi-branch federation into one unified Caisse. Change required using his gift as a communicator to influence thousands of members to vote in support of the transformation. He had to respect and acknowledge people's self-interest yet ask them to put that interest aside, and had to be truthful in saying that change at the end of the day might not guarantee survival.

The Impact of Change: Are Results Everything?

As you reflect on the responsibility Camille Thériault has to Les Caisses and its members, and how change will impact its members' lives, can you relate to his dilemma? What is your approach to balancing the importance of the organization's goals with consideration for the interests of your people? I have met managers who have told me results are everything and that people do not matter. Managers who sit on the other side of the spectrum have told me that the best results are built on relationships and employee well-being. Here's a conversation I've had more times than I care to remember, opening with a client's question about my training practice:

"Do you provide coaching for up-and-coming managers?"

"Selectively. What's going on?"

"Frankie is in a first management role and is struggling and we would like to provide some training or coaching."

"What do you mean by struggling?"

"Frankie has a great track record and is our most productive frontline worker three years running, so when a team leader job came up, it only made sense to give Frankie a try. But it's been a real struggle."

"How so?"

"Frankie is very deadline driven, but is having difficulty lighting a fire under the team around deliverables. Relationships with staff are tense and getting frayed, and we've received some requests to transfer out of that department. Staff are citing Frankie as the issue."

"How were Frankie's relationships before the promotion?"

"Good. Never the life of the party or the person people naturally gravitate towards necessarily, and a bit of a serious type, but the type of person who eventually warms up after you get to know them. We really want this new opportunity to work out. Very few of our folks deliver results as well as Frankie, but now the whole team thing is becoming a bit of a mess. Can you help?"

Here's the real question being asked in this conversation: Is it possible to teach, train, or coach people to build relationship and communication skills? The former president of Pepsi Co., John Sculley, famously said, "Stop calling it soft skills; this stuff is hard."

Are there tools and techniques that help aspiring managers and supervisors become better at relationships by strengthening their communication capabilities? You betcha. Are there approaches that can help us all become more empathetic? Absolutely. Are there tips and tools that make us better with the so-called softer side of our leadership work. Yup! And this book wants to contribute to the understanding of the people leadership discipline. The challenge? It is the dichotomy expressed in the title of this chapter: How do I balance people and results? Does one have to come before or at the expense of the other?

The answers to these questions will unfold throughout the book, but here's a hint: leaders can genuinely pay attention to both people and task through a team focus, or better yet through rigorous problem-solving. Another hint: commitment to a team approach means paying close attention to both technical skill building and fostering understanding between human beings who work together.

Pioneering researchers Robert Blake and Jane Mouton's managerial grid model of leadership, first published in 1964, has more than stood the test of time and continues to help us better understand how a leader's attitudinal concerns about people and production (relationships and results, if you prefer) translate into their behaviors.[1] Blake and Mouton's grid was also devised to better understand interpersonal conflict, and it is used extensively by practitioners. In both leadership and conflict realms, the same holds true. An approach high in concern for people and production represents the ideal achieved by focusing on sustainable teamwork and problem-solving.

Some in my profession advocate identifying people with good team and social skills, and then teaching them to be results oriented. I am convinced that (1) both sets of skills are teachable and (2) we can strengthen both our relationships and our outcomes when we are given the right tools and guidance, and when we genuinely pay attention to getting better through enhanced self-awareness that comes from robust feedback and learning. (All themes that we'll explore in the coming chapters.)

What does this mean for identifying aspiring leaders for our organizations, be they business, not-for-profit, or community organizations? Do we favor those with a proven track record of productivity or those to whom people naturally turn for guidance, inspiration, and direction? Yes, I know we would want leaders who cut across the spectrum, but given that such leaders are apparently in short supply, which type of leader would you favor? How would you describe your leadership style? Which skill set do you feel most capable of strengthening given that the other is in place—relationships or results? And how exactly might you go about it?

At this point, you might be thinking, "Pierre, if I am getting results, why would I need to change my style? I think I'm a good leader and my team gets stuff done." I say to you, "Well done. But like the hero of this chapter, Camille Thériault, there are problems that will come our way which are so nuanced and complex that one approach will not do."

Situational Leadership

From my years of helping organizations find management talent, I have vivid memories of committees attempting to hide their collective disappointment in a promising candidate, perhaps a less seasoned applicant, who would passionately identify as this type of leader or that, professing their unwavering allegiance to their enlightened approach with assertions such as "I am always participative in my approach" or "Coaching is how I supervise." While acknowledging a bias or predisposition for a certain approach is not a problem, selection committees typically look for a more nuanced answer that demonstrates a deeper understanding of what it is to be an effective leader. It calls for a variety of tools and approaches.

In our quest to determine what leadership or management style reflects the best of what we bring to our vocation, and especially which style the situation warrants, "it depends" must be our answer. Situational leadership is an acknowledgment that your ability to evaluate which approach to access and use, given the requirements of the situation, is at the core of your leadership work. As we'll see later in the book, a leader's best work is often achieved by asking questions that in time lead to a better understanding of our people and the problems they face. That in turn enables us to best align our leadership approach with what best corresponds to that person and the problem or situation at hand.

The "it depends" school, better classified as a situational approach, may sound soft or unclear, not to say wishy-washy, but it's actually more exacting, not less. A situational approach implies an openness to making a conscious choice to move away from techniques that have been successful to try other things. It means being able to move from a very directive style (i.e., a telling style) to an approach centered on questions, coaching, facilitation, and training. Such an approach holds independence, self-government, and delegation as its ideals

Leading situationally means having access to a full toolbox of leadership styles, from the most relationship centered to the most results centered. This requires self-awareness and the ability to use a variety of tools and approaches well, and we will discuss these tools and approaches throughout the book. Declaring that you are a fan of a certain approach is fine, especially if your toolbox is diverse and in good working order. Sometimes, though, what counts most is that you dampen the urge to use the tool that feels most comfortable in favor of one that might be more appropriate but feels slightly more awkward in your hands.

Situational Leadership Exemplified

In his quest to transform Les Caisses, Camille Thériault defined three challenges: getting his key people on board, waging the appropriate public campaign to bring members to vote for a unified Caisse, and confronting the gargantuan task of redesigning the organization and its systems. He knew he was the best person for the first two endeavors, but should they be successful, he wondered whether he was the right leader to take Les Caisses to new heights or if he should step away and let someone else begin the new chapter.

Thériault gathered all the general managers of the federation's then fifteen branches for an offsite away from the scrutiny of the press, who were examining Les Caisses' every move and fanning the flames of discord with members. He understood that getting everyone on the same page meant that the GMs, the very people who ran the independent branches, needed to sign off on the unified strategy knowing full well that they themselves, their staff, and ultimately their members would be asked to come out the other side of a challenging and contentious process only to face job cuts, branch closures, and the loss of customers to their competition.

We don't know exactly what transpired in that room that evening; the proceedings were confidential. But we can deduce that the CEO likely drew upon years of cultivated trust and goodwill with his people, and that those relationships allowed him to focus hard and push for the required result. We can also guess that the absence of said relationships would have made his drive for a specific outcome difficult, if not impossible. The group emerged united, supportive of Thériault's plan and cognizant that their decision was to start them on a perilous path, one that held no guarantee of their own job security and that would put them at the center of impending media storms and contentious community meetings. All of this in hopes of reinventing the institution so that it would become and remain relevant to future generations.

Thériault now had his internal people on side. Caisse populaire acadienne ltée became one unified Caisse, rebranded as UNI Financial Cooperation, and it appointed a new CEO as Thériault stepped aside, having given the storied institution the fresh start it needed to compete.

TO LEAD OTHERS requires a trust relationship, as we witnessed in Camille Thériault's quest to transform Les Caisses. In chapter 3, we discuss values and offer ideas to leaders on how to walk the talk to gain, build, and sustain trust.

Taking Stock of Your Humanity at Work

As you answer the following questions about your people leadership practice, reflect on Thériault's challenges and on ways of finding solutions in situations that may require bold action.

1. Who are those folks you have worked with who displayed an appropriate balance between relationships and results, and what was their "secret sauce"?

2. Are you more adept in building and nurturing relationships, or are you known for your capacity to deliver results?

3. What could you keep doing, stop doing, or start doing to better balance relationships and results?

(3)
What Are the Values that Shape Me as a Leader?

A RMANDO, A SENIOR executive with a private testing laboratory, was just sitting down at the baby grand piano after a delicious light dinner when the phone rang.

It was Kathleen, one of the key managers from the lab, calling—a colleague who didn't typically contact Armando in the evening. The usually calm and poised Kathleen was talking quickly, and Armando heard words about "loyalty" and "industrial espionage" and then the name of her colleague, Milan.

Kathleen and another manager had been on a business trip, and their route had taken them by their lab's largest competitor. Both labs were the product of the same university and were essentially competing in the same markets. Not unexpectedly, there was a fierce rivalry between the firms: they competed internationally for talent and research funding, aggressively tried to lure star employees away from each other, and had years of acrimony and lawsuits between them. Loyalty was prized, industrial espionage was a persistent risk in their business, and both employers became draconian in their response to anyone thinking about or actually jumping ship.

In one of the two firms, employees rumored to be departing would be confronted, and if an employee was deemed to be "unfaithful" it brought out the worst in the CEO. Threats, lawsuits, terminations for cause and without cause, and several out-of-court settlements along with the attendant negative publicity and damage to the lab's employment brand had tarnished the lab's once-stellar reputation.

The CEO resolutely felt that, in the face of the threat these departures posed to the business, swift and sudden action was appropriate to ensure the long-term viability of the company. Senior staff, corporate counsel, and some members of the board of directors had loudly questioned and criticized the CEO's stance on employees seeking work elsewhere and had deemed it inappropriate and unsuitable for a company of the lab's stature. But there hadn't been, in Kathleen's recollection, a situation of a co-founder—in this case one of the three most important people in the company—coming under scrutiny for a suspected betrayal.

Kathleen was in the driver's seat as she and her colleague stopped at a traffic light across from their competitor's head office. Out of the corner of her eye, Kathleen saw someone whom she believed to be her colleague Milan emerging from the building. He passed by the car so closely he could have tapped on the car window. In what felt to Kathleen like an anguishing slow-motion scene from an action movie, she and Milan locked gazes for what was probably a split second but felt much longer, and then he scurried down the street. Kathleen was attempting to register what she had just witnessed. Milan, in that instant, froze, looking as if he had seen a ghost, or so it seemed from her vantage point. Kathleen, in a barely audible voice, asked her colleague if she had seen anything unusual. She just looked straight ahead and said, "I think I saw something I'd rather not have seen."

The two women drove in an uneasy silence to the colleague's home, where they remained quiet as they sorted through their luggage and then wished each other goodnight. Kathleen's drive home seemed interminable. Questions raced through her head.

Did she just see one of the company's most powerful and influential senior managers and part owner emerge after office hours from their competitor's office?

When they locked eyes, did Milan think that he had been found out, or was she reading way too much into all of this?

Was he there on appropriate business? If so, why hadn't such an unusual move been discussed at senior management meetings? Maybe she was being deliberately left out of the loop? Why? Was one lab trying to buy out the other? Should she be worried about her job if a takeover was in the works?

She wondered, should she advise the company's chief of security? Could Milan be selling company secrets to the competition? They were in a highly regulated sector. She knew espionage was an omnipresent risk in their sector, but Milan would never do such a thing, would he? There had been so much in the news about spying and espionage lately.[1] She told herself to start watching romantic comedies instead of the suspense thrillers her partner loved. Maybe she was just getting paranoid.

What was her gut telling her? Could her professional ethical training in her clinical area of study help her? Could the company's stated values guide her? She had been a champion of the company's formalizing conflict of interest and ethical conduct policies, but she never thought she would find herself in this murky situation. Her spider senses were tingling, and she felt she needed to do something, but what?

Kathleen's head was spinning. She trusted her VP, Armando (although until moments ago she would have said the same thing about trusting Milan), and it was the one call she was comfortable making, even though she knew that after she shared what she thought she had seen, there would be no turning back.

She thought about waiting until morning, as her mother always urged her to sleep on things when facing complicated decisions.[2] But she reached for her phone. "Hi," she began. "I've got something to tell you. It's about Milan from the lab. Are you sitting down?"

Values Are Your Personal Bottom Line

A discussion about leadership is incomplete without a reflection on the fundamental matters of values and ethics, civility, and human decency. Any one of these subjects is consequential enough to deserve an entire book, and an in-depth treatment of any of them is well beyond the scope of this book. However, they are the very foundation of leading with humanity.

James M. Kouzes and Barry Z. Posner tell us that values are our "personal bottom line"[3] and that they shape our choices and our focus and summon our best responses when things are at their toughest. Kathleen's flurry of reflective questions demonstrates how any of us might cycle through myriad thoughts when we are confronted by a situation that tests those very values.

As organizations have more thoughtfully articulated their values and ethics and found ways to make their values a living, breathing part of their workplaces, honesty and integrity have become paramount. Some companies take the position that values are so fundamental a concept, especially for those in formal leadership roles, that honesty and integrity form the most basic of prerequisites. The requirement is akin to telling their leaders to remember to breathe. However, when it comes to integrity, or as has become common in the vernacular, the capacity to "walk the talk," I believe organizations are best served by making the virtue of leaders doing the things they say they will do a tangible, oft-referred-to core value that forms part of an organization's DNA.

Moreover, as with other values most frequently embraced by employers (accountability, diligence, perseverance, respect), integrity and walking the talk may be well intended, but they will be meaningless if tucked away in an orientation manual, mentioned only during the onboarding of new staff, or framed on the wall of the HR department. Some would suggest that the articulation and posting on walls of values is a questionable activity because those statements are strictly aspirational.

A better illustration, according to those skeptics, is how the organization spends its money. There is nothing like the annual operating budget to determine who is keeping their word. Better yet, the true measure of values is seen in how people treat others as they go about their daily work.

If you want to test a company's commitment to community, look at the number of company-sanctioned volunteer hours employees spend. Look at the number of events that were financed or partnered within the community and other tangible indicators of community involvement. Are opportunities for growth through learning and skill development maintained despite tough times? These are the true tests of organizational values.

Employers have also recognized the importance of showcasing their values to attract the right candidates. Potential new hires want to hear about a company's values and see them at work in the community. They want to understand their employer's beliefs and actions in matters of importance to them like the environment, corporate citizenship, and other realms of social responsibility like the fairness of supply chains and human rights standards in offshore factories. Employers consider these factors when making employment decisions. Don't you?

Psychologist Adam Grant in his book *Give and Take* carries the values conversation further by highlighting a generation that values "paying it forward" and mounts an evidence-based argument as to why givers, those who are *other* focused—those who are helpful and dependable, who care for the disadvantaged (an interesting notion within organizations, huh?), and who show compassion—get ahead in organizations.[4] So values are front and center, making it more obvious and offensive when we go astray.

Even the most strident practitioner of walking the talk is not immune from breaking commitments, assurances, and promises in organizational life. Situations change and the best of intentions are often thwarted by events well beyond our anticipation or control. That said, there is a chasm of difference between those who callously ignore their promises to others and are blind to the effects of this behavior, and those who, due to circumstances beyond their control, must alter an intended course of action and who do so with transparency and contrition. When a leader finds it necessary to alter course, if that altered course is explained with as much transparency as possible, leaders and managers retain—and some would argue, strengthen—their reputation for integrity given their concern and diligence when they do go back on their stated intentions.

It is impractical and nearly impossible to be fully transparent, because confidentiality must be preserved. We are not always able to divulge reasons for going back on our word when that information needs to be treated confidentially. However, leaders earn enormous credibility by letting people know that a situation requires confidentiality but that some information can be shared.

I've seen many instances of leaders cowering and saying nothing because the information was not for everyone's ears and could not be communicated, leaving their workplaces in turmoil and rife with speculation, rumors, and doubt, all the while lessening their credibility. All such leaders need to do is say that here is what can be said for now, and that further information will be forthcoming—and then return later and say what they can when they can.

Keeping Your Word

In an activity I frequently use at the end of a leadership development workshop, participants are asked to complete the following statements:[5]

1. I get worried when a leader . . .
2. A leader loses credibility when . . .
3. The personal attribute I find least appealing in a leader is . . .

In my many years of leading this activity with thousands of participants, invariably the answers have clustered around honesty and integrity. The single most common theme is captured by the response, "says one thing, then does another."

It's interesting to me that responses in this exercise never point to a leader or manager being in over their head, being poorly organized, or lacking essential managerial skills. Instead, comments tend to revolve around leaders' ethical practices and interpersonal skills.

When I press participants on whether a lack of technical competence for project management or budgeting, or a tendency to be inconsistent in problem-solving, could dampen their view of the leader, they concede that these issues matter, and when there is a skill deficiency in such areas, it is problematic. But being skilled in these areas takes a backseat to a leader sticking to their commitments and being nice.

Bearing in mind the disproportionate impact that leaders have on just about everything (people's mood,[6] the behavior of others, organizational performance), leaders doing what they say they will do has huge consequences for the accepted norms and behaviors within a workplace culture. One of the most important lessons people new to their role of team leader or manager must grapple with is the extent to which their behavior is viewed as if they were in a fishbowl.

I distinctly recall a recently promoted supervisor saying, "I'm still the same person, doing a bit of a different job than I used to. My pals should still see me the same way they always did."

"That may be true," I remember telling them, "only now they are watching your every move and weighing your every word."

Leaders not doing what they say they will do gives permission to everyone around them to do the same. Soon enough, an entire workplace culture—and even those who resist—will be compromised by all forms of disregard for what is promised, intended, or committed to, be this the big and bold commitments made to entire employee groups and then reneged on, or the smaller, person-to-person commitments we make on a daily basis. When the supervisor routinely forgets or brushes aside small, seemingly innocuous commitments made in conversation or in passing, they build a reputation no leader wants—and in some cases, one they cannot recover from.

Staff will initially give their manager the benefit of the doubt (they've got a lot on the go, lots of commitments, etc.), but when a pattern emerges, staff often become skeptical, others lose faith, and eventually the accumulation of broken commitments catches up to the offending leader, whose reputation is sealed for not keeping their word.

Can Ethical Conduct Be Compromised by Loyalty?

Kathleen had been an outspoken supporter of the company's recently updated policies on conflict of interest and ethical conduct. Ethics mattered to her, and she believed it should matter to others. She believed, too, that the largest part of her leadership role was to imbue her entourage with standards that reflect adherence to personal and organizational values. She was also committed to rewarding and recognizing those who, through their daily actions, lived the company's values. She used every occasion to role model and educate about what the company believed about its customers, its people, and its community.

Little did Kathleen know at the time of her campaigning for those policies that her visibility and tenacity in the face of some misinformed opposition on that file, and the thoughtful work done by the committee looking at this question, would later inform the gut-wrenching decision she had to make. In addition, her personal moral code and her role as a leader guaranteed that she had to act, no matter how uncomfortable the situation.

Ethical questions can be a uniquely personal matter for leaders and an important one for those tasked with training, selecting, and managing those who lead and manage. We have noted the broader implications of such questions given the disproportionate impact leaders have, yet there are other compelling considerations for the employer or organization. Ethical leadership goes beyond contributing to transparent, fair, and respectful workplace cultures, as highlighted by Professor David Mayer of the University of Michigan, who notes, "In the past decade over 100 studies with more than 30,000 employees have consistently found that employees who believe their leader is ethical are happier, more committed, perform better, are more likely to be helpful to others and less likely to behave unethically."[7]

Mayer had me at "happier, more committed," but even the most skeptical among us must get onside with trumpeting ethical leadership when we can tie better employee performance to a team leader being perceived as ethical. This is a productivity issue!

Yet this does not, in my view, happen through osmosis alone. I do believe that some employees will make better (i.e., more ethical) decisions because their supervisor casts a positive ethical shadow, but there are specific things ethical leaders do that increase the likelihood that staffers will follow suit. And there is a "feel good" and motivational lift that comes from doing the right thing and from celebrating those who do the right thing on our teams. You've hopefully experienced both situations and would agree with me that it feels great, from all perspectives.

Former member of Parliament Robert Goguen spoke to me of the sense of accomplishment he has achieved through the non-glamorous negotiations and successful collaborations he has had with other like-minded politicians. Goguen recalled fondly, from his time in public office, when colleagues of all political stripes enabled progress for Canada by setting aside their differences and, guided by what was right, quietly resolving issues successfully.

Part of casting an ethical shadow is creating the right conditions for everyday, out-of-the-limelight conversations about doing the right thing to happen on our teams, so that when we're faced with ethical challenges like the one Kathleen struggled with, we have some context and we've exercised those "doing-the-right-thing muscles," at the very least in conversation with our team colleagues and team leader.

Kathleen's reputation was that of someone who carried herself with integrity. She realized that this dicey situation was triggering complicated issues around loyalty rooted in events she had witnessed as a child. Her mom was a professional who had dutifully served a large national employer for over twenty years and was unceremoniously downsized after a corporate takeover, and difficult times ensued for her mom and the family. Her mom recovered professionally and personally, but not before fighting the shame and disappointment of being terminated at a time when companies just didn't do that sort of thing. It is now commonplace, but not so a generation ago.

Loyalty changed forever coming out of that dark period in the 1980s and 1990s. Younger workers redefined their relationships with employers, shifting away from the perspective of their parents' "jobs for life" era in favor of a different type of relationship with their employers and enjoying greater job mobility. Employers increased the use of contingent workforces and redefined the conditions, and loyalty was changed forevermore. Loyalty still exists from both employers and employees, but it looks different than it did in Kathleen's parents' time. Still, this notion of loyalties was central to her dilemma.

She was loyal to her employer, to her profession, and to her colleague, Milan. But she had a greater loyalty towards the values of right and wrong and towards her self-respect, the reputation of the company, and the hundreds of good, honest people who worked there. Her loyalty to the CEO was complicated, but to the office of the CEO her loyalty was not complicated at all. She was a loyal employee, period.

Teachable Moments for Values and Ethics

Dr. Chris MacDonald, director of the Ted Rogers Leadership Centre, Ryerson University, gets to the heart of the matter when he says that "leadership has an ethical core, and ethics means not just making good decisions, but leading others in making good decisions."[8]

There are the daily incidents and seemingly innocuous happenings in every workplace that create teachable moments for an alert leader to use in their quest to keep ethics top of mind. This could take the form of recognizing and calling out acts of honesty and integrity with individuals, using a staff meeting to showcase when an employee or neighboring department lives up to the company's values, or acknowledging a supervisor who brings in a news clipping that shows the success or failing of someone living up to or not living up to ethical standards. There is inherent value when leaders remind people of commitments kept by colleagues, by the organization or its suppliers. Underscoring the keeping of commitments through recognition and other means galvanizes that behavior far more than words in a code of conduct manual or on a poster.

Role modeling, employee recognition, and teachable moments are ways leaders can imprint their team or department with high ideals of honesty and integrity. But there is one more tactic that many have embraced with great success, and that is the adoption of a personal ethical mantra that leaders then share within the context of everyday activities.

Google famously had an informal saying that became known worldwide: "Don't be evil," which later became a formalized part of their code of conduct after being redefined as "Do the right thing." It has been widely reported that Google's "Don't be evil" slogan was intended as an all-inclusive statement—like one spelled out in countless employee handbooks and codes of conduct—that incited Googlers to be law abiding and to conduct themselves with honor and treat colleagues with courtesy and respect. Companies that experience meteoric growth struggle especially with consistency in the application of these ideals, as we saw when Googlers around the world took to the streets in 2018 to protest workplace harassment, sexual misconduct, and equity issues in their workplaces.[9]

Informal sayings and personal mantras do not supersede the need for leaders to ensure that their organizations, large and small, offer teaching moments on values, appropriate conduct, and standards of civility and human decency. This comes with the formulation and education about definitions, policies, guidelines, and mechanisms for complaints, investigations, and redress. But in the words of the widely decorated jazz trumpeter Wynton Marsalis[10] (proving you don't need to be an expert in organizational behavior to contribute to the conversation on engaged, resourceful, and productive workplaces), "Ethics are more important than laws." When leaders embody honesty, integrity, civility, and human decency, and conduct themselves accordingly, they can expect that their entourage will do the same. At the same time, if they intervene whenever these expectations fall short, it is unlikely they will need to resort to draconian disciplinary measures.

Many an employer has been satisfied to have the necessary policy and education safeguards in place and has failed to set a high enough standard for leaders to act upon said laws. In short, there has been a tolerance for looking the other way and not intervening, especially if the offending behavior comes with high output. (More on the how leaders intervene in part four of this book.)

Intervening around breaches is key, but talking up a storm about values serves everybody well. I know a young accountant who is plant manager of a four-hundred-person food processing facility. He shared that he always plucks a value off the company's value statement before speaking to employees and uses that value in an example. Each time, he acknowledges an individual in the room for having lived the value in their actions.

In one of my pre-workshop surveys, I ask attendees to respond to specific statements about ethical challenges managers face in their natural habitat:

- I have had the opportunity to work with leaders who were ethical, trusted, and respected.

- Within my leadership role, I have witnessed a situation, event, or incident that challenged/tested people's ethics.

- Within my leadership role, a situation, event, or incident has tested my personal and/or professional ethics.

In all three instances, 85 percent to 90 percent of respondents either strongly agreed or agreed.[11]

There is reassurance in the first statement. Most of us work with and learn from ethical leaders. But this is balanced by the stark reality of the second and third statements. Many of us come face-to-face with ethical dilemmas in the workplace. For example:

- A friend and coworker or your boss asks you to "cover for them" while they duck out of work for reasons unknown.
- A colleague blatantly takes credit for someone else's work in a meeting.
- A coworker is conducting extensive personal business on the employer's time.
- Abject favoritism is taking place within a hiring process.
- You are asked to cut corners on a customer order because there will be cost savings and you're told the customer won't even notice.
- You become convinced that a cloud of secrecy exists in a harassment situation with coworkers from another department.

In moments like these, leaders are often guided by a personal mantra, sometimes proclaimed as a quiet voice, that guides them as they come face-to-face with the inevitable ethical challenges we encounter in organizational life.

In so many of these dilemmas, subtle nuances need to be carefully considered, but it is in these very instances that, in addition to the company's stated values, your own personal mantra can be helpful. Here are some of the ones that my workshop participants seem to come back to, proving that a simple question keeps one's values top of mind:

- What would my children/parents think if they saw me engage in this type of behavior?
- Would I be comfortable if this was on the front page of our local newspaper?
- Will this keep me from sleeping at night?

- How will my inaction be perceived when this situation comes to light?
- What would _____ (someone I respect/admire) do?

I really like the last one. It clearly pertains to matters of ethics but can also apply to many other leadership challenges. When you encounter a strategy problem, for example, ask yourself, "What would [insert name here of a strategist you respect] do?" When a doozy of a marketing problem emerges, ask yourself, "What would [insert name here of a marketer you respect] do?" In the case of ethical issues, simply insert the name of someone you admire, someone you know to take the high ethical road, someone who casts an ethical shadow your way.

What Did Kathleen Do?

Kathleen acted that fateful night. Her efforts began with a phone call to Armando. She had to trust someone, and thankfully she made the right choice. Together, they called the other manager who had made the business trip with Kathleen. She was equally conflicted and in a quandary, and was ultimately relieved to receive the call. The trio then agreed to meet first thing in the morning and decide what course of action, if any, needed to be taken. Milan quietly left the company three months later.

ASIDE FROM TRUST, what other expectations might your people have of you as a leader? Positive motivation comes to mind, which is the topic of chapter 4.

Taking Stock of Your Humanity at Work

As you answer the following questions about your people leadership practice, reflect on the issues Kathleen faced and how she relied on her personal ethics and values to address them.

1. What is a "Kathleen's conundrum" moment you faced as a leader? A dilemma that tested your ethical foundations and your values? Would you do anything differently if you had to do it again?

2. What course of action would you have taken in Kathleen's place?

3. How does or would a personal ethics mantra serve you well?

4. How do your workplace values (stated or implied, whether you know them or not) guide you and how do they inform your leadership practice?

5. Do you lead any differently when no one is watching? Assuming you said no, how might you teach that?

(4)
Am I a Positive Force?

I'M A FAN of jazz bass virtuoso, educator, and one-person jazz wrecking crew Christian McBride. Through his larger-than-life personality and incessant global touring and broadcasting, McBride is the art form's premier ambassador.

I had last seen McBride's renowned smile when he was fronting an eight-piece ensemble at the Halifax Jazz Festival several years earlier. In the jazz tradition, the "older cats"—as soon as they are settled and can afford it—begin hiring "young lions" busting out of music schools, conservatories, and universities. McBride had come up the same way.

The danger of surrounding yourself with less experienced musicians is that, well, they have less experience. And in a highly improvised art form where communication between musicians is vital to create beautiful music spontaneously, working with younger musicians can present challenges for a touring professional like McBride.

I watched transfixed as the promising young players surrounding McBride showed their inexperience, their nerves, or the simple fact the band was new and probably unrehearsed. I was scrutinizing the habitually smiling McBride for signs of a "stink eye"—a conductor's acknowledgment of a wrong note or poor time—but none materialized. In fact, the opposite was true. The more mistakes the young players made, the more sympathetic were his eyes and smile. He encouraged, nudged, and empowered the young musicians with a positive, optimistic, smiling gaze, all the while being truly engaged in music making.

I had seen that type of smile before, in a much more somber setting years earlier in a bug-infested trailer on a mining site in Miramichi, New Brunswick. A wily veteran of Canada's mining sector named André taught me a lesson in positivity and empathy with a deliberate smile and highly communicative eyes. It was in the late 1990s and early 2000s when resource sector companies across Canada were restructuring operations, which meant downsizing or closing plants or entire sites altogether.

André was a veteran mining engineer who had worked with several of Canada's major mining companies. He had come to town to close the mine. We were sitting in a cold, damp trailer in prime moose-hunting territory—territory, not season—handy to the sprawling mine site recently purchased by an international mining company. The makeshift administrative offices would serve as the locale for the many difficult meetings we were to hold with employees whose careers with the mining company were about to end abruptly as a result of an impending mine closure. I was there to help the management team that day and to then assist the soon-to-be-unemployed with their career transition efforts.

André insisted on meeting everyone himself to impart the difficult news. He wasn't obligated to make it personal, and typically executives would leave it to the people leaders at the local mine site to carry out such difficult tasks, with an assist from local and corporate HR folks and career consultants. But with André, it was different. He wanted to look people in the eye and deliver the difficult news—to signal the company's respect for the employee hearing that news. He was also there to support his local managers who were laying off neighbors, friends, and family members.

So, along with nervous (and eventually displaced) local managers and supervisors and well-meaning HR folks, André met with workers and delivered the difficult though not unexpected news.

André smiled all day long. Not a joyous or gleeful or inappropriate smile. Smiles of understanding, smiling eyes, and a subtly nodding head that says, "I'm really sorry you are having to go through this. I'm sorry to be here under such circumstances." A smile that said, "We'll genuinely do all we can to help." A smile that says that things, in time, will be all right. A nodding, comforting smile that was not out of place despite the somber nature of the proceedings. When things got a little testy with workers, who were understandably disappointed and sometimes angry, he smiled empathetically, nodding, completely disarming and eventually calming those who were lashing out at the "big boss from away."

I watched him intently the next day as he spent time with the many employees tasked with remaining behind, some sticking with the operation for a few months to facilitate everyone's departure and others staying for years to shut down the site. People felt guilty that their neighbors were sent home while they were continuing to work. But folks were relieved the decision was finally made and the announcements were over. Now they had lots to do to assist the workers and prepare the site for shutdown.

That empathetic, heartfelt smile and demeanor, and the very way André carried himself changed after the difficult day of announcing the news and morphed into a more forward-looking attitude that signaled there was work to be done and their best bet was to get at it. (Best practice is indeed to get everyone back to some sense of routine and normalcy after shockwaves of change are sent through the systems.) He then, over the course of several hours, checked in with every individual on site, despite dealing with a blitz of international head-office calls, a local media frenzy, and the expected aftermath felt by the team after sending hundreds of people home and devastating a small community.

He reminded everyone that their neighbors in that community were feeling the brunt of the difficult news and were depending on them more than ever before to be available, empathetic, and quietly optimistic.

What the Leaders Chose to Do as Conductors

Like Christian McBride, André made a choice. Maybe you have already seen the connection between these two men: they both decided not to "go negative." Christian encouraged and empowered his young musicians, never calling out a bad note. André chose a way of being on that difficult day; he deliberately slowed himself down and put himself in the best possible place from which to lead the team and carry out its delicate work with great compassion and efficiency—a mix that can be tricky to pull off well.

Identical events were taking place at sister mines on two other continents, so sequencing and coordinating respectful and timely employee meetings, as well as quickly making public and media announcements in several countries simultaneously, was regrettably something the folks on site that day were getting good at.

Precision in synchronizing the timing was critical given that these companies are publicly traded and the mining sector is a highly interconnected, nomadic community where people know and have worked closely with each other around the world. Word travels in nanoseconds.

But in such situations, leaders like André—who feel their presence benefits the circumstances, the management group, and those most affected—attempt not to go through the exercise robotically, machine-like and devoid of sentiment, or propelled by an "it's business, not personal" mantra.

André's choice to be respectfully and cautiously optimistic in his dealings with people was in no way intended to underplay the tragic impact such closures could have on families and on entire communities, but André's subdued optimism, arguably an emotionally intelligent choice, was the only way he knew how to be in such trying circumstances. Those on the ground told me in subsequent weeks and months that they preferred André's realistic optimism and his tendency to smile, even sometimes in a really difficult situation, to other approaches they had experienced. Other senior managers, when faced with similar circumstances, often chose a stonier, more detached "it's just business" approach—not showing genuine concern other than the perfunctory. I would speculate putting on such game faces is what enabled some bearers of bad news to get through the ordeal.

From these brief snapshots of Christian and André, we may infer that both of these men have chosen to emphasize a positive approach, whether deliberately—making it a guiding principle of how they show up as a leader—or perhaps as a natural extension of an optimistic mindset. They're in very good company when they choose positivity in how they lead.

Before we explore some of the pioneering work in positive leadership to better understand Christian and André's more profound and lasting impacts, let's start by looking at the hard science of positivity that underpins positive leadership.

The Science of Positivity

Leading scholars in positive psychology have helped us understand the "forms of positivity,"[1] or how emotions like joy, inspiration, and awe impact us well beyond the temporary "feel good" effects. According to one of positivity's leading researchers, Barbara Fredrickson, "The latest scientific evidence tells us that positivity doesn't simply reflect success and health. It can also produce success and good health ... your positivity has downstream consequences for the very trajectory of your life. Positivity spells the difference between whether you languish or flourish."[2]

Fredrickson positions positivity as a "means" and not an end unto itself. The end is our ability to flourish and thrive and be happy. This view is central to the tenets of positive psychology, the scientific study of positive human functioning and flourishing that has a focus on building and leveraging strengths instead of repairing weakness.[3]

From a workplace perspective, Fredrickson's work becomes even more compelling with her "broaden and build" approach, in which positivity and positive emotions are shown to broaden people's thinking about the variety of options and possibilities available to them. Positivity makes us more amenable and imaginative.

The connections between joy and creativity are well established in this approach.[4] If we want to stimulate problem-solving and innovation, creativity's two kissing cousins, we should spread some joy! (Not specific enough? Keep reading!)

According to Christian McBride's many close friends, music colleagues, and the academics and players who commented on his performance, stage presence, and leadership, his positive, effusive, and authentic presence on stage is the essence of the man. André was much more laid back and soft spoken, but according to those who worked with him daily, make no mistake, his infectious positivity fuels a drive to see others do well in the aim of making his business unit and the company successful. Both men were described as focused and industrious.

We have established that André and Christian are both interested in creating positive emotions in their folks, but not just as a means unto itself. Positive leadership's promise is "not just to create positive emotions in people—to help people feel happy—but to dramatically affect organizational performance for the better."[5]

Kim Cameron, the co-founder of the Center for Positive Organizations at the University of Michigan, is widely regarded as one of the architects (if not *the* architect) of positive leadership. His research and that of his contemporaries has shown that "positive leadership brings improvement in organizational productivity, profitability, quality, innovation, and customer loyalty.... [T]here is published evidence that this revolutionary approach to leading and managing produces benefits in terms of individual psychological health, emotional well-being, brain functioning, interpersonal relationships, and learning as well."[6]

It gets better. Cameron and his colleagues have demonstrated over several studies in a number of industries a positive correlation between a company's performance and that company having instituted positive leadership practices.

You must be wondering how exactly we parse out "positive" leadership behaviors beyond the nonverbal cues the jazz and mining leaders demonstrated earlier and our common sense about what constitutes positive leadership. As one of my colleagues put it, "It harkens to that famous line that goes 'I'm not sure I can define it, but I sure know it when I see it.'" But while acknowledging these limitations, let's look into the subject more closely.

The Keys to Positive Leadership

Positive leadership centers on employee learning and growth, and on organizational effectiveness. It also focuses on living, role modeling, and intentionally building positive emotions in others, and it thrives on self-awareness, optimism, and integrity.[7]

The following four questions frame positive leadership nicely. To establish whether a leadership behavior or practice is positive or negative (or neutral), ask yourself,

1. Does it encourage or discourage others?
2. Does it empower or demoralize others?
3. Does it energize or drain others?
4. Does it attract or repel others?[8]

Watching André and learning about Christian, I believe they both attract others but in very different ways. One (Christian) has a remarkable physical presence, the other not so much; both smile a lot; one draws a crowd while the other gravitates to smaller "tête à tête" settings. Both are reputed for their pervasive optimism, boundless empathy, and positive energy. People are drawn to them for any number of reasons, and that likely says something about the person who is being "attracted" to them as well.

If you need some positive perspective to inject into your leadership practice, remember this: in spite of what we see on our screens or hear from the demagogues, we have never been in a better place as humans. In Stephen Pinker's exquisitely researched 2018 bestseller *Enlightenment Now: The Case for Reason, Science, Humanism, and Progress*, the Harvard researcher shows that, compared to any earlier point in history, we are better off and healthier, and that we live longer, know more, and are safer, more peaceful, and happier![9] These are lots of "bigger than myself" reasons to lead positively.

The Role of Self-Awareness

Have you ever really looked forward to attending a training event or a personal/professional improvement seminar? Were you excited? Lea Bryden has, and was. She was thrilled, though the event didn't quite start off like she thought it would. A lifelong athlete, and at the time of writing the CEO of the Prince Edward Island Medical Society, Bryden was then the vice president responsible for community engagement for the Capital Health District in Nova Scotia. She was about to enroll in a highly regarded senior leadership program, and one of the faculty there was an internationally known sports psychologist and Olympic performance coach. While this was an organizational leadership development program, she was keen to meet such a prominent figure given their decades of success with high-performance athletes.

Bryden had grown up an elite competitive varsity athlete, and while you were much more apt to see her running these past many years, her enthusiasm for all forms of physical activity because of their benefits to self and community was well known in her circles. Her positive energy, smarts, and grit were also well known.

Bryden had completed the pre-workshop psychometric testing and was about to meet the prominent sports psychologist, where her assessments would be debriefed. Things got started in a way Bryden had not expected. When she entered the room, her paragon of elite performance greeted her with "Attila, nice to meet you." He was invoking the name of Attila, the ruthless leader of the barbaric Huns and enemy to the Roman Empire.

"I'm Lea Bryden, not Attila," she replied.

"Oh no, you're not," said Bryden's instructor for the leadership program. "You're Attila the Hun!"

Bryden recalls being taken aback momentarily, puzzled by the greeting and bewildered about where this was going. Bryden does not bewilder easily.

The esteemed faculty member went on to ask her about how competitive she was, and they agreed that her training as an elite athlete prepared her well for a win–lose mentality. She really liked to win.

The burning question was to what extent her uber competitiveness, her win–lose mentality, although effective in getting things done, came at a cost. To be clear, Bryden was already an accomplished senior manager. She had been at the forefront of her chosen profession, PR, as it became the broader, more strategic area of corporate communications. Those who know her well confirm that she had built a career based on positive relationships and an authentic and welcoming approach.

Did Bryden know she was competitive? Of course she did. Was she aware that her competitiveness shaped her leadership interactions in a less than ideal way? "Not really," she told me. From her exchange with her newfound coach for the workshop, Bryden's awareness of her leadership tendencies and how they impacted what she was trying to accomplish grew deeper.

Once back at the Capital Health District, she rolled out a host of innovative community engagement initiatives, including leadership training, to all staff, not just managers and other formal leaders, in an attempt to ratchet up self-awareness, build leadership capacity, and ultimately bring about better patient outcomes. She believed strongly that we can only lead from a place of understanding of who we are.

The value of knowing one's self cannot be underestimated as it relates directly to how a leader "shows up." Because leaders are emotionally contagious (as we all are), and because of the office they hold or the esteem they garner from others, they inordinately influence the disposition and temperament of their entourage in ways that may not be evident to the developing leader.[10] Emerging leaders learn of their infectious state through early training and feedback-rich coaching, or through trial and error (aka the "hard way"), and ultimately, if they're lucky, through more robust feedback in a way that bolsters self-awareness. Again, the earlier this happens, the better.

Researchers have shown that team leaders who have greater self-awareness have subordinates with greater productivity.[11] They also have followers who are more satisfied.[12]

Let's think about self-awareness with the help of emotional intelligence pioneer Daniel Goleman, who, in his book *The Emotionally Intelligent Leader*, states, "When I compared star performers with average ones in senior leadership positions, nearly 90% of the difference in their profiles was attributable to emotional intelligence factors rather than cognitive ability."[13] And of course emotional intelligence is grounded in self-awareness, defined by Goleman as "knowing one's strengths, weaknesses, drives, values, and impact on others."[14]

Credible leadership books, reputable leadership development programs, and the popular business press value self-awareness and largely recognize that it is a foundational element of anyone's leadership practice. Yet we are poorly positioned to be objectively aware of our own behavior.

Dr. Tammy Carroll created the Self-Aware Leader leadership development program and, in her work as a psychometrician, uses reliable and validated instruments like the Myers-Briggs Type Indicator (MBTI) and others to help people better understand themselves and their psychological type by learning about their preferences around extroversion, taking in information, and making decisions as well as their response to structure and adaptiveness. She also pushes us as leaders towards robust feedback from our entourage, reminding us that at best 10 percent to 15 percent of us would qualify as truly self-aware. So, many of us have some work to do.

I think of self-awareness as being on a continuum, meaning that we and the people we work with are not either self-aware or unself-aware. It's not a binary or static characteristic. As we move through this continuum, those who are open-minded and who seek feedback are likely to keep moving along the self-awareness continuum. Do you remember making decisions at the end of high school regarding your future studies and career? How self-aware were you then? Did you get it right the first time?

Marie Andrée Gaudet was a gifted student who excelled in the sciences, pursued studies in pre-med, and did well. But the self-aware teenager knew something was off. She had been a prodigious violinist from an early age and had toyed with studying and pursuing music professionally, but she had ultimately opted for the sciences. The day she sat her parents down to explain a pending change in her studies and career plans she opened with, "I need to study music and pursue it as a career—it's who I am."

Leadership pioneer Warren Bennis famously said, "Becoming a leader is synonymous with becoming yourself. It is precisely that simple, and it is also that difficult."[15] What a remarkably simple way of framing leadership. Simply become who you are, much like Gaudet the musician did, or as you can do by continuously building better awareness of your skills, strengths, weaknesses, aspirations, and values, and using that knowledge and the best evidence-based approaches to become the leader you were always meant to be.

Gaudet's parents, both accomplished professionals, were degreed musicians with "day jobs" more or less linked to their musical training, and so were well positioned to understand the implications of their daughter's decision. They had reason to have faith in their daughter specifically because she was self-aware and that self-awareness fueled a maturity and wisdom well beyond her teen years. Gaudet changed her major to music, completed a first music degree with honors, and then completed two performing artist diplomas. Now a professional musician, she records and tours extensively in North America and Europe.

The Role of Self-Control

I once had a colleague who was temperamental but also a genius in his work. He unwittingly compelled his team to have a daily secret stand-up meeting first thing on arriving at work. The team would assess his mood each morning by sending an envoy to appraise his temperament, feigning a need to have a two- to three-minute exchange on something routine. If he was agitated and impatient, as was often the case, the news of his mood would spread, and some would argue his mood too would spread among the team. When my colleague was agitated, it meant another day of walking on eggshells for the team, especially in the afternoon, when it seemed his happiness and warmth dipped markedly (as it does for many of us).[16]

The envoy who had tested the waters with the boss would verbally communicate their mood assessment to others. In order to do this effectively and discreetly, the team devised a traffic light approach. "Red light"—avoid the manager for your sake, the team's sake, the client's sake. "Yellow light"—engage at your peril; there may be unintended consequences. "Green light"—a lineup at the manager's door was likely because the team knew his disposition was open, predictable, and calm. This system didn't ensure a favorable response to a team member's request, but it made the experience of getting a "yes," "no," or "maybe" somewhat normal and appropriate. How do we get someone like our temperamental genius to take stock of their behavior and appreciate how negative their impact can be?

A colleague who teaches anger management courses once told me about an effective technique they use to help people manage their self-control. The person is asked to visualize in detail what they look like when they lose their temper—arms flailing, red-faced, and pacing about like a caged animal. My therapist colleague says they're making progress when the individual can step outside of themselves and take account of their behavior and its impact on others. Participants are also encouraged, I'm told, to visualize the reactions of others when they are "losing it." The looks on the faces of others, especially people the angry person cares for, can provoke a powerful moment of clarity.

Don't you wish we could simply hold up a mirror to behaviors like those exhibited by my temperamental colleague and help people to see the error of their ways? My colleague's manager is in the best position to help correct the situation by intervening through robust feedback, making a case for their behavior to be different, and then holding them accountable for the change.

Exposing such behaviors does not mean resorting to a name-and-shame campaign, but what if we were able to engender a better sense of accountability by reminding people who lead that all of their behaviors are being scrutinized and their decisions are being assessed? Their entourage needs to constantly be looking for signals. In this case, they are looking for signals—traffic signals—to ensure their relative safety in dealing with their manager.

No one's value to the organization justifies temperamental behavior. Moreover, those whose behavior is unacceptable obviously haven't made the leap to understanding that to assume a leadership role is to agree to living in a fishbowl and conducting yourself like a grown-up.

Some fishbowls are worse than others. Those who dedicate their life to public service and hold public office or occupy high-profile jobs know better than most about constant scrutiny, insatiable curiosity, and thirst for information about those who hold power. Our temperamental genius may not be a premier, but for the forty people in the office, the genius is the center of attention!

People who lead are held to a higher standard because of this heightened focus. The fishbowl compels others to sit upright and take notice, but hopefully your desire to solve problems and make progress on things that matter while enjoying helping others succeed is what motivates you and not the fact that you are under constant examination.

Because you're in a fishbowl as a leader, people are constantly looking to you and then assessing your actions to see if they are consistent with your words and what you then ask of others.

If you've worked in a fishbowl type of workplace, where your actions are routinely observed, scrutinized, and discussed for better and for worse, you get the picture. Admittedly, the watchful gaze of your staff on your every move may be much less intense than when the media decide to camp out on your lawn, as is the case with those who hold public office or who live a very public life as a leader. The leadership fishbowl comes with the territory, yet the extent to which leaders, especially emerging leaders, can be oblivious to its existence and its potential for harm and for good is surprising to me. The fishbowl can feel odd when we first experience it, but some argue it can be a great motivator and a regulator of our behavior.

Positive Energy and Motivation

A long-time client called me asking if I were interested and available for an upcoming speaking assignment. The client then paid me a compliment, I think, in saying that it didn't really matter what topic I wanted to cover, as the attraction was my energy. The client was happy about the positive energy we had created in our times together.

But beyond the realm of healers, psychics, and mediums—and their claims of energy we can see or assign a color to—can we truly measure energy? Is it a viable area of examination? (Back to "I'm not sure I can define it, but I know it when I see it!") The concept of positive energy has emerged as a relatively new area of academic study.

Researchers have successfully used a series of questions[17] (answered on a scale of 1 to 5) that measure perceptions of positive energy in others:

- I feel invigorated when I interact with this person.
- After interacting with this person, I feel more energy to do my work.
- I feel increased vitality when I interact with this person.
- I would go to this person when I need to be "pepped up."
- After an exchange with this person, I feel more stamina to do my work.

The same researchers found that "when individuals are exposed to a positively energizing leader in their work, they have significantly higher personal well-being, higher satisfaction with their jobs, higher engagement in their organization, higher job performance, and higher levels of family well-being than those without exposure to a positively energizing leader."[18] Higher personal and family well-being and higher job performance—what's not to love?

Recent science supports how important positive energy can be in forecasting superior achievement by individuals. We've long known the relationship between effective leadership and influence (effective leaders influence others well) and between effective leadership and information (effective leaders are aware and gobble up knowhow). Now we have evidence that positive energy is much more powerful than either information or influence![19]

Here's the great news—we can learn optimism.[20] It is a way of thinking that enables us to see bad developments as short lived, as a function of circumstance and the actions of others and not just ourselves, and as isolated events. When bad things occur, we accept them as a challenge to learn or do something. This is the basis of realistic optimism.

The differences between realistic optimism and Pollyanna-style optimism are striking.[21] You may have already found yourself in the type of sticky situation where the reckless optimist reassures us and tells us the problem we are facing is one we'll solve quickly and easily, and that it won't be a big deal. Everything will be okay in the end. That type of optimism is dangerous in my view. It minimizes the difficulties and reassures for the sake of reassurance without accounting for the complexity of a given problem. It glosses over the effort and difficulties that may lie ahead for people in undertaking what's being asked and in maintaining relationships that might be strained by solving the problem.

When such a lack of realism is added to our brain's propensity to, at the best of times, underestimate the intensity of effort and the time something will take, reckless optimists engender doubt and fear (especially if people have seen this before) and fail to ignite positivity in others.

Let's contrast this with evidence-based realistic optimism, which holds that mindless everything-will-be-fine optimism does nothing to help us solve problems.

Realistic optimism has several important qualities:

- It is grounded in the truth that the difficult challenges, tasks, or circumstances present.

- It highlights the need for planning and a sensible assessment, and for an understanding of the determination needed to deal with what lies ahead and what that means for the team.

- It demands that the problem be clearly articulated and never underplayed, and that team members are reminded of the hard work required to solve the problem.

- It prepares us for setbacks and disappointments, which are inevitable.

In sum, realistic optimism is an unwavering certainty and confidence that all concerned are up to the task and that they will be successful together based on a proven track record of accomplishment.

Leaders who practice realistic optimism retell true stories of how that very group, the one they are currently seeking to motivate, overcame previous obstacles, suffered setbacks, and ultimately succeeded. That's realistic optimism and it sets a tone for problem-solving.

"Tone-setting leadership" is a phrase often used by Olympic and professional basketball coach Jeff Van Gundy, the vertically challenged (especially so in a game played by giants) coaching mastermind whose transition to broadcasting brought an acerbically funny, wildly entertaining, yet generous and humane color commentary to that industry. I like that very focused label: "tone-setting." It says a lot.

If the tone you decide to go for is positive, like the tone adapted by André and Christian, you're on solid footing scientifically—and frankly, it just feels right. Negative consequences are not overstepped; they add gravitas and are true to the full human experience.

It seems to me that considering the right brand of optimism as a job requirement for leadership is natural. At the very least, the behaviors associated with positive leadership are a template for learning.

LEADERS UNDERSTAND THAT they signal decisions, confidence, and action with voice and use of language. How leaders energize others by the cadence in their voice and the way they frame their speech is the focus of the next chapter.

> **Taking Stock of Your Humanity at Work**
>
> As you answer the following questions about your people leadership practice, reflect on the impact of Christian McBride's positivity on those he interacts with in his profession, and how André achieves a balance between being positive and realistic.
>
> 1. Who is your positive force, the one who by virtue of their presence, voice, and smile radiate positivity? The person people are drawn to? Who is your Christian McBride?
>
> 2. Who is a leader whose optimism you admire? If you were trying to "learn optimism"[22] from them, what would be your takeaway from that individual?
>
> 3. How do you "show up" every day? How would your colleagues answer that question about you?
>
> 4. Stepping into formal leadership roles means people are watching. How might that serve you?

5. Do you agree that a leader with greater self-awareness will have a more productive team? Why or why not?

6. What might you try to move yourself along your self-awareness continuum?

7. In your role as team leader or colleague, how can you help those who are interested in becoming more self-aware in their work?

(5)
How Do I Want to Be Heard?

As REGIONAL ENTERPRISE business awards ceremonies go, this one was noteworthy. Prizes were awarded to recognize achievement in innovation, exports, environmental stewardship, etc. This year, a new award was given to a company whose commercial activities were attracting national attention. The Achievement Across Canada award recognized those employers who had a presence from coast to coast to coast, and who were often in the running for national recognition in their sectors of business activity.

The evening is typically a glitzy and exciting night for some companies, and for a small business, a nomination means substantial media coverage and an opportunity to celebrate success with staff and others. For the larger, more "institutional" employers, the occasion can have a perfunctory feel to it, but it is important for these business and employment mainstays to be seen supporting such events and lending credibility with their presence. Thankfully, in this region the larger and better-resourced employers understand their leadership role in inspiring, role modeling, and enabling small business.

A significant moment came courtesy of the "inclusion award" and its rather astounded recipient. This award celebrates employers whose recruitment efforts focus on underrepresented groups, such as visible minorities and persons with disabilities, and the promotion of women to nontraditional roles and senior management. The recipient's acceptance speech electrified the room when she advocated for doing away with the award. She challenged the assembled business, nonprofit, and political elite to change the conditions in their workplaces so that we will eventually (and preferably soon) stop celebrating inclusion and diversity because it simply becomes the way we do business. No quotas, special initiatives, or campaigns needed.

She implored the audience to look deep into their hearts and understand that as well intentioned as we may be, we are naturally encumbered with unconscious bias. She reminded us that our unchecked stereotypes are hurting people's access to employment. She urged us all to try harder to be inclusive as people, every day, and promised that our companies and workplaces would follow—no awards required.

The stage was now set for the much-coveted last two awards. We were about to hear from two star business leaders and we waited with anticipation.

"I am extremely proud of the corporation's many remarkable achievements and grateful to have been awarded this illustrious distinction," began the CEO who accepted the evening's most prestigious award. He went on to comment on his personal vision, plans, and strategies for the company; on the firm's stiff competition and the evolving market for its products and services; and on the fact that, as a national company, it was happy to have its head office in the region. He talked about how the transition from his previous international role had prepared him for these challenges, and how he was enjoying the opportunity. He closed his acceptance speech with an optimistic outlook for the company and a call for more public support for entrepreneurs. His final words celebrated the assembled business community and heralded the region as one in which to live and do business. The full table of middle and senior managers from the winning company smiled and applauded courteously.

The recipient of the runner-up award walked purposefully to the stage to accept the award on behalf of his company. This CEO was well known: celebrated by some, disliked by others, and known as a capable orator. He began, "We, and by 'we' I mean the thousand or so people and their families who are being recognized with this award... we're proud of what we've accomplished and so thankful to have been awarded this prestigious recognition." He went on to share his take on the company's future and how the "dedicated women and men" go about their work and enable remarkable results. He spoke glowingly about the business community and the quality of the people in the region. He then turned his attention to the table where his senior and middle managers were seated, telling the audience how the quality, grit, and high character of those managers were the reasons why the company was winning awards and why its stellar workforce continued to delight its customers. The CEO light-heartedly said that if it were left up to him to guide the ship, there was no way the company would be winning any prizes.

The CEO then singled out one person and her team as those largely responsible for the nomination, given their accomplishments in the past two years and the projects she had led. The CEO returned to the table to be met with hugs, handshakes, and much joy and laughter.

Who Gave the Winning Speech?

You might say that the differences between the ways in which the two CEOs characterized their companies could not have been more pronounced, but we should not overlook the actual similarities. Both CEOs had been successful in leading their companies to sustained profitability through sound strategy, mission critical change, and ongoing systems transformation driving the modernization of their businesses. Both of them had tasted success across the country from their head offices in the region, both had been long tenured in their roles (obviously meeting and exceeding their respective board of directors' expectations), and both companies had won awards in various contests, recognizing them as best places to work and best managed companies in the country. Both firms were market leaders and deemed highly successful.

Yet the speeches highlighted one glaring difference. One CEO spoke glowingly about himself and the exploits of his corporation, whereas the other poked fun at himself while celebrating the achievements of others and the company's enviable results. Both CEOs deliver superior results, but here is the question: Which CEO would you want as your manager?

The divide for me is that one CEO made no mention of his people while the other spoke mostly of his people. Otherwise they made the same points, and both did a stellar job. You could reasonably infer they used the same template for their address, yet one ingredient, *acknowledging people*, separated them. Only one used their voice to signal people elements of their individual style and correspondingly the company's workplace culture. This public celebration is but one small example of how leaders purposely use their voice to imprint their people vision on their organization and their communities.

The Sound of Your Leadership Voice

Since the publication, in 1936, of *How to Win Friends and Influence People* by Dale Carnegie, other experts have followed with books and programs on how to develop a leadership voice.[1] Leaders themselves can get advice from the contributions of some notable thinkers and practitioners to help them find their voice.[2] There is a physical dimension to developing your leadership voice: first, from the head, which determines the choices you give voice to, and second, from the heart, where inclusivity and intent take shape.

Technique: Use the Diaphragm

How we speak and project, our body language and body placement in relation to others, and our enunciation are very important.

The next time you attend live theater, notice how an actor's whisper, when delivered from their entire body and emanating from the diaphragm, can carry to the very back of the room. They are demonstrating a trained physical dimension of speaking that some leaders work on, too. Through training and coaching, leaders blend approaches to enhancing voice, presence, and performance from the stage and the world of the performing arts.[3]

In speaking, as in all aspects of our leadership practice, awareness is crucial. Try paying attention to what "voice coaches speak of... volume, pitch, pace, timbre, tone and prosody, which is the singsong rise and fall that distinguishes... a statement from a question."[4] Noticing it in others will help you detect your own tendencies.

The Choices You Give Voice To

I marvel at how leaders use well-placed humor at just the right moments and can dial up the gravitas when the situation calls for it. Authenticity and staying within yourself is key. Forcing it rarely works, in my view, but mindfully striking just the right tone in a variety of settings is a skill emerging leaders work on.

You've likely noticed how some leaders make measured judgments about when to make pronouncements and when to ask questions. They are intentional about when to speak about what is going right and what is going wrong. They weigh their words because they know others will weigh them and be critical of what they may feel has been left out. Leaders understand that they signal decisions, confidence, and action with their voice and use of language. For example, is their language inclusive (based in "we"), which has been shown to have positive effects on teams,[5] or is it self-reflective (based in "I")?

Emerging leaders should think about when to make their voice heard. Will it be before, during, or after their colleagues speak? Hint: Develop the sense to know when to apply all three approaches. They are all necessary, and if you are always the last or the first to speak, as the leader it has huge implications on your team. Being mindful is key.

When times are darkest, how and when a leader's voice is heard is critical to helping teams move through such periods.

The Inclusivity You Give Voice To
How does a leader give voice to the values of integrity, humility, and excellence? Leaders would do well to be very aware of their voice: does it discourage, disempower, and dishearten, or does it encourage, empower, and energize?[6] How do leaders help other voices to be heard above the din? What is it about a leader's voice beyond their words that is inspiring to others, that empowers and engages? How does a leader give voice to their intentions around learning, and make others stronger and better at what they do?

We know from research that a leader's relationship with a team member influences that team member's behavior, including their tendency to speak up. This requires leading intentionally to ensure that colleagues speak up when something is amiss, or that they speak without reservation, because the "silly" idea they had in the shower could be that one creative and progressive idea needed to move a project forward. We are all better served when leaders enable what researchers call the "employee voice" and give employees the confidence to speak—especially to people in power—about the good and, perhaps more importantly, the bad.[7]

Let's close this section on voice with the story of Kari and how leaders around her eventually emboldened her leadership voice.

Pay Attention to the Differences in the Way Your Team Members Think
One company I worked with had a weekly management meeting that, along with a standing agenda, typically dealt with a specific issue that needed a decision. These issues raised in the moment allowed little prep time for discussion, but still they would be debated and viable options kicked around until consensus closed the conversation. Or so everyone thought.

Usually, in a shared moment with the president the next day, a member of the team, Kari, would bring a fact from the debate into clearer focus while assessing the problem, or would suggest an alternate option that had been inexplicably missed by the group. Occasionally, she would punch an enormous hole in the argument and decision. As a consequence, the team would sometimes reconvene briefly or the item would wait for the next management meeting. If the item could not wait, the president would make the call, to the astonishment of the other members of the team who had not been privy to Kari's assessment.

This led one member of the management team to wonder why Kari couldn't just speak up during the meetings. Kari's colleagues, however, were displaying a common misunderstanding about the quieter ones among us, the so-called introverts who re-energize and think best in conditions of calm where they have time for reflection before giving voice to their thoughts. Kari's big brain ran on another gear than did her colleagues' intellect. They absorbed and synthesized information differently and quickly to arrive at what most agreed were refreshingly innovative ideas, solutions, and strategies.

You've likely already figured out what the team needed to do, but at the time less was known and talked about with regard to introversion and what a team needed to do to ensure that all voices had an opportunity to be heard. Unless a thoughtful person (I mean anyone, not just the formal leader) ensures that others' voices are heard, the debate or conversation just moves on and the process is poorer for not having included input from sharp minds that may have a different processing timeline than others. How can this challenge be addressed?

Pioneering authors like Susan Cain[8] have offered us much-needed understanding about how we miss out on the talent, ingenuity, and enormous contributions of highly talented quieter folks. We tend to give extroverts our ear. But ensuring all voices are heard is a leader's imperative. How leaders pull it off is another element that defines their leadership practice.

Team leaders who put the tenets of Susan Cain's "quiet revolution"[9] into practice do some of the following:

- Understand that introverts and extroverts communicate, problem-solve, recharge, and manage conflict differently. All team members (and our clients) benefit from understanding the differences and working with them.

- Operate from the perspective that all voices need to be heard. An example of this is within meeting contexts, where the team leader asks for input from all team members while reminding everyone that "passing" is both respectful and appropriate.

- Acknowledge that (as Dr. Tammy Carroll told me) introverts typically *think, talk, think*, whereas extroverts typically *talk, think, talk*. Team leaders who acknowledge these differences can shape their approach accordingly and make the environment more inclusive.

- Use all types of advance notice—agendas, advance reading, prework, etc.—to engage those who need preparation time before being able to engage in a group. Team leaders do well to remember that a great number of their folks need time to think and process.

I recall the wise words of a company president who had invited me to attend senior management meetings as a career development practice for my new role as an HR manager. Three meetings later, I'd not said a thing except to comment on my departmental metrics and progress on key initiatives. The president called me to his office to ask how I assessed my performance in the meetings

I said, "I keep waiting for HR issues, but there aren't that many outside the ordinary stuff we cover in our departmental agenda."

In turn, he replied, "That's because you're listening to the words and not their messages and their meaning. You have to listen for significance, deeper meaning, and intent. Be listening for the many signals.

"There are ongoing negotiations, expressions of disappointment, requests, concessions, olive branches being offered, resources being selfishly hoarded or irresponsibly shared, and everything in between. The people around that table are communicating all of those things on an eye-popping number of issues at any one time.

Our job is to pay attention and tune in to all of that in order to be able to intervene at key moments and bring our intellect to bear and in service to what we are all trying to achieve together. I don't expect you to see or recognize all of this undercurrent yet, but you need to be especially alert to the coded conversations these get-togethers enable every two weeks."

It became clear to me in that instant how nuanced and layered these high-level discussions were and how finding my voice would take time and practice. The president went on to remind me that every good idea can stand up to scrutiny. Ask questions to enable your voice to be heard.

AS WE HAVE discussed in this chapter, being inclusive and authoritative and authentic are key aspects of your leadership voice. In chapter 6, we will focus on the undercurrent of our work, and how by asking questions we get to the heart of purpose and meaning, because this is where deep connectivity happens.

Taking Stock of Your Humanity at Work

Advances in technology mean that today a leader's voice can be heard virtually and around the world in real time. We must awaken to the influence and impact our voice can have by consciously working at developing our unique leadership voice and diligently focusing on how we want to be heard. As you answer the following questions about your people leadership practice, reflect on the conversations I had with the company president and the wisdom that the president imparted about the responsibility we all have to speak, listen, and learn.

1. You use a workplace language in your role. Do you shift the way you engage your people depending on whether they are hourly workers, direct reports, senior managers, team members, colleagues, or associates? Is their role a factor in how you engage them? Should it be?

2. How would the people who know you best describe your leadership voice?

3. How do you ensure you hear from all the voices on your team?

4. When have you found it prudent to silence your leader's voice? When else might you consider being silent?

Connecting with other humans makes work meaningful. But as you will see in this section, when work benefits others, when work is connected to personal values, when its benefits extend beyond today, and when it strengthens the feeling of community, then work has even more purpose. The benefits of purposeful work for people are many, but if your people are overloaded or not directed to the right task, you must prioritize, and that's when the art of delegation comes into play. However, even the most super-organized of leaders must also be prepared to fight against distraction. Get ready to do some serious reflection on your productivity habits so you can stay the course.

PART TWO

Know the Course. Stay the Course.

(6)
How Can I Create More Meaningful Work for My Team?

"Have you ever worked on the plant floor in a fish processing facility?" the hiring manager asked.

"Well, not really, but I've supervised workers in a similar setting," replied the young man, nattily dressed.

"Did it smell?

"Not really. Actually, not at all."

That remark unhappily concluded yet another round of interviews with no promising candidate to fill a vacancy for a night shift supervisor in one of the region's largest fish processing facilities. The industry was facing many challenges, not the least of which was finding qualified and motivated workers.

Shift 3, from 10 p.m. to 6 a.m., only operated during the peak times of the season. Called the "back shift," it was the least popular work schedule but was the entry point to much-sought-after full-time positions that worked day and afternoon hours.

The shift 3 supervisor needed to be adept at instructing new hires, ensuring they were well trained and later thoroughly evaluated for promotion potential. In many regards, it was the most challenging of the three supervisory roles and the one that required the most understanding of the production jobs and the ability to connect with a diverse range of workers, from the inexperienced to the seasoned, some local and some foreign. Above all, it meant being a "training" supervisor while meeting production targets.

The ongoing shift 3 supervisor vacancy was creating real grief for the plant manager, who was of the third generation in the family enterprise. Business was good, so the task of finding workers went from challenging during any given fishery season to an all-out emergency when catches were landing at the height of their season.

The capacity to find and keep reliable workers in a volatile (referring to the perishability of product), seasonal, and contentious sector makes the difference between the ability of Maritime communities to survive or not. There is more on the line than the business interests of fishers and processors. These communities live and die on their ability to generate enough seasonal employment in hopes of keeping residents and attracting others with a more diversified local and regional economy. Otherwise, people leave, mostly for postsecondary schooling, and rarely return except for family vacations and funerals. These resource-based jobs in the fishery are not easy; conditions are sometimes harsh, the work monotonous, and the wages barely above minimum.[1]

Community-minded businesspeople in those seaside towns and villages, who are struggling to find workers, feel enormous pressure to carry on the family enterprise, and there is a sense that the future of their town rides on a handful of business leaders and other likeminded folks to figure the problem out. A lot is riding on finding good (arguably, "good fit") people. Finding them has a profound socioeconomic impact, which explains why these regions have a complicated and ever-changing patchwork of employment insurance regimes and economic development initiatives that come and go with changes of government in that part of the world. We need only look to the example of Newfoundland and Labrador and the collapse of the cod fishery[2] to understand the devastating socioeconomic impact the closure of a fishery can have on multiple generations.

The Kid from Away

"What about the college kid?" the shift 1 supervisor asked. He and the shift 2 supervisor often had to cover the third shift and wanted a new hire as soon as possible.

"How's that working out anyway, with his courses and a night shift job?" asked the plant manager.

"Great," they both said, spookily in unison. "The kid is juggling a full-time job and a nearly full load in university. He hasn't missed a shift, is always alert and productive, and seems pleasant enough."

"He's not from here, is he?" squinted the plant manager.

"Nobody's from around here anymore. We have six languages spoken on the shop floor instead of the two we've had for as long as I can remember. This place doesn't look or sound the same, and I think the kid might just be the type to make all that work. Besides, he's the same age as the younger workers, and that might help us better understand that bunch. We've always had the highest turnover and the most absenteeism from that late shift. We need a great supervisor that can handle the job and get absenteeism under control."

They had nothing to lose, so they went with the young, inexperienced supervisor. He had a positive attitude, was eager to learn, and by all accounts seemed to be handling his studies well. Within a few months, he was meeting the demands of a full-time supervisor quite well. With his credibility established, productivity was on the rise and absenteeism on the decline.

When the university kid was asked what he was doing that was proving so successful, he simply commented that he was just doing what he had been trained to do and what he'd learned from observing the other supervisors. The plant manager pressed the rookie supervisor to understand whether his former peers, and now his direct reports, had been a challenge.

"Nothing I can't handle," smiled the young leader.

The owners were delighted and a little perplexed. In their many years in the business, they had rarely if ever seen this kind of turnaround, let alone with an inexperienced shift supervisor.

Finally, after watching hours of video of the plant floor, most if not all of it inconsequential to his quest, one of the owners saw what he was looking for. And to think it represented such a small thing in relation to the hundreds, if not thousands, of tasks completed in a workday by any supervisor. To think that tweaking only that one thing, twice a shift, could have such a meaningful impact.

Connecting Meaningful Work and Self-Motivation

The focus of this chapter is meaningful work. So you will be thinking, "Pierre, I don't understand why you chose to tell a story about a fish plant. How meaningful can work be processing fish?"

Noteworthy scholarly work has been done on the connection between meaningful work and self-motivation.[3] The distinctions among people who view their work as either a job for financial gain born of necessity; those who feel they are part of a culture that enables achievement and status; and those who have a calling—whose internal drive to do something is so strong it can come at great personal sacrifice—are informative when attempting to create work that is deemed meaningful.

If there was ever compelling evidence that we derive very different experiences from our work, the "job–career–calling" concept is helpful. The caution would be to overgeneralize based on these categories. The assumption that "job" holders would pose a greater engagement challenge than those who consider themselves in a "career" or "following their calling" is tempting, but caution must prevail. Individual differences are much more important than characteristics we assign to groups or categories when thinking about engaging hearts and minds.

Achievement, ambition, and the quest to climb the corporate ladder—in other words, always reaching for a bigger role and more responsibility—are not motivating factors for a good many people. As some would suggest, we should simply meet folks where they are. The ambitious need our help and support to grow and develop, and those happy with their roles also need our support in their choices. So our role then becomes to help make them the very best at what they've chosen to do, and to inspire an element of curiosity to improve their processes and efficiencies, if not their job progression. Those times when people are or are not "in flow" with their work give us some insight into how to help create meaning and purpose for ourselves and others. There has been a lot written in the popular business press about the "why's" of working in the last decade,[4] and some of the best thinkers on the topic suggest we need to ask ourselves questions about meaning every single day in order to attempt to engage ourselves in our work. "Did I do my best to find meaning today?"[5] is a refreshingly simple question to help us reflect on a profound topic. That question could put us on the path of discovery for ourselves, our well-being, and the well-being of our clients and colleagues. The question invokes "my best" and implies that the responsibility to achieve it is mine, not my employer's, or at the very least that we share the responsibility. Harvard University leadership expert Ron Heifetz thinks about meaning this way: "Some sources of meaning are rare; much depends on the talent, opportunities, and experiences that come our way. There is, however, at least one source available to each of us, at all times, in all circumstances. People find meaning by connecting with others in a way that makes life better.... The sources of meaning most essential in the human experience draw from our yearning for connection with other people."[6]

Connecting with other humans makes work meaningful, but there's more. When one or more of the following four factors are in play, work can be truly meaningful: when it benefits others, when the work is connected to one of your personal values, when the work and its benefits extend beyond just today, and when it strengthens the feeling of community in others.[7]

The Continuing Saga of the Kid from Away

The owner-cum-detective had been yearning for a chance to share what he discovered about shift 3 and whether those improvements were scalable and transferable to other business units of the family's considerable holdings.

"That's it?" one of the family members and recently retired production managers exclaimed at their monthly shareholder meeting.

"That's it," replied the lead investigator and first cousin of the person asking the question.

"We're getting all this sustained positive movement on all the critical metrics and KPIs on the back shift, and you're telling me it's because the kid is imitating the Walmart greeter?"

"Pretty much," replied the sleuthing co-owner.

"Do we train our supervisors to do this?" asked another.

"Nope. The kid either stumbled onto this or he's sneaky smart and figured out that the best bet for making our United Nations of a workforce work well was to keep driving relentlessly for production as we always have, but consciously or unconsciously he is making the shift more collegial and friendly. But there's much more to it than saying it's 'friendlier.' Remember, some of the workers come from a very different tradition where having a laugh, making eye contact, and even smiling on the job could land you in hot water with some employers in their homeland. People are saying that things are better and different, and that the kid is all right."

"'All right' is high praise, coming from some of our folks. What's the supervisor doing exactly that has us so impressed, besides significantly outperforming the two other shifts?" asked the patriarch.

"Within the first forty-five minutes from the start of a shift, the kid has checked in with everyone in a brief one-on-one at their work station or by bumping into them elsewhere. And this, of course, is after they've had their five-minute standup meeting at the beginning of the shift. Another thing: the supervisor is always around the staff entrance at shift start and shift end.

"The kid makes it look completely random, not like he's methodically going down the production line to chat with everyone. It's much more subtle than that. It may form part of a larger management by walking around (MBWA) strategy that became in vogue years ago, but there doesn't seem to be any rhyme or reason to it. And it's well after his daily safety tours. But while doing other things or en route to other parts in the facility, he works in a quick chat with each person on the crew. Then he does it all over again in the last hour of the shift. Maybe twenty seconds or a minute with each person. Of course, there are other interactions during the shift as always, but this 'greeter' behavior is new for us, a behavior I would have discouraged back in the day because we would have been accused of wasting our time and the workers' time."

"What exactly are they talking about when the supervisor does the one-on-ones?" asked another. "Is it personal or business?"

"It's both, the kid tells me. We talked about it. It's briefly personal, but it's mostly about seeing how the employees are today, if outstanding issues have been resolved, if they have what they need for the day and if they are clear on the day's production priorities and their tasks. The best part is what happens at the end of the shift. Remember, the kid tells the employee how glad he is to see them at the beginning of the shift and then thanks them individually at the end of the shift, while making sure everything went okay that day. If there's a problem, he listens intently and follows up the next day with a solution or a message that a solution is in progress. The kid tells me he then says he's really looking forward to seeing the person the next day and urges them to take care of themselves and get some rest."

"It sounds like he's just being nice to the team," said one shareholder.

"Yep, seems awfully basic, but I would never have thought to do such a thing when I was a supervisor," said yet another recently retired family member and shareholder. "Too scared it would impact production negatively."

If you were to ask the rookie supervisor why absenteeism is down, he would tell you he has a great bunch of workers on his team. The truth behind that refreshing humility is a style that is centered on one of the most important unspoken elements of our "contract" with our employer—that human connection is ingrained in the employment relationship. What the young supervisor was doing was going directly at the problem. He looked each team member in the eye near shift's end and said, "I look forward to seeing you tomorrow. It's gonna be another productive day just like today. See you then!"

What a novel idea. How do you stifle a stubborn absenteeism problem? Begin by explicitly telling folks you'll see them tomorrow and then validate their decision to come to work somehow, in this case with basic human decency and an attention to making real connections with folks. But that's only a beginning.

Absenteeism is a complex indicator that stands out as a significant sign of the health of any organization. You don't fix absenteeism. You fix all the things that create the conditions that allow absenteeism to flourish. We know working conditions have a direct impact on the incidence of people calling in sick when they're only "sorta sick," and researchers have highlighted the importance of improving working conditions in an effort to reduce absenteeism.[8] While some contributors to absenteeism are systemic, a key contributor is the quality of the most important relationship you have at work, the one that has a huge role to play in whether your employment experience is positive—the relationship with your supervisor or manager. The quality of the relationship between supervisor and employee impacts a lot of things, absenteeism among them.[9]

Other relationships at work can be consequential and may incite some employees to stay home instead of reporting for duty when they're not "feelin' it," but for the most part your direct reporting relationship is the one that significantly colors how you experience your job.

Do I believe a "see you in the morning" acknowledgment between supervisor and employee, followed up by deliberate steps to connect with that same person over the course of a workday, will solve unpleasant employee behavior or productivity issues? I'm not sure I would go that far. There's a lot more work to do, but that type of positive pro-social behavior sets a tone and lays the groundwork for a foundation that enables leaders to build healthy relationships and consequently productive workplaces. Understanding that many people on our teams are driven by a longing to make a human connection should inform our understanding of how people work, what motivates them, and most importantly how meaningful work matters.

Meaning in Work

We know that human connection in the workplace can create meaning. Leaders can create those connections as well as foster an environment that nurtures that connectivity. But another critical component of finding meaning in your work is seeing a long-term benefit to it, especially when it benefits others.[10] Let's examine a government agency that connects personally and professionally with its clients.

The Atlantic Canada Opportunities Agency (ACOA) is Canada's economic development agency arm of the federal government for the four "have not" Atlantic provinces of New Brunswick, Nova Scotia, Prince Edward Island, and Newfoundland and Labrador.[11] Together with provincial partners and other economic development actors, ACOA loudly touts diversification and promotes business growth for small and medium-size enterprises (SMEs). Under the energetic and recent presidency of Francis McGuire, the agency is building on a more than thirty-year track record of assisting businesses to be more competitive, innovative, and productive.[12] The agency champions growth, invests directly, convenes stakeholders, and helps clients build relationships that advance their SMEs' interests.

That success of ACOA clients is thanks to the ACOA program officers who work relentlessly to support business owners' efforts and their life's work. For many ACOA clients, a lot is riding on their risk of being in business. The up close and personal relationships these program officers have with their clients are at the heart of the agency's ability to support the region's entrepreneurs. But what if you're a head office ACOA staffer, positioned hundreds of kilometers from your SME client? You have no direct contact with the client, who is but an electronic file on your computer screen. Can that staffer derive the same meaning from enabling the SME as their local program officer? ACOA thinks so, and here's how it can work.

In many organizations, it is institutional practice to showcase their clients. ACOA has done just that over many years. Inviting the client to meet staffers whom they usually never meet has a huge impact. This can be live and in person, or facilitated by using the myriad platforms technology provides. I wonder if the masterminds of this practice appreciate how profound "putting a face to the name" can be. One ACOA client shared with me how they always knew there was a "bunch of bureaucrats" at head office backing up their generalist regional representative. Eventually, having access to more specialized expertise from ACOA headquarters—in their case, expertise in exporting to new markets—and especially getting to know the person virtually through video conferencing was central to their ability to navigate the complexities of first-time exports for a small manufacturer.

Some suggest leaders can enhance meaning for their teams by taking a comprehensive or holistic view of what team members need to know to help them create meaning.[13] This means thinking about what people *want* to know to give their work meaning and not just what they *need* to know in order to complete their tasks.

Terry and Kathy Malley are life and business partners and award-winning ambulance manufacturers who apply such a holistic approach. The Malleys have this to say about creating meaning for their folks: "Our manufacturing people love hearing about sales, customers, what we're up to, things they don't hear about in their work. And they want to hear from us." That realization gave rise to the Malleys shutting down production several times a year and having a big chat in the middle of the production floor—talking not about production but about the future, obstacles, and their clients. Their staff can't get enough of this type of interaction. It connects them to something bigger and makes them feel proud.

The Malleys have figured out the relationship between meaning and an engaged, resourceful, and productive workplace. Harvard business professor Teresa Amabile and developmental psychologist Steven Kramer drive this idea home with the central point of their exquisitely researched book *The Progress Principle*: making progress on things that we find most meaningful is the most engaging thing we do at work.[14] Our work as people leaders is to discover what is most meaningful for our employees and to enable progress on that part of the job as much as operationally possible. That requires having ongoing conversations with folks and it means being intentional about creating meaning.

THE BENEFITS OF having purposeful work to do are many. But that goal can go sideways if your people are overloaded or not directed to the right task. That's where your ability to prioritize and delegate comes into play, as we'll explore in chapter 7.

> **Taking Stock of Your Humanity at Work**
>
> Our work as leaders is to help create those connections to meaning, whether the client or person who is ultimately benefitting is nearby or an ocean away. As you answer the following questions about your people leadership practice, reflect on the success of ACOA's approach of enhancing meaning by "putting a face to the name."
>
> 1. What is the one thing you do in your work that makes time fly because you enjoy it that much? Answer the same question on behalf of your direct reports or someone you work closely with. (Be careful. We tend to project our own take on such things on others and assume everyone is just like us—they're probably not!)

2. When you try your best to find meaning, what exactly do you do?

3. Does the question "Did I do my best to find meaning today?" resonate for you? Why or why not?

4. Do you typically outline goals and objectives when declaring your intentions or do you share the meaning, purpose, and values that underpin your goals?[15] What is the difference in the impact of these approaches?

5. How might you try to enhance people's sense that their work is meaningful?

(7)
How Do I Assess My Ability to Prioritize and Delegate?

MADELEINE'S ORIENTATION PROGRAM for new hires was legendary. Her shop handled the back office for all of the HR responsibilities in a ten-thousand-employee firm. The human resources department supported the efforts of a team of recruiters assigned to various areas of the business. The company was growing, so the many units needed people in a variety of occupations, and this required well-documented recruitment files as appointments were subject to appeals, requests for access to information, or deeper scrutiny given the strict licensing regulations under which the company operated.

In contrast to contemporary onboarding programs that focus on socialization, Madeleine's process concentrated on efficient personal organization practices. Madeleine's lessons on prioritization, time management and delegation, the need to focus on deep work, and the role of collaboration to get projects done on time and on budget would influence newcomers throughout their careers. Although the tools would evolve and change with technology and personal preference, the iron-clad principles she imbued in new hires would often alter the course of a career.

Separate the Urgent from the Important

Madeleine proudly came from the administrative and executive support world. She held a degree in office management and had done post-graduate work. During her tenure, she had witnessed and taken part in the greatest-ever changes in office productivity and automation.

She would describe in some detail the "hustle and bustle" that awaited the team most days, and the management team every day. "It's crazy busy here, except when it's even busier than that," she loved to say. She took enormous pride in leading her shop so that daily activity targets and improvement initiatives were front and center in everyone's world. Her unrelenting focus on helping people improve set her apart from other managers.

Madeleine's observation that managers are busy every day is consistent with current science on the workplace. Renowned Canadian scholar and author Henry Mintzberg puts it this way: "Study after study has shown that managers work at an unrelenting pace; their activities are characterized by brevity, variety, and fragmentation, and they are strongly oriented to action."[1]

What we learn from Madeleine's "crazy busy" lesson is consistent with understanding the perpetually demanding pace of a leader's role. Her solution to the problem of excessive busyness was to proclaim "Here's your Eisenhower matrix"[2] as she pulled out a brightly colored laminated 8½" by 11" sheet of the thirty-fourth US president's famous tool for quickly assessing the difference between tasks that are important and tasks that are urgent, and what to do after you've determined what's what. (As you have guessed, there's an app for that now!) "We use that language a lot," she noted, "because every request we receive is deemed 'urgent' by the client. It's not, so we have to parse out 'urgent' from 'important' in order to establish a timeline, allocate appropriate resources and re-juggle the whole thing frequently. If everything is urgent, then nothing is urgent."

Madeleine would say, "Given that your job has this many hours of interrupted time in a day, ask yourself what can you realistically get done before you go home."

She would urge people learn to say no and negotiate priorities, as they would be pulled in many different directions from time to time. And yes, Madeleine would remind folks that there would be times when overtime is necessary.

She would then explain her version of Pareto's Law (also named the law of the vital few), where 20 percent of activities generate 80 percent of results and value. She would challenge her new hires to work with their manager to figure out the 80/20 of their job as soon as possible.

"Creating value" was Madeleine's mantra. She would take any new hire, but especially the ones destined for leadership roles, and would drill them on the need to create value by removing activities from their work that do not add value, undertake tasks and activities that add value, and invent new activities or tasks that also add value. She would then talk about quality and everyone's collective responsibility to improve the quality of products and services and workplace efficiencies.

Her next step would be to remind new employees how their recent training and experience were enviable and beneficial, and how their take on things—especially in the first few months—could be incredibly helpful for the company, its people, and its clients.

Some of Madeleine's lessons took years to take hold with those she had onboarded, managed, or mentored. She wasn't perfect, and her flaws, like everyone else's, come through when she leads boldly. She was fierce but concerned, assertive and nurturing, and demanding as hell while managing with flexibility and compassion before those words were being used to describe leaders. People willingly went to the wall for her, and not once but often and over years.

I see parallels between Madeleine's wisdom and the work of David Allen, author of *Getting Things Done*. There are many notable time management, personal productivity, and priority setting experts quite worthy of our attention, yet David Allen's work about clearing the mind and engaging to get things done really stands out for me. Like many contemporary personal productivity thinkers, Allen contends that setting priorities is critical but woefully insufficient on its own. He argues for meticulous capture of to-do thoughts and ruthless ongoing decisions about whether something is actionable or not, which then enables rigorous trashing, referencing, and task planning. I love his advice for creating trusted systems for retrieval and especially reminders to set our minds at ease by reassuring us that at any given time we are working on the right thing and are confident the oodles of other things to do are captured, scheduled, and under control. We are then free to work on something without worrying about not working on something else.[3]

Remember how fresh, shiny, and new things look when you take on a job with a new employer? Madeleine would have loved the assignment that engineer and CFO Doug Milton gave to new hires in his tenure in the gaming sector. He would insist people carry around a notebook and record all their impressions for thirty days. It was a complacency-busting exercise for Milton. After this break-in period, he would remind his new hires that all things become normalized, so we stop seeing aspects of our surroundings as new or different. Organizations have a wonderful opportunity to garner insight from those who come from away and share with the employer things that appear different or interesting. Milton also believed that rereading our own first impressions after some time has passed can incite us to address things we have become complacent about. When Milton first sprung his notebook assignment on me as a freshly minted HR person, I thought it was silly. Decades later, the brilliance of that seemingly insignificant process is glaringly evident. Want to honor the perspectives of your new recruits from the jump? Want to keep things moving by renewing and improving? Insights like these from fresh sets of eyes are pure gold.

Madeleine taught a way of being with regard to time, organization, and commitments, and left the technical choice of which tools to use to her charges. She mandated protecting and optimizing one's time, and talked about booking working meetings with oneself to "be thorough" long before it became de rigueur to investigate deep work opportunities. Consider how placing the work where it belongs through thoughtful delegation and ensuring the work is being handled by those best positioned to be challenged and complete the task checks off several very important boxes:

- ✓ Underutilization of your capability (and others' capabilities) is avoided.
- ✓ You are freed up to undertake more value-added work.
- ✓ Colleagues are provided with interesting and challenging problems to solve.
- ✓ Delegation results in identifying those who can step up to gradually assume more of your functions.[4]

Manage Distraction

With deep work comes the recognition of the value of focus and the need to protect yourself from distractions. Executive coach and author Marshall Goldsmith puts it this way: "[We] seldom plan on distractions. We plan as if we are going to live in a perfect world and be left alone to focus on our work. Although the state of being left alone has never happened in the past, we plan as if this nirvana-like world will surely exist in the future. We get down to work without accommodating the fact that life always intrudes to alter our priorities and test our focus."[5]

The extent to which we are susceptible to distraction is equally fascinating whether it is due to our impulsive nature, our incapability for self-regulation, or a need for instant gratification.[6] All three of these pitfalls stack the deck against us, especially if we don't control our environment to the extent we can in order to reduce the triggers that surround us.

Managing (eliminating) distractions clears the way for focus. Recent science once again validates that, in every instance, people who concentrate on a few priorities at a time outperform those juggling more priorities.[7] The challenge is to make the right choices of what projects to focus on, to the exclusion of other projects. If we don't get that right, even if we do great work we're potentially solving the wrong problems, which leaves high-priority items in a state of incompletion.

What does science tell us about how many priorities we can manage? If you allocate a project to your shortlist, it signals the importance of the item to your direct reports and to the organization overall.[8]

The approach of maxing out at three to five individual or (organizational) priorities[9] at any one time has a lot of supporters, and with good reason. It should also be said that the practice of carrying a larger number of priorities receives, let's say, lively criticism from credible thinkers on the topic, such as, "A leader who says they have ten priorities doesn't know what they are talking about. They don't know what the most important things are."[10] In other words, "having ten priorities is the same as having none."[11] (Communicating your priorities to a select group or team and being crystal clear on the priorities of that same group is hugely recommended and is a topic we will explore further in the next chapter.) The obstacles to focusing well boil down to a top three: maintaining too many priorities; having bosses who believe the best approach is piling it on; and giving in to distractions, digital and otherwise.[12] If left unchecked, those three hurdles will sink your efforts to bring your best to work every day, so a plan is needed. Our upcoming leadership habits conversation in chapter 8, including how to say no without sinking your career aspirations, will help you clear all three hurdles.

The Art of Delegation

One of Madeleine's favorite topics when welcoming new managers into the fold was delegation. She created value by coaching those in management roles to delegate projects ever downward to stretch teams to exercise their critical thinking and decision-making skills. The payoff was that teams rose to the occasion, were enriched by the experience, and believed the company valued them more. In the meantime, their manager was free to focus on higher-value activities.

It appears that Madeleine's way is the exception, not the rule. Eli Broad, entrepreneur, philanthropist, and the only builder of two Fortune 500 companies in different industries, famously said, "The inability to delegate is one of the biggest problems I see with managers at all levels." Why is this so?

In my pre-workshop needs assessment surveys, attendees express concerns like the following:

- "It's easier to do it myself than to organize it, explain it, and monitor it." (This I understand, but let's be clear that you're a manager, not an individual contributor, and delegation is your best hope for accomplishing your goals.)

- "I like to have things done my way." (Yes, but you're a manager, so it's not about "your way" anymore but rather about setting standards and helping others reach those standards.)

- "My staff will resent the additional work." (Yes, but you're a manager and negotiating, adjusting, and fine-tuning workloads and expectations through delegation and other means *and* helping your folks do the same is the job.)

- "My staff expect me to be the problem-solver and decision-maker." (Do they really?)

Madeleine grew up as a fan of Ken Blanchard and his pioneering work in situational leadership.[13] She is among countless others who have used his framework to inform their delegation efforts and teach it to new managers.

Blanchard's compelling notion is that as leaders we are always trying to move people through the directive-coaching-supportive-delegation cycle (see Table 7.1) in hopes of having as many team members in the delegation phase on as many processes, projects, and initiatives as possible. Even a team member who is eminently dependable needs a directive approach for new work. So the cycle is ever in motion, but the bottom line is that you are always attempting to lead people to be independent and resourceful critical thinkers.

TABLE 7.1: THE DCSD CYCLE

APPROACH	CHARACTERIZED BY...	IDEAL FOR EMPLOYEE WHEN EMPLOYEE HAS/IS...
DIRECTIVE	Tell style. One-way communication.	No experience and marginal know-how.
COACHING	Tell & Question: One-way communication, then a series of questions to engage the employee.	Some experience and know-how.
SUPPORTIVE	Questions only. The employee simply responds to a series of questions, elevating confidence in both parties.	Moderate level of experience and knowledge, but is still building confidence.
DELEGATION	Follow up and monitoring.	Fully capable of leading the initiative.

The following questions will help you understand some of the things you need to be thinking about before delegating:

- Does your task list runneth over while your staff or team members seem to have some give in their task list?
- Is the work being pushed down to the person who is best capable of doing it, or are some highly skilled folks doing low-skill work?
- Does your manager delegate well to you?

- Do you have a trusting relationship with a consistent pattern of honoring commitments with someone to whom you can delegate?

- When thinking about the right person to delegate to, do you think about not just who is *able* but also who would benefit from a particular assignment? How might it serve them with respect to their growth and development?

- Do you have the stomach and the patience to let go and watch your charges make mistakes, all the while understanding that the buck stops with you and that you are ultimately accountable?

- Do you think about clear levels of authority and clear boundaries when considering how to delegate to one of your team?

- Are you thinking about checkpoints, check-ins, and measurable milestones to help you avoid "not under leading and not under managing"?[14]

- Are you thinking about outcomes and results and not your process or your way of doing things?

A few more thoughts on delegation before moving on:

- **Delegation is potential for growth:** Leader delegation affords growth for the leader and each team member, and can be career changing. A failure to delegate will stunt your team.

- **Keep people in the know:** Employees are constrained by their lack of information in matters of delegation. Managers and supervisors have a lot of information in their heads that must be passed on to delegate well.[15] Those who keep their people informed on a regular basis are more successful in their delegation efforts. In the extreme, deliberately keeping information from people is not only detrimental to delegation, it can be rightfully called workplace bullying.[16] Managers and supervisors who constantly focus on keeping their folks in the know have a smaller hill to climb when delegating.

- **Self-awareness and delegation are linked:** Master delegators learn to surround themselves with people who have skills and strengths in areas where they do not. But that raises the dicey issue of knowing our strengths and our weaknesses—in other words, being self-aware enough to know where our gaps are in relation to the job at hand. As if we needed yet another argument for building self-awareness at every turn, here is another one. So, unless we truly know our gifts, we need to turn to psychometric testing and the feedback that teammates can provide to enhance self-awareness. Master delegators understand this and, equipped with that information, surround themselves with people who complete their skill set. It also takes a fair dose of humility to hire people who are stronger where you are not so strong, but think of all the learning that ensues and how much more effective the team becomes. Getting to this point as expeditiously as possible is key to delegation excellence.[17]

- **Clarify and communicate your delegation intent:** Is your plan to delegate born of your need to carve out time and space for higher-order and greater-value tasks? Is this purely a development exercise for a promising member of your team? In both cases, you will act as a mentor and hold the person accountable while being a sounding board as you both experiment with different approaches to delegation. Being clear with the person on why you are choosing to delegate and how you hope to go about it can be extremely helpful. All delegation carries a degree of risk. Ask yourself these questions: Is the person up for it? Do they have the skills and confidence? Are you able to let go? What is the impact if the project or task sputters along or fails? It is easier to take the chance when a solid, learning relationship is in place and intentions are clearly stated upfront.

- **Find tools that work for you:** Access training and technical delegation resources[18] to build your delegation capability. I really like Linda Hill's "Prep-Do-Review" approach.[19] The very name elicits the three key roles you as delegator must play: "Prep" represents the upfront work of sharing information and working with people to strengthen certain competencies, and speaks to the fact that there is pre-work involved before formal delegation takes place. "Do" signals who will perform the work. Is it the team leader doing the work, shadowed by the employee? Is the team leader doing the work with the help of the employee? Is the employee doing the work with the team leader shadowing? Or is the employee doing the work on their own initiative? The "Review" segment of the process is where the learning really happens, where mentor and mentee debrief, replay, ask questions, assess, self-assess, and reassess.

- **Match skills to the job:** A leader can put delegation at risk by jumping into the process without the requisite preparatory steps or by not having the best match between employee skills and job requirements. Frustration will result, and it is unnecessary. Compare this scenario to a deliberate and thoughtful exercise that, for all the reasons we have mentioned, is successful.

- **Problem-solving is a team activity:** There is something to be said for having the people with the problem become the people working on the solution, as Ron Heifetz often intimates in a variety of ways. My take is that when delegators become facilitators who guide colleagues to become involved in problem-solving, especially when those problems impact them directly, they are on the right path. Facilitating and teaching others how to tackle elements of a problem, or the problem in its entirety, is the leader's role.

IN CHAPTER 8, we will meet Rachelle Gagnon, whose story shows that daily habits (even though they are good ones) and super-organization can be assaulted by any number of circumstances. It is necessary to be prepared for anything.

Taking Stock of Your Humanity at Work

Delegation can accomplish so much, for employees who are building careers, managers who can do higher-value work, and the company whose culture speaks to its people and values. As you answer the following questions about your people leadership practice, reflect on the importance of prioritization to Madeleine's success.

1. Which one of Madeleine's time and priority management insights listed here resonated for you the most? Why?

    i. Your time is a valuable resource worth zealous protection.

    ii. "Crazy busy" management roles is the norm.

    iii. Optimize your time by delegating work to the right people.

    iv. Distinguish ruthlessly between urgent and important.

    v. What a team leader chooses to identify as a priority and place in their calendar sends strong signals to others about what is important.

    vi. Place a cap on priorities (three to five).

    vii. Aggressively manage distractions for yourself and your team.

    viii. Deciding on the few priorities is just the beginning.

    ix. Follow up!

(8)
What Are My Leadership Habits?

I F YOU TOLD a shy, retiring teenager who loved to frequent the school library that she would one day be vice president of administration of an Atlantic Canada–based financial institution with brokers and clients across North America, you might wonder what her response would be. Even today, Rachelle Gagnon will evince a degree of disbelief, but this belies the character and work ethic that has propelled her career.

Admittedly, being reserved and finding solace in a library are perhaps not reliable predictors of anything, certainly not of professional success, but Gagnon will refer to her affinity for books and learning when she speaks about her career. She frequently tells her story to young women and girls.

Gagnon began her career with the Assumption Mutual Life Insurance Co. in human resources, where, progressing to a middle then senior management role, she was greatly respected for her high degree of organization and for achieving results. She guided Assumption through successful recruitment efforts, and the company's achievements spoke to its policies, programs, benefit offerings, and so on being best in class. Her work received public recognition when Assumption was named one of Canada's best employers.[1] Gagnon radiated positive energy, a lot of which she devoted to community involvement.

It wasn't surprising that she was offered a vice president's role, but the fact that it was completely out of her area of expertise startled some within the company. Her challenging role as VP of administration involved overseeing claims, which are highly technical, contractual, and legal aspects of the insurance business. This intricate work with policies, customers, and the company's network of agents across Canada entailed a complex and constant learning curve. Understandably, highly specialized claims staff speculated about Gagnon's proficiency, coming as she did from the world of HR. But let's dive into her background and see what it reveals.

As a rookie in HR, Gagnon had put up her hand at an organizing meeting for a local chapter of a new HR association. She wound up guiding that association locally and provincially as its president and then moving on to other roles at the provincial and national level. But that success was in HR, where she was knowledgeable, experienced, and confident, and she admits that this new role in administration made her apprehensive. After all, who wants to be known as an example of the Peter principle—to be promoted to your level of incompetence and fail in public fashion at such a senior role?[2]

But Gagnon was not one to run from risk. She forced herself to do a weekly reading in church to overcome her fear of speaking in public. Most important, though, was her approach to learning her craft through community volunteerism. Gagnon's university business studies had been complemented by volunteer work in the same way that she nudged her university-age daughters into volunteerism. Now, she looked once again to community work to hone her ability to be an active and engaged board member, learn how to chair highly productive meetings, and master having difficult conversations. She understood the subtle art of influence and persuasion that all leaders need to be great at whatever they do.

Let's add into the mix that she juggles a busy home life against demanding professional roles and a busy life of public service, plus devoting time to being with her siblings and their families throughout the year and on most weekends in the summer to enjoy life at the shore. Did I mention the Gagnons like to travel as a family? She takes regular vacations as well. How does she pull it off? Some would call her a superwoman. She disagrees.

The one thing Gagnon knows she can count on, the one thing that has never let her down, are her habits around organization and systems. She believes that being on top of things is imperative to her success and that of her team, so systems matter and tools matter. But habits matter most of all.

One of the more interesting revelations from Gagnon was her statement that she was "somewhat undisciplined." I wasn't expecting that. How could someone so intent on a high degree of organization be undisciplined? This personal reflection gives credence to Daniel Levitin's observation, "[W]e have to trick ourselves or create systems that will encourage us to stick with the work at hand."[3]

Gagnon, like many of us, uses certain tools from her digital office suite, and contrary to the common preference for carrying around an entire office in a small handbag nowadays, she prefers a bulkier paper-based agenda, tasking, and follow-up mechanisms. She blends, as I observe so many well-organized leaders do, up-to-date tech-enabled tools with time-tested paper systems. She swears by her system and encourages her direct reports to adapt it or use whatever will work for them. Rachelle admits to having a great memory but relies on her system for recall. If her daily and weekly habits with her system are intact, she's on top of it, follows up with amazing consistency, and has the mechanisms that keep her priorities and tasks front and center.

The argument is that if these habits become, um, habitual, they become nearly automatic, freeing up necessary brain power to solve more complex problems. But are systems and habits sufficient to deal with the complexities of our work today?

Multitasking: The Blight of the Contemporary Workplace

Multitasking is a charade. It gets us nowhere. Researcher Ron Friedman notes, "Chronic multitaskers—those of us who can't help but read emails while talking on the phone, for example—are especially prone to experiencing boredom, anxiety and depression."[4]

Switching between tasks is expensive as it taxes our precious and finite neural resources. The brain is built to do one thing at a time and to stay on it until the work is done. We are deceiving ourselves by thinking that fast switching can be done without paying a price. McGill University's gigging musician turned professor of psychology and behavioral neuroscience, Daniel Levitin, put it this way in his 2014 book about the organized mind: "When people think they're multitasking, they're actually just switching from one task to another very rapidly. And every time they do, there's a cognitive cost in doing so.... Even though we think we're getting a lot done, ironically, multitasking makes it demonstrably less efficient."[5]

Some jobs are legitimately laden with switching. I've marveled for years at top-notch CBC radio hosts I have worked with who switch in the flash of a red recording light from one topic to another that is completely different, drawing from their impressive breadth of knowledge, then applying their journalistic sensibilities, and also going in a matter of seconds from one emotional state to another when shifting from story to story and from one guest interviewee to another. I see leaders do this as well, and many do so with ease, moving methodically from one demanding task to another, but clearly, as with my esteemed radio colleagues, this is after much training and practice. They are *not* multitasking. They're progressing purposefully from one task to another—finishing, then moving on in rapid succession.

I get that we have information overload, and so we multitask as much as we do, tricked into thinking it helps. Plus, we get a shot of dopamine that is like a ray of sunshine in our brain every time we multitask. Levitin puts it this way: "Multitasking creates a dopamine-addiction feedback loop, effectively rewarding the brain from losing focus and for constantly searching for stimulation from external sources."[6] We get a short-term benefit every time we squander our focus. And our brains really like those benefits.

Our electronic devices are delivery systems for opioids our body manufactures naturally. Levitin advises that we are better off enjoying cannabis than multitasking. Pot causes less cognitive loss in the moment than multitasking does.[7] Multitasking is the enemy of focus. When focused, you get more done and you're less weary when you're done. The absence of focus hurts our ability to problem-solve and impairs creativity and innovation. The argument I get all the time—"You just don't understand. I have so much to do!"—is precisely the reason we need systems that trick us into maintaining our focus and all the requisite aids to keep us on task.

Conquer Email Overload through Batching
Want to feel like you've done a day's work in just a few hours? Want to eliminate one of the single most corrosive habits our endorphin-dispensing technologies have foisted upon us? Try beginning your day with the most challenging thing you must do today, and avoid email. The sense of accomplishment that comes from making progress or completing a high-priority, high-value item and the momentum it creates sets up a positive start to the day.

The link between frequency of checking email, which produces anxiety and stress, is well documented. Checking email less frequently reduces stress.[8] Instead of checking email sporadically, set up a time to check it and put this in your calendar. Also consider having a set time to check phone and text messages.

I liken moving to an email batching mindset as the same thoughtful sequencing we all use—with hopefully much less deadline and efficiency pressure—when planning our Saturday (or whichever morning) routine for acquiring provisions. Think of your thoughtful sequencing of your outing. You probably cluster and aggregate those tasks to certain parts of town where they can be accomplished together to save gas, time, and energy. What if you practice batching on something that isn't mission critical, like your errands, and then build that discipline and muscle to resist the urge to check your email constantly? A colleague who wisely uses the function in their calendar to book fifty-minute meetings (never sixty-minute meetings) or twenty-five-minute meetings (never thirty-minute meetings) then uses that five or ten minutes left over for quick email checks, and never does so more frequently unless the work requires it.

Focus Tricks of the Pros
Tech entrepreneur and chief technology officer for hire (and monster jazz bass player) Simon Gauvin, who sold the mobile platform he created based on his PhD research, delves deeply into his latest project on screen for forty-five deliciously uninterrupted minutes, then tunes and plays his six-string electric bass guitar for fifteen minutes, has a quick bio break, and returns to the work. He explained to me that getting just beyond the forty-minute mark is his target, and then he engages the other side of his brain, leaving him refreshed to get back at it. He can maintain the 45/15 loop all day with stretch, bio, and replenishment breaks. People who manage their energy well are aware of the restorative power of breaks and other pauses the body and mind need to function at high capacity.

Alternatively, the so-called Pomodoro technique of alternating twenty-five-minute blocks of focused concentrated effort with five-minute breaks of free time has its adherents.[9] These techniques trick us into focusing for an allotted time.

Unplug to Focus
Now, wouldn't it be great to have a little voice in our ear reminding us to stay focused at those times when our ability to stay on task wanes? Uninterrupted periods of quiet and concentration are more difficult to justify to those who equate being busy with being productive, but the benefits are incontrovertible. It is your job as a people leader to know that periods of deep concentration bring value and meaning to people's work.

Unfortunately, contemporary office layouts are not conducive to helping us concentrate. That's why we take work to a nearby coffee shop or even home, where we can concentrate. Although workplaces are being designed and redesigned with collaboration (and cost reduction) in mind, people like computer scientist Cal Newport of Georgetown University suggests knowledge workers require access to a distraction-free workplace in order to add value.[10]

People are taking a hard look at their internet use as a leading distraction. No wonder folks are experimenting with internet sabbaths (one day off per week totally unplugged from all technology) and internet sabbaticals (unplugging for longer periods of weeks or months). Also increasingly popular are internet batching, where professionals batch all internet usage in specific time blocks through the day; company-wide email-free afternoons or meeting-free Mondays or appointment-free Thursdays; and the practice we have already discussed of booking meetings with yourself.

We also know that an effective tactic is to schedule your priority tasks in your calendar instead of on your to-do list, to ensure you provide yourself with an adequate block of concentration time.

Daily Success Habits for You and Your Team

When Martine Savoie, director of human resources for the burgeoning city of Dieppe, New Brunswick, took me on a tour of the new municipal office building, I was struck by the planning calendars that were visible in all of the areas where people gather. City council meetings and other relevant information were noted on the calendars. Martine explained, "Our citizens are our priority, but our focus is always a function of when our city leaders meet. Having everyone in the building focused of those key outcomes supports that we are here to provide the best advice and information to our elected decision makers on a predictable schedule."

Martine went on to say that keeping meetings front and center enables city staff to plan better, avoid major scheduling conflicts, and most importantly smooth out the work for staff in a more predictable and routine way, creating space for the unexpected demands on city officials that inevitably arise. While the tactic may seem simple, it is one that has deep meaning. Our brain tricks us into believing we have all the time in the world to get things done.[11] The planning calendars enabled city staff to begin to see time differently, to emphasize that time is finite, to see patterns that can assist with forecasting and thoughtful planning.

While we are on the topic of calendars, let's note that we should all use time tracking to constantly improve how we manage ourselves and our energy, which leads to efficiency.

Tracking where you spend your time from week to week is extremely helpful in figuring out the nature of your work, where you bring the most value, and how you might improve your use of time. Remember the 80/20 rule? Some stuff just needs your attention every day, regardless. How you work that into your daily habits is a personal approach, but it is vital. Here are some key ways to do that.

Build a Dashboard, or Build a Better Dashboard
A daily dashboard diet gives you a snapshot of the most important metrics and key performance indicators (KPIs) that are relevant to the health of your business. Leaders must know the numbers regardless of their role. It role models for others the value of measurement and elevates data as the driver of our decision-making.

Improvement numbers, sales performance against targets, budget updates, market share, production stats, turnover, absenteeism, balanced scorecard results, and recent employee engagement results are examples of data you have at your disposal. What you must decide is which three to five factors are the most critical and are those you should have at your fingertips every day. (This needs to be a quick daily hit. Analysis and problem-solving around the numbers is something else, but a daily diet of numbers sets you up nicely.)

Mark Symes, one of the founders of the wildly successful organizational design firm Symplicity Designs, describes his early love of improvement numbers, and the value of making them visible and an ongoing topic of conversation. A forester by training, he tells the tale of breaking tree-planting records as a teenaged crew supervisor by posting the numbers and specifically the requisite improvement numbers for his team on the open back doors of a beat-up Econoline van. He would hold early-morning and late-afternoon talks about improvement and getting the numbers moving in the right direction. The planters loved it and they consistently beat their own records.

Symes explained to me how those early experiences shaped his philosophy of "measuring to improve" and not "measuring to prove." Measurement is meaningful and much easier to digest for those whose work is being measured when it's clear the focus is on helping them improve, not prove their worth.

Learn to Say No
Repeat after me: "*No.*" Practice saying the word, absent of any emotion, aggression, or ill will. It will protect your focus, sanity, and time. Experts suggest we say no in low-risk situations to build up that muscle. Rachelle Gagnon learned the skill of saying no to the unimportant requests that would compromise higher-value work.

We want to be "yes" people, saying yes to opportunity, learning, and career-building possibilities. By our nature, we like to be optimistic and to please others. But we cannot be all things to all people.

My take is that we need a comfort level in saying no, a rehearsed easy automatic phrase that is at the ready for a spontaneous request for help. Here's a technique that can serve us well:

- "I'd love to say yes, but I can't, and here's why...."

- "You know I want to say yes, but I'm not able to, and here's why...."

- "Thanks for asking, and in another instance I would say yes, but I'm afraid I have to say no. Please let me explain."

We spend lots of time training for and generally encouraging collaboration in our workplaces, and with good reason. However, we also have excellent science on the importance of selective collaboration—in other words, the need to be more discerning when asked to participate in collaborative efforts.[12] (A meeting is a collaborative effort; or should I say, at their best they can be.)

According to global researcher and respected workplace soothsayer Marcus Buckingham in his superbly researched book *Nine Lies About Work*, we can be a part of and contribute effectively to no more than five groups, projects, or teams.[13] Five even sounds high, but how we define groups and teams will differ. If you are actively a member of more than five groups, projects, or teams at any one time, Buckingham argues it is a recipe for ineffectiveness.

Focus on and Communicate a Few Priorities
If you've worked with a team in which the leader is unclear or indecisive about the team's priorities, or if priorities are constantly changed or are not talked about much, you know first-hand the confusion and inefficiency that result.

An effective people leader is

- ✓ always assessing and carefully reassessing the key priorities of the day, week, month, quarter, year, and beyond, in some roles;
- ✓ making the right directional choices, setting aside all the temptations and distractions that beset a team;
- ✓ keeping the list of priorities short for themselves and their people to facilitate focused, high-quality work and successful completion of projects and tasks; and
- ✓ bringing clarity to daily tasks and expectations.

Leadership Habits to Nurture Well-Being

Authors and researchers have been attempting to get us to slow down in order to be more productive and achieve more, but the change is counterintuitive for many of us and may raise questions about what it means for our practice. Won't I lose my edge? Can I rebuild the momentum? Will people think I'm less committed? When I first met Mario Allain, he did not take vacations. He ran and grew his specialty construction business FundyPros to the largest of its kind in the province. Allain leads with intensity, enormous dedication, and drive. As the business grew, he put capable people in key roles and then decided the best thing he could do was start taking vacations and watch his people grow.

His slowing down, if only slightly, would give his senior people a chance to flourish, but tearing himself away for a few days was no small feat. The temptations of staying connected tugged at him, and the first vacation or two of gradually increasing duration were more stressful than being on the job!

Allain became more adept at getting away. He's the better for it and he'll quickly tell you, as he told me, that his people and the business are the better for it. FundyPros continues to grow and thrive, and Allain is as committed and engaged as ever, and maybe more so because he has incorporated slowing down into his practice as a leader and business owner.

Techniques to help us slow down can take only seconds and may be effective at any time, but they're especially so when we feel overwhelmed. One technique is pause, prioritize, and refocus. *Pause*: Breathe in, breathe out, and repeat as needed. *Prioritize*: Look at what's really urgent or important in the moment that is the best use of your time. *Refocus*: Devote time to one thing.[14]

I've noted while attending management meetings recently that the chair begins by having all participants take a deep breath and enjoy a moment of quiet to clear the mind and be thankful to be in the presence of thoughtful, well-intentioned, and capable people. This practice is becoming widespread in workplaces, and rightly so. Many employers, like New England's not-for-profit health benefit provider Harvard Pilgrim Healthcare, are offering short meditation recordings that can be downloaded by staff and members of the public to their phone or desktop to allow for a quick reset, after which they resume work with vim and vigor!

Positivity can be felt and appreciated only when people slow down.[15] I believe the movement towards mindfulness and other contemplative practices in workplaces signals a quest to insert a bit of time and space in our day to deal with the often frantic pace we experience.

The stress management and wellness benefits of mindful meditation are now widely understood, and the shift towards a holistic approach to thinking about health, safety, and well-being by employers is overdue and welcomed by both HR professionals and their accounting counterparts. Employers are motivated at least in part by reducing costs related to health benefits and insurance. That's fair play. And there are always legitimate productivity concerns related to incidents of short- and long-term absences, so for employers to be supportive of the most inclusive definition of a healthy workplace is simply good business. Thankfully, employers are playing a leadership role on issues of mental health, specifically depression and anxiety, not only within their companies but also within the broader community. One has only to look at the work that Bell Canada has done with Let's Talk, the telecommunications company's annual campaign to destigmatize mental health issues. It's a shining example of how improving the health of employees can have a broader societal implication, albeit with commercial considerations.

Daily Rituals

We all bring little habits to work, habits that open and close our workdays. One of the clear signals we benefit from at the end of our day is a "shutdown ritual" that tells our brain that any unfinished business (our brains like thinking about unfinished things) will be done tomorrow.[16] Some folks make a grand motion in shutting off the lights or in placing their chair just so as they leave their work station, while others utter a ceremonial phrase to end the day. For others, the signal is a change of clothes at home or an activity that clearly signals the work is done.

There are accounts of Rolling Stones drummer Charlie Watts always placing his drumsticks just so, at a specific angle on his snare drum to signal the end of his night's work.[17] It's been reported that in the excitement of the end-of-show curtain calls, and leaving his kit too quickly, he'll sometimes double back while leaving the stage for the last time to adjust the sticks. Some speculate this act has a spiritual component, others that it signals a heightened attention to detail; either way, I think it's his end-of-work ritual.

ONE OF THE reasons I wanted to tell Rachelle Gagnon's story was to highlight how she takes on the demanding role of a senior leader apparently without feeling the burden and weight of a hugely responsible position. It is refreshing to witness someone's habits enable them to view the mountain of challenging work that awaits them and say to me, "It's fun, bring it on!"

Rachelle Gagnon has thrived in her non-HR VP role. She began a two-year exercise of flattening the division, offering opportunities for managers to swap jobs for six months as a cross-training initiative, and using her fresh status as a non-expert to ask thoughtful, silo-busting, and forward-thinking questions. After the initial two years and many structural, process, and management changes in the division, a period of relative calm was ushered in, allowing for the integration of new ways of working. At the time of this writing, Gagnon has changed roles once again and is overseeing the group insurance side of the business. The former HR professional is now going to tackle sales and marketing and more.

In the meantime, Assumption continues on a successful path in the hypercompetitive insurance and financial services sector. It successfully transitioned to a new CEO in 2018 and distinguished itself by being certified as a B Corp, a certification that promotes the triple bottom line: people, profits, and the planet.

IN PART THREE, we discuss building leadership within the team. As we shall see, fundamental to this is giving feedback; rewarding and recognizing people for their achievements; and setting the right expectations so that they are realistic and perhaps even ambitious, but never self-defeating.

Taking Stock of Your Humanity at Work

When I asked Rachelle Gagnon, who was now more than three years into her VP role, how she had pulled it off, how she had averted the Peter principle, and what she had learned through that process, she was effusive in her praise for her CEO, the management team, and the people on all of her teams, many of whom she had hired in her previous role. She was also quick to emphasize the systems she created that have turned into the leadership habits that enable her success. As you answer the following questions about your people leadership practice, reflect on Gagnon's organizational habits and how they have served her well throughout her career.

1. Which elements or aspects of your personal organization serve you well? How could they serve you even better?
2. How do you fulfill your daily dashboard diet?
3. What helps you say no? What's your go-to phrase?
4. On a scale of 1 to 5, how would you assess your ability to stay focused on a task?
5. On a scale of 1 to 5, how would you assess your team's ability to stay focused on a task?
6. Do you make it a regular practice to mentor your team on daily success habits?
7. Do you insist that your people take their holidays?
8. What are your opening and closing daily rituals?

The practice of delivering effective feedback or intervening more strenuously is at the heart of part three. And foundational to this is a leader's ability to focus on goal-setting and setting clear expectations. Although feedback is crucial to instilling a learning mindset, fueling innovation, and fostering improvement, many companies fall down on this essential aspect of teamwork and collaboration. This section will help you determine how effective you are at communicating feedback, both positive or negative, and why it's imperative to get good at doing it if you want people to become self-reliant.

PART THREE

Awakening the Leader Within Your People

(9)
Do I Set the Right Expectations for Myself and the Team?

THE EXECUTIVE VICE president was a rocker. Not a Led Zeppelin kind of rocker (although he was a fan), but the kind of rocker who, while standing in place, in a line, or with a beverage in hand, would rock gently—toes up, toes down, heels up, heels down, backside in, backside out. They have special shoes for that kind of thing now, but Thomas would use his pointy and freshly polished shoes *du jour*.

Early every morning, folks would find Thomas gazing at the vista from the twentieth floor, coffee in hand, rocking gently. Depending on the tides of the world-renowned Bay of Fundy and the season, the view of the Petitcodiac River could be nondescript or spectacular. Being "from away," Thomas would rock as he marveled at one of Mother Nature's gifts that the locals drove by, around, and over without giving it a second thought. Those who worked on the twentieth floor would wander over to Thomas as part of their morning routine.

"*Salut*, what's going on?" Thomas would ask. For others, he would begin with "*Allô*. See the game?" Then, after praising the Montreal Canadiens, win or lose, Thomas would eventually ask his colleague what was on their agenda for the day and would sometimes inquire about their family. This was all good-natured good-morning banter, or so they thought. Thomas frequently spoke of his past failures and poked fun at himself, which made him vulnerable in front of his folks. It had ingratiated him with the team.

Thomas was attentive to people and things. Everything he did, he planned out, especially when strategy and tactics mattered. The rest of the time, he was simply mindful of his surroundings, sensitive to the energy of those around him, and intentional and authentic in all his dealings.

Thomas was a savvy senior manager, who in his few short years with the company had fulfilled his mandate: to energize and revitalize the management group, help the brand-new CEO change course for the agency, and bring some rigor and discipline to the management group. He had led projects, teams, and eventually entire business units in defense contracting, the chemical and paint business, and food processing. He talked a lot about projects that went well, always parsing out planning from execution, and painstakingly teaching his team of managers the importance of a good start in any type of initiative. He reminded his crew, "You never have to make up for a good start," and he valued the "fresh starts" that author Dan Pink writes about.[1]

He loved that built-in bounce that came with the fresh start of the day, week, month, fiscal quarter, hockey season, dandelion season, or flu season. Reigniting people's energy was important to Thomas. He introduced "sprints"—borrowing the IT developer term for short bursts of intense activity with ridiculously tight deadlines to bring small initiatives into being in days or weeks instead of months. Staff loved the momentum and specialness of the "sprint." Thomas, however, was judicious in his use of the approach.

He spoke a lot about purpose, the alignment of the company's mission with top-line objectives, and goal setting. He set out his expectations front and center, frequently revisited them, and insisted managers do the same in their departments. He worked quickly from a plan and stated objectives, and was the best follower-upper his management team had ever encountered. To be on "Thomas time" was to be ahead of schedule: early to work, early to complete projects, the first one to get things in. . . .

Thomas's penchant for following up assertively had been tagged as micromanagement when his soon-to-be direct reports had done a bit of reconnaissance work on their new manager. He wasn't in fact a micromanager—not by a long shot—but he knew which questions to ask of anyone in his division. He knew the numbers and understood processes, and this knowledge enabled him to ask the uncomfortable questions a leader should ask about the intricate running of an operation. (We'll talk more about what constitutes micromanaging and consider its insidious impact in chapter 13.)

His initial set of expectations upon taking the job, which the team had bristled at, was what they labelled "Thomas time," which meant you might as well set your watch ahead by ten minutes because, with Thomas, if you arrived right on time, you were already late. If you arrived last, you were expected to entertain the group with a poem or song. (Trying to be punctual—and always early and never last—became a game that infused joy and camaraderie. It also established timeliness as a core value that spoke to respect of others' time.[2])

His team had several relatively new managers, so Thomas assiduously differentiated activities from goals, a distinction that was sometimes lost on the newbies. There was also a robust process for highly productive two-hour management team meetings that served as a model for others in the company. The management group met bi-weekly with a standing agenda and rigorous attention to ensuring their meeting process worked for everyone. Thomas also met with each member of the management team every week.

With Thomas, like everything else in business, every meeting had to have a clearly articulated purpose, so people's meeting objectives were clear and roles were understood. Each item in a meeting was assigned an action point, as either (1) for a decision; (2) for your input; or (3) for your information. (And yes, sometimes an item initially identified as one thing morphed into another, but that was okay if it was the will of the presenter of that item.) There was room and encouragement for spirited, organic discussions to happen. Decisions were made and items were often taken offline to optimize the use of everyone's time.

The role of chairing the meeting rotated among members of the team, with Thomas chairing only once every seven weeks. The ever-rotating chairs learned to facilitate, knew their place, and were strong when they needed to be as facilitators, but they gave others the floor on matters of substance.

Then the day came for Thomas to move on. The team was sorry to see him go, but he had prepared them well for his departure. In their first bi-weekly management meeting without him, the acting executive vice president, a colleague—and until Thomas's departure an equal to her assembled counterparts—asked if everybody thought they should continue the morning standup meetings in the kitchenette on the twentieth floor. There was a silence in the room until, one by one, everyone realized what had been happening all along. Every morning, within the space of a matter of minutes, Thomas had held several one-on-ones, one-on-twos, and one-on-threes or fours. Sometimes the entire gang of seven was gathered together. Quietly and serendipitously, Thomas was validating, coordinating, and bolstering people's focus on purpose, key divisional priorities, and individual objectives and daily activities. It was so loose, so conversational, so "Thomas," his team thought they were having a coffee together, and they were, but they were also being set up for success. The team agreed these informal meetings should continue. The captain may have left the wheelhouse, but he ensured the mechanisms were in place and instilled leadership and management habits in his team that kept the ship on course.

Goals, Alignment, and Outcomes

During my many years of helping managers overcome issues that led to problematic team performance and behavior, it was startling to me how many of those instances of subpar performance or problematic conduct occurred because team members were not clear about what was expected of them today, this week, this month, this quarter, or this year. Boundaries were not set to define accountabilities; behaviors were not described to govern activity. The process, action steps, and outcomes were not aligned. Folks may start out well intentioned and with some understanding of what is expected of them, but then everyone gets busy and conditions change. When a leader fails to check in, projects go adrift.

Thankfully, some people do ask, speak up, and inquire with their team leader so that they are not making assumptions as to what they are required to do. Without a leader's clear direction, people will fill in the blanks.

Goals are the language of business and organizational life. We speak of goals and objectives that are strategic, operational, or tactical, or that focus on innovation and learning and development. We speak of goals that are SMART (specific, measurable, agreed-upon, realistic, and time-based);[3] or big as Everest[4] and hairy;[5] or, from management's early writings, something you manage by.[6] More recently, we have been speaking of goal-setting systems like sophisticated OKRs[7] (objectives and key results), the new darling acronym of the goal-setting set.

Achieving goals requires that everyone is aligned to what is strategically important and really adds value, and what must be done to delight clients. Perhaps our greatest fear as team leaders, owners, and managing partners is that everyday busyness—all that work we see every day in our workplaces—is not aligned to our purpose and our larger goals and objectives. All that busyness does not equate to value, productivity, or success.

Achieving goals also requires that those goals are realistic. Setting poorly considered, badly designed, and unrealistic goals will confuse workers and cause them to disengage, especially those on the front line. And if there are no goals whatsoever, outcomes may be worse.

No wonder misalignment keeps people up at night. Well-intentioned hard-working people doing their very best at a task when the purpose is not clear or the right tools have not been provided to them is one of the great wastes of our people talent that we must guard against as leaders. What is the solution?

Connecting Goals to the Real Work

The cascading of goals is an activity that organizations use to create alignment. Larger organizational goals are broken down to roughly equate with the number of layers a business has. Divisional goals are broken down into departmental goals. Managers break them down for their departmental people, who in turn break them down to the front line of the organization. The theory is that the cascading exercise provides the alignment that is so critical.

Marcus Buckingham and Ashley Goodall, in their recent book *Nine Lies about Work*, argue that we're better served by cascading meaning and purpose than goals.[8] I agree. Providing a context as to why goals are important and a purpose for focusing on them as guiding lights of our work makes imminent sense. This context provides an anchor for goals workers co-create with their managers, which is much more valuable than the broader context of an organization's overall goals.

This is not to argue against the value of moving goals through a company. Quite the contrary, it simply raises the question of what the leader's work is during that critical exercise. Mechanically pushing down a series of SMART goals, as brilliantly as they may have been formulated, may not serve up the sizeable benefit that effective goal setting can deliver.

For a leader and employee to arrive at a mutual accord on clear, achievable, deadline-driven expectations takes work and is a great beginning; but relatively speaking, it's the simpler piece.[9] How those two people will then join forces to work towards the employee's success, and what role each will play in the monitoring and assessing of progress, is where goal setting comes alive.

Resistance is likely when the process of goal setting, tracking, and evaluation is static and distinct from the fluid flow of daily work, and especially when it is part of an administratively driven performance review mechanism or strategic planning process that lacks the appropriate connections to the work.

Contrast that with goals (daily, weekly, monthly, quarterly—whatever makes sense for the situation) that are at one with the work;[10] that are integrated into a management approach, style, and systems that are living and breathing; and that frame virtually every weekly coaching conversation, management meeting, and project initiative.

Thomas's favorite questions were, "Are we adding value? And are we doing so in a way that helps us reach our objectives?" In time, these queries were imitated by many others in the company. Thomas used those questions to put the never-ending choices managers make in allocating their focus and resources and those of their team into a larger context of value and objectives. He instilled in his folks a concern for how everyday actions added value and advanced their larger priorities

That kind of goal setting, when central to the conversations, communications, and daily stream of what we do, can galvanize commitment to making progress on what matters most.

Thomas was the type who would connect those dots during the team's morning get-together with comments like, "Your remarkable work on the client relations file connects to our corporate goal of community engagement well beyond our usual client base, and that broader role is what the founders of this company had in mind."

I hope you have someone on your team who is inspired to achieve a goal simply because it's there. It's the equivalent to mountain climbing for these folks. The power is in the goal itself. They love striking tasks large and small off their lists. Others need to connect a goal to something bigger to contextualize the work they are being asked to do. They internalize the goal, accepting it as their own. People leaders sensitive to this reality are always seeking out specific examples in their employees' work and using those moments to connect the task to larger objectives and ultimately to purpose. Leaders who employ this type of commenting style seek to build a through line between the individual's work and the company's raison d'être. It is foundational work for people leaders, and it's the best outlet for examples and stories.

Finding the right combination of complexity and volume that potentially propels each worker into a flow state is our shared objective. Working with staff to find the "just right" level is a combination of trial and error, constant communication, and a willingness to nudge the person beyond their comfort zone to facilitate learning and engagement. "Set it and forget it" doesn't work in goal setting.

Objective setting and virtually all other aspects of our leadership practice benefit greatly when we provide rich examples and stories to bring our expectations to life. You needn't be a gifted storyteller to lead, but the ability to provide examples is paramount. And wrapping the examples in stories that compel people's attention, curiosity, and learning is a skill well worth developing.[11] Objectives have the potential to carry that motivational, focusing, and action-inspiring quality right off the jump, but only when they're thoughtfully crafted and when we generate the essential data needed to fuel robust monitoring of where we stand against the target. Be they the goals we create for ourselves, the ones we co-create with our team, or those we establish for our entire organization, committing to making them central to our work and to how we manage and improve is the key.

A Retreat Tactic for Better Goal Setting

Serial entrepreneur and highly sought-after entrepreneurship coach Ray Hebert conducts an annual goal-setting retreat at a hotel within an hour's drive of his home. With flip charts in hand, he locks himself away with his business for a goal-setting session for his business and personal pursuits. He emerges with clarity and a short list.

He's not alone in employing a grand gesture to inflate the objective-setting bubble from which people emerge with a greater sense of purpose and with a manageable number of SMART objectives broken down into practical pathways[12] or specific action steps. Organizations of all shapes, sizes, means, and purpose seek out a variety of settings that will serve as the backdrop for a retreat where, distanced from the contained chaos of the workplace, they can find the quiet for reflection and the perspective needed to bring people together around a shared purpose and objectives with action plans that will guide their progress. Getting away from the daily din of the familiar helps put people in a different frame of mind. Patterns are broken, greater learning is possible, and team building is often an intended consequence.

Shared purpose does not in and of itself transform a relatively small group of folks with different but complementary skills into a team. However, add goals, some ideas on how to achieve them—and, oh yeah, for the high-performing ones, a climate where holding each other accountable is a met expectation—and voilà, a team is born.[13] No goals, no team. Great intentions, great people—not a team.

The Link between Self-Awareness and Goals

The relationship between self-awareness and goals is a healthy one. People who are self-aware typically know where they are going and why.[14] Of course, we all want people who can figure things out on their own and intuit what needs be done and jump to it, but Thomas would remind us to be vigilant. It is precisely when people are resourceful—able to divine what's expected of them and find the resources they need and get to it—that we sometimes go to sleep on setting expectations. "They'll figure it out on their own" is a risky assumption opening the door to misunderstandings that can lead to some nasty surprises. Tempting though it may be to leave people to their own devices, even those who are self-sufficient and seem to know (sometimes before you do) what needs to be done still need the value-added activity of agreeing on the why of what's expected and applying some SMART rigor to the process. Remember, it's not enough that employees know what's expected of them; the real work is in how you then collaborate to ensure their success.

Why Fairness Matters

Some goals, standards, and worker expectations are not negotiable. Agreeing upon those types of objectives is more about the *how*. Ideally, it involves recognizing the value of engaging the employee in what they can improve to consistently meet and exceed expectations, and determining how the supervisor can best support those efforts. Explaining the reasoning behind the immovable or non-negotiable objective is critical. People are more likely to agree to the objectives and make them their own if they perceive the method used was fair.[15] Even better, when fairness is present and people grasp what's expected, office politics wane, preferential treatment subsides, and people can concentrate on the work.

My take is that we set an important tone in how we negotiate goals and objectives, especially the non-negotiable ones. Thomas invoked fairness often: "Is it fair to all concerned?" he would ask, citing one of the Four-Way Tests from Rotary International, the global service network.[16] He was an advocate of beginning any negotiation with "All we're looking for is for what's fair. I'm sure you're looking for the same." That sets a tone.

Expectations and Self-Fulfilling Prophecy

People live up (or down) to the expectations that are set before them.[17] Thomas had a painful example he often told of how challenging it was to get expectations just right and how he still had regrets about a situation from years before. Essentially, he had set someone up to fail by levelling expectations that were right for the job but not right for the skill set of the individual. That person deserved expectations that were in keeping with their learning curve. The young Thomas had learned that expectations or objectives co-created with direct reports need to take into consideration the complexity of tasks, quality requirements, and speed of execution when arriving at metrics, targets, and standards. Setting expectations for an employee is ultimately about meshing the established job standards, requirements, or quotas with the capability that the individual presents at the time of setting objectives.

Thomas, a SMART goal fan, hammered away at the "R for realistic" component a lot. He felt it was the most important aspect of goal setting, and that it had oodles of significance because it was really about trust.

Thomas loved European football—the *real* football, he would tease. He would quote people like Sir Alex Ferguson, legendary manager of the Manchester United Football Club, who said, "Setting realistic expectations and communicating them clearly... to bring a team along with you ... is one of the hardest leadership skills. It is easy to brim with enthusiasm, establish unattainable goals and leave everyone feeling deflated if the targets aren't achieved."[18]

Setting realistic goals means getting down to tactics and the task level, and understanding how much elasticity needs to be built in to respect present circumstances, including the employees' skills, marketplace conditions, and other internal or external factors that fair-minded people would enter into the calculation and definition of a specific objective. Stretch goals—those that are ambitious and get people to extend their limits—still have to be realistic and reachable. Setting aspirational goals that are unrealistic such as arbitrarily increasing sales quotas in a declining market for a product or service, will set a sales team up for failure.

When I think of stretch goals, I think of a game of tabletop hockey, in which each player is only able to skate along the vertical groove cut into the table. You control the speed at which the player moves and spin the player to shoot the puck. The player cannot move outside its dimension.

Contrast that to the way real-life players move on the ice. They have complete freedom of movement and, as their skills develop, can stick to or deviate from their assigned positions and choose to ignore passing and skating lanes that are assigned to them. Imagine thinking of your team as tied to their role and position with only slight predictable movement from where they are versus the enormous potential presented by live skaters capable of diverging a little or a lot to make a play. If you approach your group with the latter in mind, your objective-setting process, especially in areas of learning, can unlock enormous potential. But be careful: if you stretch the goal too far, something will break. Unreachable is not realistic.

Thomas spoke of goals as "the stuff perseverance is made of." He encouraged breaking goals down to the daily task and activity level in order to create the best climate for employees to persevere and be tenacious in accomplishing their objectives. Among the qualities he looked for in new hires were tenacity, perseverance, and grit.[19] Science validates grit as a predictor of productivity and effectiveness.

Thomas felt these qualities, combined with a role the person found meaningful and coherent goal setting, were a recipe for successful job performance. He advocated working hard at monitoring the progress of goals with regular high-quality data and celebrating mini-triumphs along the way, or having the conviction, gumption, and humility to change course when needed and adjust expectations while recalibrating objectives as required.

Thomas pressed his team to invoke legitimate meaning for the employee when speaking of goals and objectives. He claimed that co-creating SMART goals is much easier when we have an employee's interests and strengths on the front burner, together with the knowledge of what is really important for that employee to achieve individual progress along with operational objectives. He would often exclaim enthusiastically, "And you're really good at that!" after reviewing an objective that was in line with what someone did well and not so coincidentally enjoyed. When objectives are meaningful to the person, everybody is off to a great start.

Lastly, Thomas would speak very much from the heart about the realistic expectations leaders needed to have for themselves. Perfection was off limits. With notable and very limited exception, the standard was "excellence." That's perfection less 5 percent or 10 percent because objective setting for perfection, he believed, was fundamentally unrealistic, unattainable, and guaranteed to discourage and disappoint.

How We Work Together Is the Most Powerful Tool

Setting goals is how we set and raise standards, and is one of our core functions as a leader and manager. But working hard at co-creating objectives and task-centered work plans does not guarantee success. How team leader and employee work together is key to goal achievement, learning and development, and productivity. SMART improvement-focused objectives are where it's at, especially when they are properly aligned with something bigger: strategic and operational priorities, something in the business plan, anything that provides context for your area's objectives.

Co-creating objectives is a tone-setting activity. Setting objectives is one of the first things we do with new staff, so the impressions we leave with them are substantial during onboarding. As the employee learns and grows, look to put the emphasis on the "co" in *co-creation*. Objectives and expectations are so much more valuable when written by the employee and fine-tuned with you.

Let's take an example. You've just returned from a workshop you expect will be very helpful in your new role as a front-line manager. This is the first time you attended such a session under the guidance of your new leader, so upon your return you are looking forward to debriefing the workshop with your manager. You knew before you left that you would have to lead a twenty-minute mini-workshop at the next management meeting to share and teach three specific actionable takeaways. But you weren't expecting how thorough your new manager would be in ensuring the transfer of knowledge. She has four very specific questions she wants managers to answer to ensure the learning that takes place is shared and folks are accountable for changes in their behavior. She wants to see results based on the investment that was made in the learning. Her questions are:

1. What did you learn (i.e., what are the specific takeaways)?

2. What behaviors should I, as your manager, look for to indicate that you're doing things differently?

3. What are the outcomes that you and I should be looking for based on what you've learned?

4. What are the indicators that will enable us to know whether or not you accomplished the objective of transferring what you learned in the workshop to your job?

Through discussion, you agree with your manager that the SMART objective coming out of this learning experience is that you will now hold weekly check-ins with each of your employees. The longer-term outcome should be signs of better employee engagement based on data generated by tools like employee engagement surveys. Lastly, there will be indicators based on absenteeism and productivity after implementing the weekly check-ins to see if a targeted increase of X percent in productivity with a Y percent decrease in absenteeism is reasonable. The questions that will guide this activity are as follows:

- Is the objective specific? (Yes: It's about weekly check-ins.)

- Is the effect objective measurable? (Yes, both in the short term in the number of weekly check-ins and in the longer term with some of the metrics that have been identified.)

- Is the objective attainable? (Let's assume this is a "yes" based on past experience.)

- Is the objective realistic? (This question asks you to examine your ability to make the changes to your work schedule to accommodate weekly check-ins.)

AN IMPORTANT ASPECT of how we work with one another is feedback: the kind of feedback, how it is delivered, and what it is meant to accomplish. Employers fall down on this essential aspect of teamwork and collaboration. It is the subject of chapter 10.

Taking Stock of Your Humanity at Work

Thomas ran a tight ship, with a focus on clarity of goals and providing the right support to enable his people to reach them. Yet he also brought an aspect of humanity to his role as leader—a vulnerability and a recognition that *perfection* was not in his vocabulary. As you answer the following questions about your people leadership practice, reflect on Thomas's leadership and why he was able to inspire his people to do well.

1. When you think of the people you work with, do you think of yourselves as a team? Have you been brought together as a group of individual contributors to do similar work and report to a common team leader? Or are you part of a truly interdependent group—your objectives are dependent on other people meeting their objectives and collectively a group of you are striving towards a larger objective together?

2. How important to you and your team is purpose, alignment, and goal setting?

3. Do you regularly set and revisit expectations for yourself? For your team?

4. How often do you think about the language you use to define and describe expectations? Have you changed your language over time?

5. How might you seek clarity when expectations of you are ambiguous?

6. Do you offer your team the opportunity to take on stretch goals?

7. How might you teach the co-creation of performance objectives?

8. How do you ensure that objectives are realistic?

9. How do you know if you have your expectations for your direct reports just right?

10. What happens daily to ensure and reinforce alignment between your organization's larger goals and your tasks? What about the tasks of your front-line workers?

(10)
How Can Receiving Feedback Well Make Me a Better Leader?

YOU ARE CORRECT to expect that a chapter on feedback within a book intended to make the lives of team leaders better would focus on *giving* feedback. We'll get to that, but let's begin with a foundational skill you can easily work on to make giving feedback easier, even when it's negative and you (like anyone) find the conversation difficult.

The skill is that of *receiving* feedback well. This is easier said than done, but first let's look at feedback generally before looking at this particular skill.

It is understandable that people avoid seeking feedback, because doing so might invite a critical assessment. The science is clear, however, that the more we are interested in learning and in achieving our goals, and the more exposed we are to feedback, the better our relationships are. But achieving those improved relationships means setting our ego aside and exercising a little humility, or we risk not hearing some good advice.

The situation is even more complicated for older leaders. The evidence clearly shows that the longer we've been with our employer and in our job, the less likely we are to go looking for feedback.[1] Folks with an abundance of confidence in their ability to perform lose out when they underestimate how useful the intelligence gained from feedback could be.[2] This is not to say that you should accept all forms of feedback at face value, but denying what another perspective could mean for meaningful self-development is a shame.

Our ability to receive feedback graciously is a function of our deciding whether to give it credence or importance.[3] And whether you determine that the feedback you've received can be helpful depends on your having a clear understanding of what exactly is being communicated to you.[4] We've already established how wobbly that process can be.

How the feedback makes you feel, its accuracy, and how it is delivered (e.g., in an email, virtually, or in person) are all factors that will weigh on your decision to accept and act on that feedback, to reflect on it and defer acting, or to dismiss it outright.

In the aptly titled article "Find the Coaching in Criticism," Sheila Heen and Douglas Stone, researchers at the Harvard Negotiation Project and authors of *Thanks for the Feedback: The Art and Science of Receiving Feedback Well*, remind us that we've been receiving feedback for our entire lives and, as a result, have developed certain predispositions—a way of acting that runs the gamut from listening gracefully to lashing out to discrediting the sender or focusing on the sender's motives instead of the message.[5] I like Heen and Stone's advice to "disentangle the 'what' from the 'who'" and, with detachment, determine whether the feedback is valid and helpful, and then to make a thoughtful choice to accept it or disregard it.

Brené Brown frames the subject quite colorfully when she refuses the feedback of those who she feels lack standing or qualification: "If you are not in the arena getting your ass kicked on occasion, I'm not interested in or open to your feedback."[6] So we need to assess not only the feedback itself but also the person who is delivering it.

During a 2018 interview on Sirius XM's Business Radio, General Motors CEO Mary Barra made a fascinating statement about the responsibility we all have to seek out robust feedback. She stated, "The power of feedback is with the receiver, not the giver." She went on to explain that while many of us receive feedback through formal systems like performance management, the most important feedback she had received as a young engineer was that which she sought out herself. Barra made the point that we all have the power to elicit information on our work from any number of sources. Armed with such information, we have the power to ignore it, simply acknowledge it, or have it inform our future choices and performance, our learning, and where and how we decide to grow our careers.

The Clash of Feedback, Assumptions, and Expectations

One of the great clashes in the modern-day workplace is between "no news is good news"–type supervisors and workers whose schooling and upbringing was feedback rich. The disconnect is highlighted in a 2016 video by the award-winning international employee recognition company Terryberry. The century-old American family-owned business run by the fourth generation of the Byam family has a global footprint with a who's who client base of well-known corporate giants. The video, which accompanied Mike Byam's 2016 book *The WOW! Workplace: How to Build an Employee Recognition Culture that Engages Your People and Produces Big Results for Your Organization*, juxtaposes how stark the feedback landscape can be for an employee who is in their first job and who has had a feedback-rich upbringing from teachers and family members.

So, feedback clearly plays a central role in our learning, but according to Heen and Stone, it does two other things of note. They assert that, beyond learning, feedback also tells people how they are doing against standards, and sometimes it's simply a vehicle for showing appreciation. Interestingly, a single piece of thoughtful feedback, well delivered, meets at least one of its three purposes, or sometimes all three! Talk about getting lots of bang for your feedback buck. One carefully timed and delivered piece of data can let me know how I'm measuring up to expectations, teach me something, and make me feel valued and appreciated. I don't think it's about going for the trifecta every time, but carefully crafted feedback will lead to positive outcomes.

And the learning can be multifaceted. Receiving feedback from a credible source can help people learn in a very technical way in relation to a specific task or skill, but from a leadership perspective the richness of feedback comes from the self-awareness it fosters. Former Medtronic chairman and CEO and faculty member at the Harvard Business School Bill George famously says, "Leadership skills start with self-awareness."[7] So, while many focus on building the capacity for leaders to deliver feedback effectively, George has championed an approach that says that to lead effectively you must lead with authenticity, and the cornerstone of developing your authentic leadership style is aggressively seeking out honest feedback to build your self-awareness. Leading well means developing your ability to deliver thoughtful and effective feedback that inspires and influences others. Leading well also means that you avidly seek feedback to build your own self-awareness and learning.

The Power of Unsolicited Feedback

Have you received a piece of feedback that had a profound impact on the completion of an important project or even on your career? Maybe it was a comment that really hit home, brilliant for its insight (even though not seen as such by the person who delivered the insight). Feedback—whether positive or negative, deliberate or off the cuff—given at the right time can produce enormous results and be surprisingly memorable.

Take the case of Bonnie, whose mid-level HR position focused on recruitment in a multinational company. She was ready for a change and wanted to grow her career into a management role. She had been passed over for a few managerial roles and told that, to be a manager, she needed to understand the business context more, learn operations and the numbers, and be less HR-oriented. She took the advice to heart and quietly began to study the business, having coffee and lunches with other managers and asking questions to understand their operations. She took on her recruitment assignments with a different zeal, now wanting to better understand the role and the systems and processes they work with in that part of the business. Bonnie was eventually promoted—several times, in fact. In her capacity as a vice president with that same multinational, now based in Europe, she harkens back to one piece of feedback she received when she was a fledgling individual contributor.

The company was interviewing for its chief information technology officer. Bonnie played her usual role in guiding a selection committee through a painstaking process to identify their next senior executive. Once the competition was over, one of the candidates who was eventually hired pulled her aside and commented, "It's a good thing you had given me your business card, because after three sets of interviews I had no idea you were in HR. I was convinced you were the head of one of the business units given the way you spoke of operations, the business objectives, and our financials." That single piece of feedback, Bonnie would explain, gave her the confidence to keep learning the business, and ultimately she broke through, rising to executive levels and having a stellar career in middle and senior management roles. For the feedback provider, the exchange was likely unmemorable and they may not even remember it, but for Bonnie it was life (work) altering.

Most people yearn for feedback, but many people leaders are deemed "inept" at providing it.[8] And although we want to encourage what researchers call feedback-seeking behavior in others, if we as leaders hold out on providing feedback, this does not stimulate in our teams a desire to receive it. So, if feedback frugality doesn't increase people's appetite for feedback, what does?

Creating a climate where feedback is perceived as valuable, helpful, and without risk stimulates people's appetite for feedback.[9] Leaders who develop and promote that type of curiosity for feedback in their teams have been shown to increase their leadership effectiveness.[10] Added to this, team leaders who actively seek out negative feedback from their team are more effective. We can only assume that a leader with the openness and humility necessary to look for negative feedback is also of the ilk to take that information and seek to improve their approach, thus enhancing their effectiveness.

The Positive Rewards of Feedback

When employees see their manager use feedback for their own self-improvement, it has an impact. Working with someone who uses feedback purposely to get better at what they do and increase their impact tends to motivate us to do the same.[11]

Leaders create feedback-rich environments by consistently reinforcing positive views about feedback and by emphasizing its role in promoting self-awareness, learning, and improvement. Employees should be reminded that sound feedback can substantially shift a team towards an improvement mindset for each person, the team, their processes, and the organization.

That type of leadership, if found within an organizational culture where feedback is valued and supported and where coaching is used to help people work with the feedback, has multiple rewards.[12] In smaller organizations, one feedback-rich manager can positively infect an entire company or department. A manager who is friendly towards feedback for themselves and towards their own learning is rated as a better coach when evaluated by their employees. Who doesn't want to be perceived as a better coach by their folks?[13]

Active Listening: Feedback's Enabler

Active listening has been shown to be a manager's principal communication asset, and it's vital to both receiving and giving feedback well. It's also an ability that managers tussle with a lot, and one you would do well to master.[14] Who among us doesn't believe we are well skilled at listening with our eyes, leaning forward, and nodding only at just the right times; using pauses to elicit more comments; honoring the other person by using their words when paraphrasing;

and leaving people utterly convinced they were heard? Those of you who have experienced this have been in the presence of masters, perhaps inspired by Eastern wisdom.

The Chinese character *ting*, meaning "to listen," is profound and tells us a lot about active listening.[15] The ancient character, or *hanzi* symbol, depicts an ear to hear, eyes to see and make eye contact, undivided attention to focus, the heart to feel, and the mind to think through what is being heard. The symbol has similarities to the character representing virtue and is interpreted as the ability to listen quietly without interrupting.

We think we've got this active listening skill down, but do we really? Recent Gallup data report that only 25 percent of employees strongly agreed that their opinions count at work.[16] This suggests that not only are leaders missing out on actionable ideas that could have an enormous upside, but that active listening stimulates the much-sought openness to feedback by employees.

You've likely picked up, through osmosis or through training, some active listening basics. Leading with humanity is not only about demonstrating those abilities but about always teaching and modeling them. Crucial aspects are the slight tilt of your head, eye contact that communicates concentration, and intent listening to truly understand what's being said. You might then paraphrase what you heard, using the person's words to honor their message. Equally as indicative of active listening is responding with questions that incorporate the notions that the speaker has been using. All useful tips, but what about active listening under more trying circumstances?

Robert Goguen, whom you met in an earlier chapter, was the parliamentary secretary to the minister of justice as well as the attorney general of Canada's forty-first Parliament. I think of him as a lifelong political volunteer and active participant in our democracy. Defending a government's position on contentious matters was in his job description.

Goguen mastered active listening while at the same time being committed to not yielding. He spoke to me of defending contentious legislation that was particularly unpopular in his riding, and of knowing that no amount of pushback from his constituents or from him would change anything but that his job was to listen well and respond. Think about it. Sometimes being unyielding, inflexible, or unbending is exactly what a situation calls for. You've been there, and so have I. I know I'm not at my active listening best under those circumstances, and I've witnessed many a team leader struggle to listen well while tempted to simply shut the discussion down because it won't change anything in the end. But we should all know, as Goguen has mastered, that listening well—intently and actively—does matter in the long run, especially when the going gets tough.

Intentionally thinking about and building our active listening game in situations that are not terribly critical or volatile builds our capacity for when it really gets tested. And listening is a learnable and coachable skill.

> ### Active Listening in a Diverse Workplace
>
> We are fortunate to have an increasing number of cultural newcomers in our workplaces. We'll talk more about inclusion and diversity later in the book, but for now it's important to acknowledge that the notion of active listening when working with cultures and traditions that are not our own can be daunting. In a Western tradition, eye contact is considered a sign of active listening, but this perspective is culturally specific and we should be mindful that other cultures may not regard eye contact the same way.
>
> So, how can you know that aspects of active listening are culturally appropriate? Mirroring, or in essence assuming the mannerisms of the other party, can be very helpful here. Listening and communicating well with people from other cultures and traditions can be simplified through this practice. For

> example, if the other party tends to avoid your gaze, you may want to do so in return. If you notice they speak in a quiet tone of voice, you may want to do the same. If you notice they do not extend their hand to shake your hand, you will not insist that they do. Mirroring helps us to be respectful of other traditions and cultures within our communication practices in general.

Mentors: Find Many, Be One

Mentors and coaches are in the feedback business. If you want to strengthen your ability to receive feedback well, seek out mentoring or coaching.

When I think of coaching, I think of a task-focused relationship in which skill building, behavioral change, and accountability are key. Questions are at the heart of the development strategy, and the inherent assumption is that the "coachee" has most of the answers or at least an inclination as to what the answers are. The coaching role is defined by helping people come to a better understanding of things they largely already know but on which they need prompting, reframing, or maybe a different perspective.

When I think of mentoring, I think more of a relationship in which there is guidance and knowledge transfer but also emotional and psychological support and a longer-term provision of advice, especially with careers in mind.

Whether you think of the process as coaching or mentoring, let's agree that in both cases helping the person get a better view of themselves, their actions, and their behavior will contribute to enabling them to be more self-aware, to take stock, and to grow.

I believe that one of the misconceptions that people have is that they can find that one special mentor who will guide and shape their careers. Consider yourself fortunate if that happens. A more workable approach to mentoring is to identify multiple individuals who have specific gifts, skills, and experience that they may be willing to share. Mentoring need not be an all-encompassing lifelong relationship; it's about having either an informal or formal arrangement with one or more people who can help you question your assumptions and push you to see things from a different perspective.

Building a network of mentors and subsequently becoming a mentor to others is truly how we fulfil this leadership project of ours. Here are a few practical suggestions for effective mentoring:

- **Get clear on what you need,** what you're looking for, and how a mentor can help. You may want to seek out assistance in validating your needs (with your team leader or ally or colleague). We've already established that we benefit from help to get an accurate view of our capabilities and our own needs.

- **Establish goals** to indicate progress or completion if it feels appropriate. In some instances, when the mentoring relationship is informal, such goal setting can feel out of place. However, in other settings, if you are to approach a business acquaintance senior to yourself with the express intention of requesting guidance, then being very clear on objectives, as well as on how mentoring is to be facilitated, is appropriate.

- **Set the parameters.** Prescribe how often you will meet and how long it will last if it's going to have some legs to it. Alternatively, a single mentoring session can produce meaningful results. Coaches speak often of someone being just one conversation away from a breakthrough or substantial progress, and if so, that conversation needn't be a series of conversations.

- **Mix up the settings.** If your mentor suggests a monthly get-together at a local pub on a Friday afternoon, then go with it. Alternatively, think about doing different things, from attending a reception together in the business community, to meals and drinks, a round of golf, or an outing that truly resonates with the mentor.

- **Show gratitude.** Indicate your thanks in a way that resonates with your mentor; and most importantly, become a mentor yourself.

NOW THAT WE have covered your side of the ledger when it comes to receiving feedback, let's turn to the other side. In the next chapter, we'll discuss the process of providing feedback and how to determine your degree of effectiveness at communicating feedback.

> ### Taking Stock of Your Humanity at Work
>
> Feedback is central to learning, and that's true for everyone. As you answer the following questions about your people leadership practice, reflect on Bonnie's story and how her active response to feedback made all the difference in her career.
>
> 1. What has receiving feedback meant to your development, professionally and personally?
>
> 2. Would you say you have received sufficient feedback, inadequate feedback, or so much of it that you feel micromanaged?
>
> 3. As a leader, do you sense an emotional charge around giving and receiving feedback, or is it neutral—i.e., "just business"?
>
> 4. Think of the best active listening leader you know. What makes you go "Wow!" when you watch them listening actively? What might you incorporate from their practice into your own?

5. When was the last time you brushed up on or experimented with your active listening skills? When you very consciously used the tools and pushed yourself to really put your active listening on display for examination? Try picking a day, an activity, or meeting where you can check in on your active listening. (Here's a tip: Count to three after the person with whom you are conversing stops speaking, and then and only then begin to speak. If you're an interrupter, this will torment you and eventually cure you.)

6. Have you ever considered being a mentor? Which of your capabilities or insights do you believe would be most helpful if taught to others?

(11)
How Well Do I Provide Feedback, Especially the Difficult Stuff?

HAVE YOU EVER wondered about what effective leaders notice and pay attention to? I have. This is the critical difference between a leader who engages their people as a matter of course and a leader who does so only when a process requires it of them.

I think a lot about a conversation I had with a financial services client who had been promoted into a key administrative middle management role six months earlier. When I asked how things were going in the new role, she responded, "I think I'm doing okay. Why? Have you heard anything?" Her question didn't come from a place of paranoia, but understandably she was looking for signals, likely from her manager and other influential people within her team. Knowing that I had a relationship with the managing director, she sought an opinion from me.

I happened to know that the firm was delighted with her progress, yet she was uncertain, and this was not a feeling that was normal for her. In her role as a veteran lead administrator, she found the work intrinsically motivating and understood full well where she stood against expectations. The nature of the work was also such that she saw the results of her work relatively quickly and could assess those results.

Now, in her management role, that type of feedback was longer in coming and more subtle, and it also required context from her manager. She faced a learning curve and needed training and coaching. At the very least, the manager needed to be paying attention. My client was not the type to be caught up in her own insecurities; however, she clearly needed signals around how she was doing. And yes, she had asked for feedback and received a cursory "Everything is fine." Her follow-up questions were met with equal ambiguity. She needed specifics.

Sadly, there are still those folks who believe that biannual, quarterly, or annual reviews (heaven help us) are sufficient. They're not, and we as leaders must pay attention to our people and respond with the feedback they seek. My financial services client needed a strategy for getting meaningful and robust information from her immediate supervisor and other members of the management team whom she served in her role.

Displaying the kind of initiative that got her promoted in the first place, she identified key individuals from whom she required feedback and devised an approach that would solicit the feedback she needed by asking questions. She seamlessly wove these questions into her ongoing conversations with people so she would receive the type of feedback on how she was tracking well ahead of her biannual reviews. Her approach to feedback supports exactly what the folks at Gallup discovered.

Gallup's 2019 magnificently researched *It's the Manager* states that "employees who receive daily feedback from their manager are three times more likely to be engaged than those who receive feedback once a year or less.... As a rule, managers should give their employees meaningful feedback at least once a week."[1]

Some interpret this as an administratively burdensome process that requires forms and the like, when what we mean by feedback is in fact the normal daily interactions between a leader and a team member. It is the ongoing and, dare I say, continuous process of evaluating results against expectations, and then coaching, teaching, and showing appreciation. The only formality is the documentation of that process at periodic intervals.

My client would let her manager off the hook when I asked her about his reluctance to share feedback. She spoke to me of how busy he was. In addition, his need for feedback was limited (or so he claimed), and as a result he likely assumed that others too could do just fine without it. Many a new team leader has had to come to grips with the fact that the people they provide feedback to as part of their role may need much less or much more than they themselves do. How is the new team leader to decide the adequacy of feedback and how it ought to be delivered? What is the proper timing for delivering it? The appropriate setting? This chapter will address these questions.

The story of my client is deeply relevant to today's workplace. She is highly visible given her role. People do not wonder what she does as she goes about her work. Think of those employees who are not visible and who are never given a stretch assignment or a chance to grow. Leaders and their firms are throwing away so much potential by not paying attention. The question is: Why?

Why are so many of us so frugal in giving feedback? Why do so many of us believe feedback is negative and that it always needs to entail a difficult conversation? Why do those who immerse their colleagues, direct reports, and even their managers in meaningful feedback stand out? And, for the purposes of this chapter, what do master feedback providers do that is in keeping with the best evidence that we should learn from and emulate?

It's been my experience, from watching team leaders of all stripes, that we're more likely to speak up and provide feedback when something is wrong or not up to standard. Rightly so. Setting, monitoring, and raising standards is central to a leader's role. But many people don't see that their role also includes providing affirming comments that recognize standards being met or exceeded, for teaching purposes, or simply to have the person feel valued and appreciated.

Why is this seemingly so hard to understand for so many? No wonder that in the largest study of the future of work ever undertaken by Gallup, the researchers reported that slightly less than half of employees receive any type of feedback from their manager "a few times or less" per year.[2]

This chapter's opening narrative told the story of a director and her manager who was unsympathetic to the role and merits of feedback. The notion of mentorship shows how vital feedback is, but what if we think of it as something less formal, as a form of paying attention to one another? How do you feel when others notice and commend you for your efforts? Exactly.

Why Are We So Reluctant to Give Feedback?

Noted MIT Sloan School of Management professor emeritus Edgar Schein reminds us that "the reluctance we display when someone asks us for feedback mirrors the degree to which we are afraid to offend or humiliate."[3]

Those who are looking for excuses for not noticing, not paying attention, and not providing feedback will find them, and I hear such excuses all the time: "I don't want to interrupt someone's work flow" (a well-intentioned but a flimsy argument); "I don't want to spoil people with positive reinforcement" (this one makes me laugh); "It's not my place to commend subordinates, colleagues, or my manager" (this excuse makes me ask, "Why not?"); or the clincher, "Why should I provide feedback when people are simply doing what they're paid to do?" (okay, this one makes me slightly ill, but it drives home the point that feedback is an alien concept for some).

Let's examine these excuses. It is necessarily our role and our job to interrupt others with data that can enhance their performance, better our collective efforts, and improve outcomes. As we will see later in this chapter, it is nearly impossible to *spoil* people with feedback when it meets the criteria of being specific, genuine, and true. And I believe that we all play a part in contributing to healthy workplaces with the kind of constructive and affirming feedback that people thirst for, and, when it is appropriately delivered, that people respond to. This is not solely the work of supervisors and managers, though admittedly those folks do bear heightened formal accountability for providing feedback. Lastly, commenting on what people are paid to do, when they do it well, is at the heart of how we can strengthen engagement and signal that we notice and value their efforts.

Noticing and validating people for "simply doing their jobs" is what lays the groundwork for people to be engaged and creates the climate for them to go above and beyond. Saving praise for only exceptional performance or breakthroughs is a misguided approach that squanders opportunities. Commenting positively and often on people doing their job well, especially when they're making progress and continuously improving themselves and their processes, opens the door to our creating healthy and exceptional workplaces.

Emotional intelligence expert Daniel Goleman positions feedback as organizational lifeblood and reminds us that there can be more nuanced reasons for a lack of regular feedback in a particular situation.[4] In some ethnic cultures, for example, speaking openly and criticizing the behavior or performance of others, and even offering sincere flattery, is frowned upon. Or it could be the case that the team leader simply does not have the skill and confidence to give feedback. Whatever the reasons behind the frugality of feedback, we can do better.

Weekly Feedback and Other Real-Life Suggestions

I've asked hundreds upon hundreds of managers for their top piece of advice on giving effective feedback. Participants do a survey of every other participant in the training room and thereby learn what the others' best trick is for delivering feedback in a way that works. Over the hundreds of times I have done this exercise, invariably when I ask my accomplished audiences how long feedback can sit on the shelf, the answer is days or a week at the most.

Coaching or feedback sessions are scheduled around a weekly schedule in many organizations, and yours may be one of them. There are experts who argue that a weekly session is essential for leaders to reconnect with our people on expectations and provide feedback, followed up with any coaching that might be required to ensure progress is made.[5] They also suggest that the span of control, otherwise known as the number of people reporting directly to one supervisor, should be determined by how many people you can reasonably sit with in a week. Let's appreciate that the nature of the role—its complexity and impact—determines whether a weekly session makes sense and what length of conversation makes sense.

Workplace motivation master Bob Nelson stresses that a person's motivation is connected to time spent with their team leader. That seals it for me.[6]

Here are a few other gems related to feedback that should be kept in mind:

- **Ask permission before offering feedback:** "May I share an observation on how you led the discussion with our team?" This type of question conveys respect, provides control to the other person, and allows them to prepare themselves for what they are about to hear.

- **"I'm here to help":** If you have lived in a university residence, you'll have interacted with "proctors" or "residence assistants," the students who take on a leadership role with their fellow students. They find themselves in every conceivable challenging situation typical for a den parent or older sibling to young adults, many of whom are away from home for the first time, with all that involves. They are drilled to clearly state their intentions and begin every situation with "I'm here to help" to make crystal clear that what is about to happen is in service of helping the individual in question. This practice is at the heart of the ability to deliver effective feedback or to intervene more strenuously, as we'll see in part four.

- **Feedback is to be offered, not imposed:** I have witnessed many an exchange between supervisor and employee where the supervisor feels compelled to drive the message home through repetition and restatement, when, judging from the response from the individual, an offer to share and say it once would have sufficed. To be fair, some situations and some individuals welcome critical feedback more than others; yet when it comes from a nonthreatening place, as information to be shared and not shoved down someone's throat, the receptiveness to the data appears to be significantly increased.

- **Feedback dialogues outperform feedback monologues:** Senior HR executive Diane Allain's training as a coach always comes out when she provides feedback. Allain routinely opens an exchange with "How do you think that went?" She then steers the person towards what went well by suggesting what she observed that went well, while asking the individual for more of their own thoughts and then ultimately asking what they learned and what they might try differently next time. Allain asks self-reflective questions and turns a conversation that lasts only a few minutes into robust feedback by urging meaningful responses and chiming in thoughtfully at all the appropriate junctures. For her, appropriately worded questions are central to any feedback offering, and their use ensures a two-way conversation built on the belief that the individual has some sense of how they performed and that her role is to round it off, identify blind spots, and put a point on things.

- **Details matter:** Being told we did a great job may make us feel good, but it's not enough. Sharing the specifics of what exactly the person did to qualify the job as great makes the feedback uber useful and substantially increases the likelihood it will be repeated. When we provide details, examples, and specifics, the feedback becomes authentic, honest, and extremely valuable. It's pretty difficult to come across as phony when the details are rich and when they resonate with the person. Providing this type of detailed feedback also signals that we are paying attention.

Delivery doesn't have to be perfect. Sometimes feedback is delivered in less than ideal ways, but if the intent is correct, the receiver can get over the fact that the delivery may have been awkward or clunky. The feedback is in itself able to change the course of events in meaningful ways. That's encouraging for those learning to get better at giving feedback in a variety of circumstances, even to a group.

Composer, musician, and academic Dr. Richard Gibson speaks of being in recording sessions with some of the world's greatest symphony orchestras led by top conductors. He has done so in recording studios as famous as Abbey Road—seat of creativity for the Beatles and their producer George Martin—and others not as famous perhaps but their equal for quality.

Gibson quietly tells the story of how a recording session he witnessed was not going well. The conductor left his perch to speak privately in hushed tones to the first violinist, who in the orchestral world is the equivalent of the chief operating officer. The first violinist wielded a hefty bow.

While the conductor went to freshen up in his dressing room, the violinist took center stage, cleared her throat, and addressed her comments to one of the sections in the orchestra, reminding the musicians that playing in time and in tune were critical to the success of the recording. Her use of expletives and the cheeky tone of her feedback to the trombone section brought a smile to the faces of the dozens of professional musicians and guffaws from the "bones" section (who heard nothing out of the ordinary). She then thanked the orchestra. The maestro returned and the recording was completed without difficulty. This story underscores that feedback is context specific. What works in one workplace may be inappropriate in another, and while we all aim to deliver highly effective information to others, sometimes we're clumsy and not in line with what the experts would advise. But effort is worthwhile even when it's a little wobbly. Better to make some mistakes in giving feedback awkwardly and learn from it than shy away, which is so often the default approach.

Let's agree that the informal practice of continuously noticing and paying attention and speaking up defines our daily work as people leaders. Not paying attention is not leading.

The Praise-to-Criticism Ratio

In my work, the one piece of the feedback puzzle that always stops practitioners in their tracks is the praise-to-criticism ratio. The question is, how much positive feedback or praise do you need to hear on a relatively regular basis to increase the likelihood that when you receive constructive or negative feedback—the pointy, uncomfortable, "bad news" kind—you'll take it well and hopefully act on it?

We have clear evidence that constructive criticism is more likely to be accepted and acted on when it's part of a steady diet of acknowledgment and positive feedback. In their excellent *Harvard Business Review* article "The Ideal Praise-to-Criticism Ratio," researchers Jack Zenger and Joseph Folkman state that the ratio is 5 to 1 (actually it's 5.6 to 1, but let's not quibble).[7] If I am to drop my defenses and act upon constructive criticism from my team leader, colleague, or direct report, that one incident of criticism needs to be accompanied in the preceding days by five or so relatively positive comments.

The startled look on the faces of many managers I work with when they internalize how often they need to be focusing on what people do well is something to behold. Getting to a 5 to 1 ratio of praise to criticism as part of an ongoing way we work with others is very challenging for some, though less so for others. Let's explore why this is so.

Gallup senior scientist and best-selling author Tom Rath, in his 2015 book *Are You Fully Charged?*, reminds us how much weight our daily interactions have on our state of mind and well-being. Rath explains the physiological response we have to criticism, noting that it stimulates the stress hormone cortisol, which "shuts down much of your thinking and activates conflict and defense mechanisms," whereas positive interactions "boost your body's production of oxytocin, a feel-good hormone that increases your ability to communicate, collaborate and trust others."[8]

He goes on to explain that three to five positive interactions are required to outdo the impact of one negative exchange. Rath, Zenger and Folkman, and others make a very compelling argument that, given the additional importance our brain places on negative information, we need to, in the words of Ken Blanchard, "catch people doing things right,"[9] and per Tom Rath, have "80 percent of conversations focus on what's going right."[10]

Not-So-Difficult Conversations

How, then, are we to think about how we approach negative feedback and the difficult conversations it often entails?

We've thankfully started talking about difficult conversations when training emerging people leaders. Approaches to dealing with such tough conversations are now considered a key component of a people leader's toolkit and, in some enlightened workplaces, a part of all their people's toolkits.

The huge success of books like *Fierce Conversations* by Susan Scott and *Difficult Conversations: How to Discuss What Matters Most* by Douglas Stone, Bruce Patton, and Sheila Heen highlights the appetite folks have for getting help on how to carry out the stickiest of conversations well. The latter work has the best take on what a difficult conversation actually is: anything you find uncomfortable to talk about.

In the workplace, meting out discipline or terminating an employee can be trying for the most experienced of leaders, but also challenging are coaching conversations with a team member, a chat with a colleague about a touchy interpersonal subject, or pushing back against your manager on a point of principle. We've all had to summon the courage to face such exchanges. Hats off to those of you who have the poise and discipline to go into such conversations when they are called for and pull them off well. Some of us only do so when dragged into them by obligation or we avoid them all together.

The bulk of my experience in difficult conversations came from being an HR leader in the career transition business, where we were called upon to sit in on difficult chats having mostly to do with employment terminations. I have come away from a decade of doing that work with a few beliefs and suggestions about difficult conversations:

1. **Start early:** Conversations are easier when relationships are sound. Establishing those strong relationships starts long before any kind of a hard talk takes place. Ask yourself whether the rapport you have with your colleagues and direct reports would provide a foundation for having the various kinds of conversations you will need to have. If not, what needs to be different?

2. **Be prepared:** Before going into a difficult conversation, ask yourself some hard questions about what the reaction might be, how you will respond, and what the likely outcomes are. Have the facts, know the data, and be very clear on what your objective is and the ideal outcome.

3. **Be a problem-solver:** No matter how fierce, crucial, or difficult a conversation might feel, dialogue (not monologue) promotes learning, another essential component of feedback. Asking questions helps promote a balanced dialogue and moves the discussion towards problem-solving.

4. **Be real:** I watched hundreds of managers, business owners, and executives struggle through difficult conversations with employees. When their approach was devoid of judgment, demands, or denials, they had better outcomes. When they were able to steady themselves and work through whatever script or agenda needed to be expressed, and were able to be themselves and convey a genuine empathy, they had better outcomes.

5. **Be respectful:** When emotions, people's identities, and differing perspectives are in play, things can get messy. However, the diligent people leader's role is to navigate through such conversations

with resolve, humanity, and a commitment to move forward and make progress. Responding and not reacting is the order of the day. People leaders role model, teach, and insist upon respectful and dignified conduct.

Negative feedback hurts and has the potential to discourage, which explains why leaders shy away from providing it. But when negative feedback is thoughtfully delivered it serves to lessen the emotional downside, strengthen relationships, and propel improvement.

Negative Feedback and Motivation

Beyond the relationship-destabilizing concerns of sharing negative feedback, there is an ever-present risk of demoralizing and demotivating the receiver regardless of how well planned and executed the delivery of "bad news" feedback is. No supervisor wants to mess with someone's intrinsic motivation, that highly sought-after desire to achieve that bubbles from within because the task or the work is personally satisfying, pleasurable, and interesting.

Negative feedback diminishes how people see themselves, threatens their sense of competence, and lessens internal motivation. Positive feedback builds intrinsic motivation largely because it emphasizes our capabilities.[11] Thus, we can see where the temptation towards the "feedback sandwich" likely came from—that is, the belief in surrounding negative feedback with positive feedback before and after, creating a sandwich of sorts. Softening the blow is a human instinct, as is trying to leave things on a positive note.

I'm thinking people know intuitively that they need to build someone up if they are going to "knock 'em down a peg." The science and the sentiment behind the statement are correct, even if the expression is a little dated. What the sandwich metaphor does not consider is the timing of those two ingredients of feedback.

Culture maven Daniel Coyle[12] considered organizations that achieved positive outcomes through feedback and reported witnessing distinct approaches to providing the two types of feedback. The organizations clearly separated the positive from negative, the latter being addressed in dialogue with a focus on learning and the former being locked on acknowledgment and celebration. (We'll have a proper chat about rewards and recognition in chapter 15.) Most importantly, the two processes didn't happen at the same time and place.

Finally, an educational, non-confrontational approach to providing clear instruction is a crucial part of negative feedback.[13]

After Giving Feedback—Then What?

We all learn differently, and science suggests that accommodating learning styles is beneficial to achievement.[14] That knowledge can inspire us to shape feedback in learning-centered ways that speak to individuals' learning styles, our surest bet for lessening the potential harm of bad news feedback.

Let's assume you have a diverse team of learners. One member learns by doing; another needs to understand the theory behind the lesson; a third is very practical and needs to see how it works in practice; and the last team member (rounding out all four learning styles)[15] needs to observe from afar and reflect. Knowing the learning style of each person just made your preparation and your life a whole lot easier, as it gives you your best shot at assuring uptake of what you must deliver.

Getting your hands on the right data in the form of goals and objectives (agreed-upon expectations or targets), getting yourself face-to-face with that person, and getting a grip on their learning style so your delivery matches their preference for learning are the evidence-backed practices that deliver the best outcomes in relation to minimizing the impact on people's intrinsic motivation. (Or, as Jack Donohue, the late coach of Canada's national basketball team, used to call intrinsic motivation: *Wanna!*)

Angela Duckworth, commenting on what experts do after they receive feedback, says they need to "do it all over again, and again, and again, until they have finally mastered what they set out to do, and until what was a struggle before is now fluent and flawless. Until conscious incompetence becomes unconscious competence."[16]

The Role of Candor

When I started in this business, I mistakenly believed my purpose as a human resources professional was to contribute to a workplace that made people comfortable to a degree reminiscent of the 1980s REM song "Shiny Happy People,"[17] thinking this evidence of employee satisfaction meant people were effective. Wrong! Happy, shiny, and laughing are great factors in a workforce, but engaged and productive are better objectives, and much easier to measure as well.

In working with scores of managers and HR professionals, I've noticed that many still carry a misunderstanding about workplaces. Daniel Coyle puts it this way: "One misconception about highly successful cultures is that they are happy, lighthearted places. This is mostly not the case. They are energized and engaged, but at their core their members are oriented less around achieving happiness than around solving hard problems together. This task involves many moments of high-candor feedback, uncomfortable truth telling, when they confront the gap between where the group is, and where it ought to be."[18]

One could have guessed, given her political lineage, that Lisa Merrithew would ascend to one of Canada's most sought-after roles as a political strategist and communications whiz. Like many before her, Merrithew converted her extensive political experience into a coveted role with one of the country's corporate heavyweights, Bell Canada. That's not the surprising part, I grant you, but that she would devise a leadership style grounded in candor and transparency is a testament to her very interesting journey.

Merrithew grew up in a political household. Her father, Gerald Merrithew, a much-beloved teacher and man of the people, ably represented his constituents in Saint John, New Brunswick, as a minister in both the provincial legislature and in Canada's Parliament. Lisa's ascent to the role of principal communication advisor to New Brunswick's thirtieth premier, Bernard Lord, is not surprising. However, to know Lisa Merrithew is to know that her approach differs significantly from others, and this is what made her highly sought after in the corporate world.

By the time she moved beyond the political realm to an executive role with Bell and then Emera, a $32 billion energy company, Merrithew's leadership style was well developed and had served her well, and it helped her shape strategy in some of Canada's most important communications campaigns in a wide array of settings.

"It's about finding a better way," Lisa replied when I asked her how she frames the sometimes blunt, candid feedback she's known for. She's apt to meet resistance when telling a colleague senior executive or chief executive things that are uncomfortable and disconcerting and that they'd rather not hear.

"Remember," she continued, "I've worked with lots of guys with processes, facts, and models" for whom the woman purveyor of the soft arts of communications speaks another language. The strategic communicator says many of these colleagues have been a dream to work with, and others make tremendous progress in understanding the highly nuanced communications work required to grow valuable brands to exceed customer and investor expectations with publicly traded companies. I'm thinking her direct style helps, especially when armed with the most recent data on company reputation, brand awareness, the reach of their communication strategies, and how the company is perceived in the marketplace by customers and would-be customers. She relishes data.

As we discussed her approach for delivering feedback to individuals and groups, and whether her delivery had changed over time, she admitted that she was as bold early in her tenures as later and, given her highly intuitive style, was also data driven in order to avoid just being the "one with strong opinions."

Lisa Merrithew reminds us that backup matters, data matter, and eventually a track record of results speak loudly, enabling her to benefit from the trust she earns. "In time, you can be even more direct, and it all takes less time," she says. People quickly get that she cares, and that enables the directness that defines her approach.

Merrithew concedes that candor can be hard and exhausting. I agree. We sometimes take the more expeditious, less risky polite approach or go along to get along, but for her it's the search of finding a better way that makes the sometime harder road of candor worth the effort.

Merrithew's approach is well explained by author Kim Scott in her boldly titled and informative book *Radical Candor: Be a Kick-Ass Boss without Losing Your Humanity*.[19] Its premise is that we can provide others with pointed, direct feedback if our motivation is clear and if the receiver understands that we are doing it in their best interests. When the receiver of challenging feedback is clear on its intent, Scott argues, that enables the provider to be as direct and challenging as the situation calls for.

IN THE NEXT part of the book, we turn our attention to the workplace and assess what it takes for leaders to ensure that people feel their organization is safe and inclusive.

Taking Stock of Your Humanity at Work

As we have discussed, the approach to delivering feedback is as crucial as the learning that is being communicated through it. As you answer the following questions about your people leadership practice, reflect on Lisa Merrithew's story and how she developed her ability to provide direct, candid feedback.

1. As a leader, on a scale of 1 to 5 (5 the highest), how adept are you at paying attention and noticing employee behavior and performance?

2. What might you do to increase your praise-to-criticism ratio?

3. How do you prepare for a difficult conversation?

4. Do you coach your team members on having difficult conversations? What tips do you offer?

5. Do you draw a link between feedback and a learning culture?

No organization is immune from tension and conflict, but how a leader chooses to intervene defines their leadership. Do the people in your organization regularly contribute ideas and opinions without worrying that they will be punished or embarrassed? This is psychological safety par excellence, and is the ground floor to getting intervention right. In this section, I explore how leaders can create safe, healthy workplaces and deal effectively with conflict and other challenging people-related organizational problems.

PART FOUR

Getting Intervention Right

(12)
Do I Practice Psychological Safety?

Nوvember 9, 2016. Around the world, people were numb from the overnight news. A combination of disbelief, dread, and concern for the future was pervasive, even in the far reaches of Atlantic Canada, remote from the corridors of power in Washington, DC.

The day after the 2016 US presidential election, Terry and Kathy Malley, life partners and business partners in Malley Industries of Dieppe, New Brunswick, joined many others in worrying about the implications of a Republican presidency. On the campaign trail, Donald Trump curried favor with voters by promising to renegotiate NAFTA, making those who did business in the United States very nervous. The Malleys have overcome many challenges—some that seriously jeopardized the company's survival. But the challenge of a renegotiated free trade agreement promised to be one of their most significant.

On that November day, the Malleys told me that they had recently reached an important tipping point in their business, growing their export sales of ambulances, retrofitted vehicles for people with disabilities, and assorted plastic automotive accessories for the US industry. You may have seen a discreet Malley sticker on the back of an ambulance, school bus, or retrofitted vehicle. Those stickers and the vehicles to which they're affixed can be seen in many US states and coast to coast to coast in Canada and Mexico. These state-of-the-art modular ambulances are a long way from the company's initial product line. Terry's father, Archie, began the business as a sideline while working at the Canadian National Railway in the 1970s; he converted panel vans into recreational vehicles such as campers by installing, among other things, neon lighting and deep-pile carpeting. Terry worked in the family business, eventually taking it over with Kathy after going to business school. They grew the business into an award-winning manufacturer of ambulances and other emergency and commercial vehicles, specializing in conversions for people with physical challenges. Malley Industries now distributes throughout North America and increasingly worldwide, and they've expanded into design engineering and plastics manufacturing for the automotive industry.

Terry is very open about what has enabled the company to meet challenges. A crucial aspect is that their people have a clear understanding of what is required of them. Terry tells me, "People know exactly where they stand, and I am never afraid or reluctant to ask the very hard questions." The same can be said of Kathy Malley, whose positive disposition and way with people allow for comfortable two-way conversations. Kathy's keen business sense and astute ability to read and engage people has been passed on to their son, Myles, a director of the company who, like his father, is a low-key, exceedingly bright, and reflective individual. This has always been a family business in the true sense. Maudie Malley, Terry's mom, worked in the business well into her eighties, and Myles's sister, Kayla, brings her artistic flair to the company's graphic design needs.

Although the Malleys present a rich case study on building and sustaining a successful family business, this chapter will consider their story as an example of the need for leader intervention during company challenges. In the Malleys' case, and likely yours, the need to respond to competitive or external threats is common. Another threat that requires response can be a dip in productivity or teams that are on a collision course. Often, issues that require intervention are related to employee performance or behavior that is subpar or inappropriate. Whatever the reason, when you need to intervene, you must ask the hard questions.

In describing this process, Harvard's Ron Heifetz and Marty Linsky use the analogy of controlling the temperature, which is equivalent to knowing when to raise or lower the level of discomfort. Asking questions is but one way leaders can adjust the temperature. Heifetz and Linsky put it this way: "Changing the status quo generates tension and produces heat by surfacing hidden conflicts and challenging organizational culture. It's a deep and natural human impulse to seek order and calm, and organizations and communities can tolerate only so much distress before recoiling."[1]

Turning up the heat is a leadership imperative to keep any operation running. But before we explore a leader's options for regulating and adjusting temperature, we must first consider the prerequisite that supports all our efforts in effective people leadership—namely, psychological safety.

The Importance of Psychological Safety

In chapter 1, when we spoke about safety at work, our focus was on hard hats and Maura McKinnon's pink boots. However, government-mandated health and safety committees have expanded beyond a traditional manufacturing, industrial, or construction safety definition to one that today includes a broader definition of both health and safety.

The health component continues to expand to include the promotion of healthy lifestyles and healthy choices, including mental health and wellness. Health and safety committees have evolved from focusing on ever-important accident prevention training and investigation to include education and activities related to smoking cessation, healthy eating, and stress management. Lunchtime walking clubs and contemplative practices like yoga and meditation are now common workplace features. Promoting a healthy lifestyle is a way a company can mitigate high healthcare benefit costs and do right by their folks.

So, our contemporary definition of health and safety is now a more holistic one in workplaces. Thankfully, we're talking about issues like psychological health and psychological safety, which, though related, are not the same thing.

The World Health Organization defines mental health or psychological health as "a state of well-being in which every individual realizes his or her own potential, can cope with the normal stresses of life, can work productively and fruitfully, and is able to make a contribution to her or his community."[2] The above-mentioned initiatives by employers with respect to employee well-being are clearly directed towards the improved psychological health of their workforce.

Part of that larger concept of psychological health is the more recent notion of psychological safety, defined as the absence of harm or threat to a worker's mental well-being. Scholar Amy Edmondson has helped us to fully understand what psychological safety is and what it isn't. First, what it is: "In psychologically safe environments, people believe that when they make a mistake or ask for help, others will not react badly. Instead, candour is both allowed and expected.... [People] offer up ideas and ask questions without fear of being punished or embarrassed."

Edmondson goes on to remind us that psychological safety means that "new ideas are welcome and built upon, not picked apart and ridiculed," and that colleagues will not "embarrass or punish you for offering a different point of view," nor "will they think less of you for admitting that you don't understand something."[3]

I also really like Edmondson's take on what psychological safety *is not*. Being pleasant, comfortable, or agreeable, especially when operating in a climate of low performance expectations and lax or nonexistent standards, is not what psychological safety is about. Psychological safety means that people should not be fearful about contributing an opinion or idea, even if it is contrary to a workplace's norms, and should always be supported when wanting to learn. Psychological safety fuels learning, especially when high learning or performance standards are present.

High standards and psychological safety are the goal to which all workplaces should aspire. In such an environment, people are free to be themselves, and as a result they will create, learn, and perform challenging yet realistic work.

Psychological Safety and Asking the Tough Questions

I've had the privilege of watching and learning from both Terry and Kathy Malley in one of their many board of director roles. As leaders must, they've worked diligently to bring volunteers—emerging community-minded business people—into board of director roles to ensure the ongoing success and sustainability of needed community development and economic development agencies and organizations. If you've had the responsibility of hiring senior staff in your capacity as a volunteer board member, you understand the finesse required to address difficult people-related problems with agency CEOs or senior staff or fellow board members. As often happens, sensitive issues are avoided, efficiency therefore suffers, and the organization ceases to be relevant. This occurs unless people in leadership roles are willing, as the Malleys are, to tackle the elephant in the room.

No volunteer board member wants to have to discipline or terminate people, or to address messy people challenges in their volunteer board of director roles, yet that is the work that the Malleys are always willing to take on—work that has benefited many organizations.

The Malleys successfully guided a number of their volunteer community organizations through considerable turbulence, and in all cases they were a grounding force unafraid of the most difficult of questions and the stickiest of interventions that in the end benefited the purpose of the organization, its clients, and the community it was attempting to serve. For the Malleys themselves, their biggest challenge may lie ahead as their business has become more dependent on the US market.

As we know, after Trump's election in 2016, the US and Canada engaged in a lengthy and rancorous free trade negotiation that in time produced an agreement. Nearly three years to the day from our first conversation immediately after the election, the Malleys confirmed in an email that "business has been wonderful. In fact, the next fiscal year will be among the company's strongest in our history." The company keeps a close eye on activities in the US, where their business has continued to expand organically, and they are expanding into other countries, such as Israel, where you'll now see that discreet Malley sticker—no minor feat for a small manufacturer. Terry Malley stressed that he and Kathy continue to ask themselves hard questions, make changes to the management team, and refocus on the basics, which in their case is ambulances, vehicles for people with disabilities, and thermoformed plastic products.

So, why do some leaders, like the Malleys, willingly ask the hard questions, make the pointed observations, and take the harder route of intervening and raising the heat when others might not? Some would contend it is all a matter of leadership courage, the clichéd ingredient that seemingly allows managers and supervisors to have the gumption to face difficult challenges and overcome them. I believe there is more to it. Raising the temperature and lowering it again—and doing so skillfully, respectfully, and with excellent outcomes—takes clear intention and the ability to create safety and to sense and read the energy and climate within a group of people.

Adept people leaders adjust, raise, and lower the temperature by availing themselves of effective technique as observers and interpreters of human behavior. They follow that up with how they coach, intervene or stay in, get involved, give voice, speak, engage, or butt in. Add to that a diet of constantly building emotional intelligence and they pull it off because they are constantly learning from their experience and adapting how they raise the heat and bring it back down with intentionality and finesse. How we pay attention combined with how we get involved defines our leadership.

Alongside: An Example of a Culture of Psychological Safety

Yves Boudreau looks the part of a chill San Francisco–incubated tech entrepreneur. Six-foot-five and lanky, he's just as comfortable at a poker table in Las Vegas as he is in Berlin, Germany, at a Rammstein heavy metal concert with his wife. And he's equally—some might say more—at home when plunked in the middle of his ten or so Alongside Inc. colleagues in their oh-so-funky dog-friendly shared and open office space in a fixer-upper of a hundred-year-old Moncton, New Brunswick, warehouse that was a historic hat and cap factory in the 1910s and is now called home by table-tennis-playing tech entrepreneurs. A flight of stairs takes you to Passages, a groovy New Age shop for your incense and other like needs. The whole building smells fabulous!

Alongside—the company Boudreau co-founded in the HR technology space—grew from an idea of offering the next generation of employee recruitment technology-aided solutions—this in an age when so many employers struggle to fill key positions, some of them critical to the survival of their enterprise. Boudreau's previous entrepreneurial venture and his work in the economic development field helped him understand how to be successful in business, especially in the startup world, and exposed him to the harsh recruitment realities faced by employers big and small. He also knows only too well how the highs and lows of surviving and thriving in small business can destroy people. His previous venture did not end well, as is the case with many entrepreneurs, and the loss took a huge toll on Boudreau and those closest to him. He learned a lot about business and himself.

Boudreau tells me, "I've been known to give a chance to a few folks who were quite deserving but maybe would not have typically been perceived as well-suited for our line of work. They brought something unique that fit and it worked. I'm happy we spotted their gifts." He then speaks openly about anxiety, depression, and suicide prevention, all represented by his semicolon tattoo just above his wrist, which he sports in solidarity with Project Semicolon, the global non-profit that tackles suicide prevention. He wants Alongside to be humane, responsible, and open in all its dealings. Candor is critical to its success in his view.

"I'm not sure how long this whole thing will continue, but in the meantime, you work with us you know you can be yourself and speak your mind and be respected and appreciated. How can we innovate quickly and keep people engaged otherwise? Using cool tools like Slack for mobile internal communication and the latest tasking capabilities like Asana can make you ultra-connected and productive, but the real magic work happens when we solve problems together and we are candid enough and feel safe enough to get at the real client issues, and learn and innovate."

For Boudreau, that means creating a work culture where his people are unafraid of making blunders (he reminds me he's made a few along the way) and surfacing difficulties, and where they feel comfortable turning to colleagues for assistance and know their unique contribution is welcome. His take is in keeping with our best thinking and evidence from scholars[4] and practitioners.[5]

Making a Commitment to Psychological Safety

The way a team leader behaves has the most significant influence on the team's sense of psychological safety, but there's more to the equation.[6] Psychological safety thrives in organizations where learning is central to the way of being. (We'll delve more deeply into learning as a defining element of your leadership practice in chapter 18.) You might want to look around to get a sense of how psychologically safe your workplace is today. Here are a few things to look for:

- Respect is paramount. It is a way of life.

- People speak up: they offer ideas, make suggestions, and call out what needs to be called out.

- People don't walk on eggshells: they can tell the truth without concern that they will be perceived as trouble-making, inept, or uneducated.

- People willingly ask for help and talk openly about errors.
- Humor and laughter are present.

So, how can you create or enhance the sense of psychological safety on your team? Here are some suggestions to achieve that goal.

1. **Spend time with your employees:** As the saying goes in basketball, "Availability is the greatest ability," meaning that approachability and access are key. As a people leader, you never want to hear "My boss is always so busy I rarely ever get time with her." And please refrain from using the words "My door is always open." It's a passive cop-out that puts the accountability on employees for you to be approachable and accessible. Successful people leaders diligently work at their access and approachability, understanding that one of the greatest motivators for people is the time spent with their boss, no matter how brief. Frequency is the key.

2. **Show the limits of your knowledge**: Try saying "I don't know" instead of trying for the "smartest person in the room" award. Peter Amirault, former president of Swiss Chalet Canada and now the CEO of a privately held Canadian commercial development company, credits his personal growth and decades-long success to the moment he decided to approach his leadership from a place of humility. Amirault explains that his approach had much more profound implications than he might have originally imagined: "Employees felt empowered and that their voices were being heard by the leaders of the organization for the first time!" But the personal shift Amirault made also signaled a deliberate cultural shift for the entire organization. His listening created the type of space for people's voices to be heard and for those voices to stimulate improvement and better results.

3. **Create boundaries:** A leader must be willing to intervene when people cross the line. When individuals humiliate, bully, or disrespect others, the leader must act immediately and decisively in a measured capacity to protect the climate of safety.

4. **Try team coaching:** Any type of team coaching that enables a group to move through a process together to create the hallmarks of psychological safety is a worthwhile investment.[7] Team coaching looks and feels like individual coaching and follows much the same processes of assessing where the group is at, identifying change or improvement objectives, and working to close the gap.

I recall a cohesive seven-person unit in a hyper-fast-paced professional services environment. The group chemistry was right, but the team felt they were not living up to their potential. They were right. The starkest manifestation of the problem was an unproductive relationship with another similar-sized unit comprised of field staff. The two units had the potential to grow sales by cross-selling and by sharing clients. This was not happening.

Their ask: "Help us work better with the field team. It's not them—it's us!" Their view suggested a very mature take on the problem. Other team leaders would have handled this performance gap in any number of ways, many of which have their place: compel the field unit to work better together by working team leader to team leader; have everyone go bowling together; or have a facilitated training workshop to learn together and seek opportunities to collaborate better. This unit opted for team coaching, with the premise that they were the ones needing a bit of a reset to work more effectively with the field staff.

They did individual personality assessments to determine the team members' communication styles, which were then boiled down to establish the team's preferred styles. They then identified objectives, including milestones of effective partnering and collaboration with field staff and others, as well as what they needed to learn or change in order to be better business partners.

The team then met for ninety minutes every two weeks for three months and worked through a number of challenging issues raised through tough questions and discussion. It was sometimes messy and often hard as issues of trust and bias were surfaced with great candor. There was always homework between sessions and lots of dialogue about trust and how to relate to others, because this team had its main challenges in relatability.

They agreed to undertake to change their behavior and wrote a team charter that captured their resolve in seven specific ways, with mechanisms to monitor their commitment to making the team better.

Things improved in time. The team did eventually go bowling with the field staff unit and then launched a series of workshops with them and other units to identify opportunities, but only after they had traveled a journey on their own related to trust, safety, and their commitment to make their team better before engaging others.

The connection between psychological safety and trust is a real one, but I think of trust as a component of relationships, whereas psychological safety really speaks to how a group *feels*.[8] A trusting relationship with my colleague or my team leader may well enable me to speak freely; however, we also know that there is a connection between psychological safety and people feeling comfortable to speak up regardless of their level of confidence or their personality. Environments with a high level of psychological safety enable people with lower confidence to speak up. The notion of speaking up is important around issues of employee health and well-being, shedding light on inappropriate behavior or issues that need to be surfaced. Employees' ability to speak up with confidence that they will be heard and that they never need to be fearful is related to openness on the part of the group as well as psychological safety.[9]

NO ORGANIZATION IS immune from tension and conflict. In the next chapter, we will explore leadership styles and how to find the right balance when intervention is needed.

Taking Stock of Your Humanity at Work

A key takeaway from this chapter is the importance of the relationship between psychological safety and performance. As you answer the following questions about your people leadership practice, reflect on how important psychological safety was for Yves Boudreau and how he leads.

1. Think back over the past quarter, two quarters, and year. How many times have you had to intervene to deal with a situation that was impacting business? What were the circumstances? Are there common factors or trends that point to systemic problems in your organization?

2. How attuned are you to the external factors impacting your industry and sector and to the internal climate of your organization? How might related factors suggest the need for intervention?

3. Do you pay close attention to your inner voice that raises the question of whether you should intervene in any given situation? Before deciding to do nothing or let the situation play itself out, ask yourself this hard question: What is the real reason for *not* stepping in? If it's because you're not sure what to do, you don't have time (translation: you're choosing not to make time), you're fearful of the person and/or their reaction, you believe it won't change anything, or you want to avoid conflict, you may want to think again whether inaction is really what the situation calls for. Is the scenario in question best served by doing nothing, or are you best served by inaction?

4. How would you rate your ability to go against the status quo and raise issues that will make people uncomfortable?

5. How would you rate your organization on the attention it pays to psychological safety and well-being?

(13)
Do I Find the Right Balance between Situation, Judgment, and Action?

"I'M JUST GOING to take a step back and monitor how the situation unfolds" can be the approach of an astute people leader who chooses not to intervene in a situation as a wisely considered decision and legitimate strategy. In medical terms, it's called "watch and wait," or WAW. An individual (1) senses a need to act and is committed to act, but first needs more information; (2) senses a need to act but does not know how, and hopes the whole thing will go away; or (3) knows only too well what needs be done, but chooses to avoid facing the complicated and sometimes emotionally loaded issues that come with getting involved or stepping into a situation.

But "watch and wait" should not be confused with laissez-faire leadership, which is a style of leadership that allows teams to make their own decisions given that they have processes and structures in place that with proper training enable them to be self-guiding. The concept of laissez-faire (from the French term for "leave it be" or "never mind") was first articulated by legendary researcher Kurt Lewin and his colleagues in 1939.[1] They referenced the terms *autocratic*, *democratic*, and *laissez-faire* as a way of thinking about three states or styles of leading others—the first, a directive, one-sided approach; the second, one in which decision-making and control are participative and inclusive; and the third, one in which leadership is turned over to the team members. Where teams have deliberately set up a self-managing regime with all requisite processes, laissez-faire is workable. But in most instances, it isn't.

When a laissez-faire style of leadership is invoked, it can be code for inaction or avoidance on the part of the leader. Or it can signal an emerging leader who may not recognize that the situation calls for them to take a more active role. Their reluctance to do so may be a function of their not seeing the situation for what it is, but it also may be attributable to their just not knowing what to do. They may be caught up in the notion that they must either intervene or do nothing—a false dichotomy.

Leadership scholars lump in laissez-faire leadership, as it is commonly practiced, with a host of negative leadership behaviors, such as dishonesty, opportunism, and dictatorial control.[2] Laissez-faire leadership is not in very good company. To me, it sounds like avoiding responsibility and under-managing.[3] Is that what it sounds like to you? It should. And I'll bet you've seen laissez-faire leadership at work. I've seen it all too often.

When We Don't Intervene

Passive approaches to leading and managing are linked to intimidation, harassment, and bullying, and are anathema to a culture of psychological safety. Research published in top management journals has equated the harm done by a passive approach—characterized by under-managing and not intervening on matters of direction, morale, and key decisions—to the more apparently autocratic or dictatorial styles we associate with workplace unhealthiness. Passive leadership paves the way for bullying among colleagues.[4]

Over the course of hundreds of workshops with leaders and aspiring leaders, I have asked the question, "What prevents you from intervening in situations where your better judgment is telling you that you should?" The top five answers that come back with amazing frequency are these:

1. **"It's difficult. I am not sure what to do."** This is a fair comment. Lots of folks have yet to benefit from training on "difficult conversations," feedback delivery, or the grey area of when one should intervene. It's sometimes murky business. We need to know the *how*, and I hope this book may help. There may be those in your entourage who do this well and are willing to help.

2. **"I'm so busy; I don't have enough time."** This can be a dodgy excuse—there's always busy work that can conveniently need our attention just when a sticky situation we'd rather avoid is presenting. Or it can be a truthful statement, and I am sympathetic to those who struggle with managing the high demands of leading in our warp-speed world. But postponing or avoiding messy but needed interventions while putting out fires reveals an urgent need to master time management and personal efficiency habits. This serves as yet another reminder of the importance of learning to negotiate well and being watchful over our time—our only true inventory.

3. **"I'm afraid of the person and/or their reaction."** This response is a common one. I find that what helps in this situation is to give the hesitant leader a script of what needs to be said. The leader thinks through both the obvious consequences and the unintended consequences of intervening, and is coached to be comfortable with the discomfort that comes with doing so, whether with or without sound practices.

4. **"It is useless; it won't change anything."** An HR colleague of mine refers to this response as "managerial impotence"—pointing your finger at a cumbersome bureaucracy or other external factors and saying, "Why should I bother?" The generous view is

that tools and practices will help this type of leader. Perhaps past attempts did not have the outcomes that had been hoped for, and maybe that was because of the method, the timing, and potentially a host of other circumstances. The less generous view is that such a perspective—that it's useless to try to improve a situation—raises the question of how appropriate it is for that person to be in a leadership role to begin with. We are in the business of solving people-related problems, and the day that this becomes "useless" may be the time for questioning person–job fit.

5. **"I want to avoid conflict."** Don't we all? Dr. Tammy Carroll, whom we met in chapter 4, reminds us that interpersonal conflict and its resolution can be messy and not fun, especially when left unattended to fester. Yet a leader's role is to shed light on things. Role conflicts will emerge often, but that doesn't mean they are interpersonal conflicts. People leaders learn that the magic comes from an ability to move through daily truth telling, making sometimes uncomfortable interventions. It also comes from surfacing conflict in a responsible, respectful, and deliberate way so that we achieve a creative and highly effective problem-solving way of working. All conflict is not to be avoided. Role conflicts raise issues of "turf"—which responsibilities, tasks, budgets, and people are yours and which are mine. Moving through those types of differences well and with dignity is the work of leadership. Interpersonal conflicts, on the other hand, need to be paid attention to with measured urgency, timely response, and confident assuredness of exactly what to do and try, just like a skilled team of fire fighters works to extinguish a fire.

When managers and supervisors can call upon specific tools or approaches that they've tried and that have proven successful, they can take a measured approach to intervening. But there are also those who seem fearless. If rarely getting involved is problematic, what about the flip side of measured action?

Micromanagement

Have you noticed how micromanagement, the over-involvement of a supervisor or manager in the work of their direct reports, is often referred to as a disease? It's referred to as a "contagious infection," something that requires diagnosis and a cure.[5] This comparison is apt given that a micromanaging boss can make workplaces, teams, and individuals noticeably unhealthy.[6]

Micromanaging as a style of intervention is not always caused by ill intent or by a supervisor's insecurities, perfectionist tendencies, or control/trust issues, although admittedly these are the top contenders to help us understand micromanaging.

Take the example of Ryan, an outgoing and upbeat IT manager known for his ability to spot talent. Ryan cares about his people's learning and their progress, and cares a lot about results. He sets high standards. The generous interpretation of Ryan's management tendencies would be to say that he hovers, figuratively and literally. Though appropriate in the early going, this approach becomes problematic when Ryan doesn't pull back as his new charges get stronger, demonstrate confidence, and become more accomplished. Ryan was candid in describing his leadership challenge:

> I don't mean to micromanage. I worked for a controlling, perfectionist micromanager once and hated it. He was a pleasant enough person, but I learned nothing except how to be a micromanager, and it robbed me of my confidence.
>
> I know micromanaging kills initiative and drives people out of their jobs—I know that. But I like to monitor, and I like details. I've learned there are often not enough limitations or constraints on the delegated piece of work; people crave direction, so I make sure to establish clear boundaries for decision-making. I know having too many hindrances and limitations will not give people freedom of thought or movement. Getting that balance just right is never easy, but now we work at it.
>
> Otherwise, I'm curious and want to be helpful, but I accept that I'm probably just in the way with a few too many comments talking

about the *how* when I know I need to be talking about the *what* and leave the details and minutia of the *how* to my very capable people. I get really uncomfortable when I don't have control. If I'm clear on our progress, I can let go and shut up more!

We've devised a signal that enables my team members to tell me very directly when they feel my *helpful* nature and concern is creeping up on micromanaging, and it helps me catch myself and step back. Their feedback has been instrumental in my becoming a recovering micromanager and inching along to being a much better delegator. Okay, I'll never be great at it, but hopefully it won't stall and divert my career again.

As Ryan explains, he found a way to catch his micromanaging urges so that he could counter them by (1) setting clear expectations with measurable progress indicators; (2) consistently coaching but not constricting unnecessarily; and most critically (3) managing outcomes, results, and deliverables.

Knee-Jerk Reactions

Micromanagers drive away good people and hurt their organizations in numerous ways. Less troubling but worthy of mention are the knee-jerk reactions that leaders sometimes exhibit.

Some supervisors and managers combat leadership knee-jerk reactions better than others. Do you ever give a quick answer to a colleague's question, only to realize on further reflection that providing a bit more of an explanation, or maybe better yet posing a question to the colleague, might help them learn and become less dependent on your sage advice next time around?

Equally as concerning are managers and team leaders who, at the first sign of trouble, reel in assignments that have been entrusted to a direct report with a fair amount of independence. Their knee-jerk reaction, pulling back delegated work when it is not going as planned, can have long-lasting effects.

Only after paying very deliberate attention, seeking out robust feedback and data, thoroughly discussing why we're off course, and reviewing people's roles and work plans should we consider pulling back delegated work.

When a leader steps in, seemingly out of left field and at the first sign of trouble, it signals a frailty of confidence and trust in the other person's abilities. Sometimes it's the right thing to do; however, it needs to be done selectively and thoughtfully. Leaving the work where it belongs is a critical leadership and management function.

Our work as leaders requires thoughtful responses, not reactions born of an inability to temper our urge to jump all over a situation. And thoughtful responses require an informed choice.

Do Not Limit Your Choices

Choosing when to step in makes a difference. Humans are not great decision-makers at the best of times, and when dealing with people issues, we can really get in our own way. Researchers have narrowed the problem down to a few things we do that are not very helpful.[7]

For starters, we tend to restrict the number of alternatives when important decisions are before us. Have you found yourself in a situation where coming up with those first two viable options is relatively easy but finding a third option is incrementally harder?

Maybe it's the yin-yang, heads or tails, up or down, left brain-right brain split that forces us down the path of these false dichotomies. There are always more options: curiosity and questions lead to human ingenuity. Pushing beyond the obvious and sparking the creative thought process is the highest order of work that leaders do. It doesn't have to be the idea of the century; simply a boring old third viable option is brilliant creative work!

Tough choices narrow our field of vision, and being aware of that constriction gives you an edge. (Hint: Always be the one who pushes for the third viable option—you may have to go through quite a few ideas before you get the *viable* part taken care of.)

Some choices people leaders make can have sweeping ramifications on the lives of employees and their families. We owe it to ourselves and others to find a host of creative alternatives, especially when messing with people's work, jobs, and careers.

Second, both conscious and unconscious bias kick in, and we narrow our range of information and data to prioritizing the ones that agree with our initial position or our first choice. If I initially thought that I should deal with an employee's interpersonal conflict on my team without calling my pals in HR for guidance, I am apt to favor any information that agrees with my own position and discard information that doesn't. (Hint: Get a second opinion to combat the confirmation bias described above, someone who will give it to you straight to correct some of your self-serving bias.)

Unconscious bias is a big deal. Bias is evident in our decisions about most things, and we're not yet an evolved enough species to shed our unconscious bias or "mindbugs," as the authors of *Blindspot: The Hidden Biases of Good People* so aptly call them. "Debugging" ourselves from our human need to categorize and stereotype is a big ask, but awareness is our starting point.[8]

Third, your emotions can color your decision-making. We've all learned to count to ten or go for a walk or take deep breaths to prevent ourselves from letting our trying emotions derail our better judgment and potentially our well-being or reputation. Choosing calm is an imperative when leaders get involved, and such techniques can help you assess where you are emotionally as you make decisions.

Lastly, many leaders are prone to overconfidence, as exhibited in their choices and decision-making, which are typically overly optimistic about the future.[9] That overconfidence is no more helpful in the decision-making realm than it is anywhere else. Realistic optimism is the goal, allowing decisions to be taken against a backdrop of facts, data, and a consensus around what the facts are saying. Human resource information systems, performance data, and valued opinions of trusted colleagues can tame our natural inclination to overestimate how much can get done by a particular deadline. When faced with challenging choices on whether you should get involved, be the one pushing for facts and data and for securing as accurate and unbiased a read of that information as possible by putting several heads together.

Leaders are faced with choices related to intervention every day. We interject and sometimes disrupt, we purposefully say nothing, we coach, we coax, and we sometimes use silence to compel others to step up. We intentionally move the critical thinking and reflection along by joyously jolting people with a thoughtful and timely observation that alters their assumptions, surfaces their biases, stimulates their curiosity, and moves the creative process along. Those are the insights we need to cultivate, the ones that, when shared, help us all make progress. That's the work of leaders, and that's how true leaders get involved.

Tension and Conflict

Veteran professional basketball coach and likely future Hall of Famer Mike D'Antoni was asked about the prevalence of conflict in the groups and teams he had led in his forty years of managing individuals, coaches, and other personnel. He replied, "There's always tension. That's okay—that can be a great thing. Once in a while there's conflict, and you have to deal with it."[10]

I really like Coach D'Antoni's take on tension. It concurs with what researchers have demonstrated: when workplace conflict is moderate and related to tasks, processes, and how we get the job done, the normal tension level can be positive. This type of conflict is indeed positive and needed, but only when it's at most a 3 on a conflict intensity scale of 1 to 5. Such conflict is purely about the work—and oh yeah, we have an environment of high psychological safety and nothing is ever personal![11] The moment conflict does not fit into that framework, the moment it becomes about personality, is the moment it's no longer positive. In fact, it can be as bad as we might fear it to be.

You probably don't like conflict, and I don't either. People thinking about the usefulness of conflict from a management and leadership perspective have long said that the avoidance of conflict is a management behavior, whereas working with conflict to make progress is a leadership behavior.[12] Conflict avoidance by managers is in part understandable; as they are on the hook to deliver a good or service on time and on budget, they want to minimize conflict. In fact, they want to minimize anything that will get in the way of their team meeting its objectives.

Let's be realistic. Managing interpersonal conflict and conflict in general is difficult—certainly one of the most difficult things we undertake in our team leadership and management roles. I believe many of us, especially as emerging people leaders, are caught flat-footed in our first such situation, and because we are sometimes hesitant, scared, and reluctant, we default to highly mechanistic disciplinary policies and procedures—we become heavy handed.

In my years of working with supervisors, managers, and team leaders, they've often expressed their inability—or more precisely their perceived inability—to deal with interpersonal conflict on their teams as one of their greatest concerns, and they acknowledge it as one of the greatest opportunities for growth.

I can't tell you how often I heard the well-worn yet brutally ineffective response, "I told them they had to work it out—they don't have to be friends, just work together." There is wisdom in having people attempt to resolve their differences unassisted, through conversation. But telling two people or a group in full-blown conflict to simply work it out, without assistance, guidance, or tools, is imprudent.

People leaders need to know what they don't know, especially in matters related to highly contentious and loaded conflict management. Dr. Tammy Carroll can help us understand the requisite nature and power of self-awareness and has been doing research on a too-frequent outcome of escalated conflict: workplace bullying. In her conflict management practice within the Canadian federal public service, Dr. Carroll quickly figured out with her team that their best shot at reducing escalated and intense conflict situations was to focus on prevention—because, let's be honest, mediations are typically grueling. Yet many would likely prefer a mediation or a few conflict coaching sessions than a case (or alleged case) of workplace bullying.

If there's one thing that the 250 client managers Dr. Carroll works with in four Canadian provinces can likely agree on, it's that they, more than most, have a vested interest in creating unfavorable conditions for unresolved conflict. People leaders may feel overwhelmed by the complexity of intervening in conflict, managing it, and bringing about resolution or making progress, whether with or without the help of HR folks or conflict resolution specialists. But the stuff of successful conflict prevention is the stuff of good leadership and of being a credible employer.

The federal government is the largest employer in the country, and its workforce has access, by law, to conflict management and mediation services. Dr. Carroll believes that her team's focus on prevention delivered via training, workshops, and coaching is starting to pay off, noting that it has led to "fewer mediation interventions, and those we are involved in are less severe and entrenched. And let's face it—doing a team-building exercise is way more fun for clients than a three-day conflict resolution group process."

Carroll adds another important focus: organizations that foster a prevention-rich climate—in which people leaders facilitate self-awareness through robust feedback, pay close attention to team dynamics, and deal with tensions and conflicts quickly and actively—put themselves in the best position to be inhospitable to interpersonal conflict. Given that most of us don't have access to our own conflict resolution practitioner, we can benefit from Carroll's five actionable suggestions for people leaders in relation to conflict management.

1. **Seek knowledge:** Self-awareness is pivotal, not only for leaders (as discussed in chapter 4) but for all team members. Consider investing in assessments such as the MBTI, Insights, or EQ-i 2.0. They are valuable and accessible. Most critical, as we know, is a robust feedback regime that is led and modeled by team leaders. Destructive conflict can be minimized when an entire team is aware of its members' individual and team preferences and mindful of the team's inclinations (abilities, shortcomings, and triggers).

2. **Emphasize prevention:** Meaningful team-building matters. The annual company barbecue is still a great idea, and even more so the weekly debrief over seasonal beverages on Fridays, but imagine adding to these measures training that really builds teams with the use of psychometric assessments such as the Thomas-Kilmann Instrument or the MBTI. Any credible team assessment that helps members understand each other better and appreciate diversity and generational differences at work is worthwhile.

3. **Deal with it!:** Difficult conversations are what team leaders, managers, and business owners have to do. The problem won't go away, and if action is delayed, things will just get tougher. Still not sure? Consider the cost of doing nothing.

4. **Check perceptions and assumptions:** Don't assume that one person's impression and understanding is accurate. Deal with it—times two!

5. **Remember that the problem is not yours:** It belongs to those in conflict, but your role is to provide support and ensure that something is being done. Consider your likely indirect or direct contribution to the conflict and intervene accordingly.

The White Paint Outcome

What happens after conflict? How do you put the pieces together after parties have worked through their friction? How do you find a new way of being after the harshness of hurt feelings, painful mediation sessions, and perhaps even a formal investigation? What happens when we reintegrate those who've had to step aside for whatever reason? How do teams become whole again post-conflict? In addressing these questions, people leaders need to be vigilant and to continue to seek out advice and reflect diligently on how to best get beyond the difficulties. Sometimes it's simply about taking the first step.

Henri Mikhael had been warned by his superiors about the state of the hundred-employee plant he managed, which was owned by a large industrial group. Graffiti on walls and machinery was evidence of the toxic work climate. The place was filthy, was losing money, had a poor safety record, and was subject to labor strife. The plant would be mothballed if things didn't improve.

The most glaring symbol of the rancor and conflict was the supervisors' office, which, equipped with a lock and buzz-in mechanism to prevent unauthorized entry, looked more like a military-style bunker than an office. Supervisors felt safer behind locked doors, protected from their direct reports.

Mikhael knew that, to turn the situation around and move beyond years of conflict, he needed to instill among all affected parties a shared sense of purpose for the plant's long-term viability. He started with the union president. Using an approach the wily GM calls "tit-for-tat baby steps," he told them, "You don't know me, but I'm here to take the first step. When you then take a step, I'll take another, and so on."

The union president agreed, and the duo began modestly. Time was allotted for employees to clean their work environment at the beginning of their shift, encouraging them to build a sense of ownership and pride for the cleanliness of their station from the start to the end of the shift. It worked. Employees liked the attention of the many small but not insignificant changes made after Mikhael and the supervisors met everyone at their work stations in a series of one-on-ones. Such meetings had previously happened in the supervisor's office or at a table in the kitchen when there was a new GM cycling through. Every time Mikhael took another step, the union leader reciprocated. Graffiti disappeared, the supervisors' office was de-bunkered, and production and safety eventually improved.

Mikhael knew they had come a long way in a short time when employees requested an unusually large amount of white paint. Workers were determined that, with a white floor instead of the customary industrial grey, everyone would see they had the cleanest and therefore the best plant in the company.

BUILDING ON THE takeaways from this chapter, chapter 14 presents intervention strategies. How a leader chooses to intervene defines their leadership, as we see almost daily in public life. This principle applies on the shop floor, too.

> **Taking Stock of Your Humanity at Work**
>
> Do you agree that managing interpersonal conflict and conflict in general is difficult, and that it is certainly one of the most difficult things leaders deal with? As you answer the following questions about your people leadership practice, consider how you might apply Dr. Carroll's five actions when dealing with conflict.
>
> 1. Have you avoided intervening in a situation that you know called for an intervention? Why?
>
> 2. Have you intervened too early when you should have waited? Recall why that happened.
>
> 3. Is there currently a situation in which you are unsure whether you should intervene or not? What would be the advantage of you getting involved?
>
> 4. What are some of the signals of psychological safety you've witnessed? What are some signals of psychological safety you attempted to send?
>
> 5. On a scale of 1 to 5, how psychologically safe is your work environment? What might you try in your leadership practice to enhance psychological safety among your immediate colleagues?

6. What strategies might you use in attempting to transform your team or workplace into one that is even more inhospitable to interpersonal conflict than it is now?

(14)
How Do I Know If I Am Making the Right Call?

As we've discussed, the ways a team leader takes action are varied and the possibilities are many and nuanced. Some challenging conversations will likely take place along the way. The four approaches we will outline in this chapter—paying closer attention, sharing your observations, asking insightful questions, and ultimately taking action—are all intended to get leaders to think about how they intervene. After all, the way a leader chooses to intervene defines their leadership. Understanding that we have options when that inner voice tells us that we should do something, and having a nuanced way of thinking about how to intercede, increases the likelihood we will do something appropriate and meaningful. It also helps us choose an alternative that raises the heat not for its own sake but with the clear goal of achieving better outcomes.

Four Ways to Get Involved

Leadership scholars argue for small and straightforward leadership interventions that are situationally based.[1] Although the following four approaches are described as separate for our purposes, in real life they will overlap and can be powerful mechanisms on their own or blended together to best suit the situation.

1. **Pay Closer Attention**

Our first option for stepping in is getting involved by not getting involved. We've already established the imperative of paying attention. Now it's time to pay *closer* attention.

Norbert Poirier—successful businessperson in the gaming sector, sailboat builder, airplane pilot, builder of drones used by the Canadian and US military in the 1970s, and trouble shooter extraordinaire—doesn't miss a thing! I accompanied the septuagenarian to a Thunderbird sailboat regatta at the historic (circa 1875) Savin Hill Yacht Club in Dorchester, Massachusetts. My job was to take in the sights at the yacht club while Poirier mingled with his brother and sister sailors and builders. Thunderbird racers are a labor of love for their owners, with many like Poirier having purchased a set of drawings and consequently spending four to five years, amounting to thousands of hours, constructing their dream boat.[2] There was a lot to take in on a blustery day on the bay that is home to the spectacular John F. Kennedy Presidential Museum.

We later compared notes. Poirier observed everything in the setting—things I missed completely, not solely because I'm a landlubber and he's an experienced captain, but because I *saw* while he *observed*. He could have spoken at length about the salt air infused with gasoline and diesel, the wind gusting due east, the striking colors of one remarkable sail in the harbor, and the fleet of power boats bobbing from their moorings in the harbor. He could then have told you several very specific details of each boat he had got up close and personal with. That level of observation is a skill honed by a deliberate and conscious exercising of your observation muscles.

The United Nations sends trained observers to witness an election in fledgling democracies. Here are some proven ideas on how you can become a trained observer as a people leader. These are a blend of the best of the scientific method and other insights. What other ideas might you add?

- Scan the big picture, then quickly look at important details and zoom in even more.
- Engage all your senses.
- Take notes.
- Count things.
- Look for patterns and textures.
- Ask yourself how it works and come up with an assessment.
- Demonstrate curiosity and inquisitiveness—ask questions.
- Share what you believe is really going on, and be prepared to be wrong.

The role of the observer is to discriminate. Often the difference between the novice and the expert is the expert's ability to quickly determine what's relevant and what's irrelevant.

2. Create a Learning Moment by Sharing an Observation

I trust you've had the joy of working with conscientious folks for whom a simple observation based in fact can be a powerful instigator for change. Notice that this influence takes the form of a sharing of information and that it is left up to the individual to reflect upon and process the feedback. Armed with your observational superpowers, you are now in a position to provide an observation without judgment as a way of intervening. By way of illustration, this leads me to introduce Katherine d'Entremont, former commissioner of official languages in New Brunswick.

Provincial and territorial legislative assemblies appoint auditors general and independent statutory officers to report directly to the legislature and the public on matters of financial and operational efficiency. There are a small number of such roles in most areas, such as child and youth advocacy, elections, and citizens' privacy, and most areas have an ombudsperson to field complaints from citizens. In New Brunswick, one such officer, tasked with auditing and investigating whether government is following Canada's laws and constitution as well as its own rules and procedures, was Katherine d'Entremont.

You would be forgiven for assuming that someone who made public proclamations to hold government to account, held press conferences, and publicized her office's annual reports and investigation findings would believe that the way to mobilize others is to report observations, findings, and interpretations of events publicly. d'Entremont agrees this is part of the process and would tell you, as she told me, that her favorite way to intervene was one-on-one, armed only with facts and her observations, because that's where real traction happens. She shared with me that "intervening one-on-one is how you can have the most impact. It's slower, more tedious and time consuming, but potentially leads to better results."

When Madame la commissaire sat privately with whomever, often speaking truth to power, she intervened by making observations and simply presenting the facts. It must be said that she also brought to her role a reputation of untarnished personal integrity, being called to public service and devising and implementing the very first policies, training programs, investigation processes, and redress mechanisms to tackle bullying and harassment, sexual harassment, poisoned work environments, and the lopsided hiring and promotion practices in relation to women, visible minorities, Indigenous peoples, and people with disabilities. Commissioner d'Entremont brought personal and professional credibility to her interventions, as well as an immense capacity for empathy.

Yes, d'Entremont was tough, gritty, and unrelenting, but she was also defined by her uncompromising humanity and was confident in letting facts and her observations be the catalyst when she intervened.

3. **Use a Question Combo**

You may have noticed that one of the central threads throughout this book is the multifaceted value of asking good questions that are intentional, ideally suited for the situation or circumstance, and useful to all. Questions are a meaningful, intentional way to intervene, and they can stand alone or alternatively be the equivalent of your favorite side dish with which you can combo anything.

Has this happened to you? Your colleague asks for a moment with you, asks an insightful question, and then leaves without giving you time to answer! I worked with a fascinating person who would ask a colleague a question and, upon finishing, would say, "Just something for you to think about. End of story." There was no follow-up in a task-related sense, but every question had a purpose and a lesson if you unpacked your answers upon further reflection.

This person's questions came as a result of their noticing something in the other person's approach. Sometimes a question was all that was needed to set the tone for further conversations. Their favorite leadership device was the question: a simple question that would lead to reflection and self-insight for the person being asked.

My favorite approach is the "observation and question combo." If I want to turn up the heat a notch, I share my observation—my take or interpretation of what's really going on—and then ask a question. For example, I might say to a fledgling team leader, "I've noticed you meet with your team members for a one-on-one coaching session once a month. Is the monthly schedule for your sake or do your team members feel the frequency of your meetings is appropriate to get what they need from you?"

A people leader who makes effective questions one of their defining strengths and something they consciously work on does so much more than sharpen their team leadership and coaching chops. That leader is able to shape the workplace climate; create the crucial dimension of psychological safety and eliminate questions that seek to blame, disempower, and humiliate; and role model the curiosity and inquisitiveness that fuel questions that help solve problems. A team defined by questions that empower and teach, rather than questions that judge, is a learning team, not a judging team. There is a huge difference between "What happened that led to this problem?" and "Who is responsible for this mess?" There is a huge difference between "What can we do about this?" and "Whose fault is this?" There is a world of difference between "What can we learn from this?" and "Why can't you get this right?" If the question generates curiosity and reflection, it's likely a learning question.

4. Take Action

We've come 180 degrees from the last chapter's starting point, when I bemoaned the common and insidious problem of people leader inaction. We are now at the next step. You've intervened as a conscientious leader should, by paying close attention, sharing your take, and asking all the right questions. In some instances, it will be necessary to move in a little deeper. Let's look at the increasingly controversial concept of progressive discipline and an innovative practice called the "turnaround interview," which is intended to avoid progressive discipline.

When we as managers and supervisors think of taking action as a form of leader intervention, we often think about progressive discipline, which is a formal way of addressing job-related behavior or performance that does not meet agreed-upon expectations. The goal of this approach is to help an employee comprehend that a problem is present that offers an opportunity for improvement, and that over a specified time the situation needs to get better—otherwise, there are consequences up to and including termination of employment. The actions of the employer are formal and progressive, the latter meaning that the steps in process become increasingly severe. Critics suggest this harkens back to the antiquated punishment-based approach of the Industrial Revolution, and that it does nothing to help team leaders better manage inappropriate behavior or bad performance, other than in extreme cases.[3]

How quickly or reluctantly employers resort to progressive discipline is a function of their workplace culture. And though executing successfully on formal discipline takes skill and is no fun, it is by and large a technical HR issue that most organizations get right if they put their mind to it. I often hear from managers and supervisors how challenged they are in their ability to correct, redress, or alter behavior, and they are usually talking about how to intervene before the last resort of progressive discipline needs to be applied.

But progressive discipline—a process that includes a verbal warning, then a written one, then suspension with or without pay, and ultimately termination of employment—is increasingly under scrutiny. Progressives now advocate a problem-solving rather than a punitive approach for the policy or procedural breaches that occupy the most time of unfortunate team leaders who are caught in a spiral of having to write people up and document their files. But legal advisors continue to insist that the practice still has its place, especially with regard to the most egregious of employee discipline and termination issues.

The Turnaround Interview

One way of taking action is through something my friend and colleague George Raine, a pioneer in HR and labor relations in Canada, created: the Turnaround Interview® (TI).[4] A tool for managers and supervisors to use when other forms of intervention have not succeeded, it provides an opportunity to avoid the weighty succession of events that comprise formal progressive discipline. As Raine explains, the TI is an informal conversation that has as its foundation a framework where an employee is presented with detailed evidence and in response acknowledges the problem, generates their own options for dealing with the behavior or performance shortcoming, and then commits to redressing the issue and to subsequent follow-up conversations.

Raine and his company, Montana HR (named after a Swiss boarding school—not the US state, as he'll quickly tell you), have successfully trained thousands of employees in unionized and non-unionized environments. Many employers, with full support from their unions, include the TI as part of their core curriculum when training supervisors. It offers users the comfort of an established and thoroughly researched procedure that is trainable and easily learned, and that, through practice, serves as an invaluable tool for managers and supervisors who want to intervene by taking action that lands just shy of invoking formal discipline. It is a thoughtfully designed way of turning up the heat.

Knowing When to Lower the Heat

The act of lowering the heat comes to us much more easily, so easily we might not even know we are doing it. We have all been at a gathering when the elephant in the room is broached or something thought of as off-limits within the workplace culture (aka a sacred cow) is challenged. Instantly, there is silence of the pin-dropping variety, perhaps an audible gasp, a sense of the air rushing out of the room, and a collective lowering of the eyes towards the floor and squirming in chairs. In an instinctive bid to decrease the discomfort in the room, someone—whether the person who elevated the temperature or someone else—says something to soften the remark, negate it, or change the subject, and the tension is released. They may even make a wisecrack, or "name what is happening" by exclaiming "Awk-waaard!"

What happens next in this situation depends on many things and reveals much about that group's workplace culture. On some job sites, a healthy if uncomfortable exchange takes place to air out or resolve an issue. High-functioning groups have developed that ability. This isn't always an easy path, but hopefully you've been part of a team or group of folks where such awkward conversations can take place.

In other settings, full-blown avoidance behaviors take hold. In some situations, it is appropriate to lower the temperature if only to assure civility and appropriate conduct or to allow the best chance for a productive exchange. What strong leaders do, however, is take note of the tension, discomfort, and energy in the room at that moment and decide consciously whether to address the issue in spite of how uncomfortable it will be or to lower the temperature temporarily and then deliberately revisit the issue in a matter of minutes or days.

Read the Energy Levels

A leader's ability to sense the temperature can be compared to an accomplished facilitator's skill in "reading" energy levels in a group. Master facilitators, at any point in their work with a group, can tell you on a scale of 1 to 10 what the energy level is and know when they need to do something to bring it back up when it is waning. Watch how the good ones will interject an unscheduled stretch break, move people to different locations in the physical space, or quickly refocus the group through provocative questions or humor to re-energize the room.

Strong leaders do the same thing. When a comment, remark, or impromptu event raises the heat in a group or a one-on-one, they are conscious of where things are at and are always taking the temperature to know how and when to do something about it. Let's look at an example.

When Ali accepted the role as head of his department, he did so with full knowledge of the challenges his predecessors had experienced when dealing with four middle managers, a situation that he gave serious consideration. Yara, one of the most experienced managers, was the division's comedian, quick with a joke and, though competent, sometimes much more interested in scoring a laugh than getting down to business. The other manager of note was the division's self-appointed "caller outer" of elephants in the room. If there was a topic people generally wanted to avoid, you could count on MJ to raise the issue, always appropriately but usually provocatively as well.

Ali knew management meetings would be a challenge. The psychometric testing he had done always pointed to his having a pleaser personality. Striving for harmony and wanting people to get along was very important to him. Ali was now trying to view healthy conflict as a means of making progress and solving problems, so taking on this new role meant tempering his urge to always smooth things over and keep the peace. As fate would have it, he was blessed with two individuals on the management team—Yara and MJ—who would test the limits of his newfound focus on not shutting things down at the first signs of disagreement, discomfort, or strife. On some days, that blessing felt like a curse.

Management meetings would typically play out in the following fashion: MJ, who was also relatively new to the team, would challenge or question a long-standing approach or process. The more contentious the issue was, the more Yara would distract or divert the team with one-liners, puns, and clever wordplay. Yara's sense of humor was whimsical and ingenious. Everyone in the room enjoyed the levity but was also relieved to not have to broach what MJ was bringing out in the open. "Old Ali" would have used Yara's diversion tactics to gently shut down MJ or placate the issue with a "let's take this offline" avoidance strategy when the comments risked taking the group to an uncomfortable place.

"New and improved Ali" would now pay close attention to moments when pleaser chimes rang and peacemaker tendencies were set off. Striving to assess the temperature in the room (using a 10-point scale) and ensuring the discomfort was allowed to persist through the ensuing dialogue (always within the bounds of respect and appropriate behavior) was now the order of the day. Over time, Ali and the team were becoming increasingly comfortable with the requisite unpleasantness some issues surfaced, and Ali was not giving in to his internal default settings when things were heating up. Ali realized that, subconsciously, he was placing his chin in his hand and had his forefinger over his mouth as if to silence urges to lower the temperature prematurely.

WITH TACTICS FOR intervention now under our belts, in the next section we move on to another way a leader can motivate people to get things done—through reward and recognition. When approached meaningfully, this can be a strong binding agent for a thriving culture.

Taking Stock of Your Humanity at Work

The four approaches outlined in this chapter (paying closer attention, sharing our take on things, asking really good questions, and taking action) are all intended to make leaders think about how they get involved in workplace issues. After all, the way a leader chooses to intervene defines their leadership. As you answer the following questions about your people leadership practice, reflect on Ali's newly developed awareness and his work on not jumping in at the first sign that things are uncomfortable for him or for members of his team. Consider how developing such powers of observation and self-control could serve you.

1. The next time you're in a group setting, take the temperature (i.e., assess the level of discomfort) on a scale of 1 to 10 (10 being so hot it's dysfunctional and 1 being so cool it's not evident that people have a pulse). What happens next that raises or decreases the temperature?

2. In what setting might you be very attuned to a raising or lowering of the temperature?

3. How do you react to triggers or chimes in your head when the temperature is being raised one-on-one or in a group? Can you assess the temperature on a scale of 1 to 10?

4. Do you lower the heat with humor, avoidance, or another diversion tactic, or do you assess the temperature and strategically respond?

When done meaningfully, recognizing and rewarding people can be a strong binding agent for a thriving workplace culture. And who doesn't want the people in our organizations to be more industrious, engaged, and creative? This section explores how leaders can nourish the sense in people that they are valued so that they are not shy about connecting well-being to clear expectations and high standards. Critical to this element of humanity at work is the relationship between leaders and their HR colleagues (or the HR part of their brain), and how that partnership can work wonders.

PART FIVE

Recognizing and Rewarding

(15)
Do I Reward and Recognize People Appropriately?

WHEN THEIR FRIEND lost a family member to depression, four running buddies decided to host a run in support of mental health. John Dallaire, Patrick O'Brien, Robert LeBlanc, and Richard Bennett are nothing if not resourceful. Over the course of ten years, and initially with no corporate backing or marquee sponsor, they have raised, with the help of the local community and the generosity of local enterprises large and small, well over $300,000 for depression and mental health programs by organizing the Three Mountain Relay.

The event is purposely kept low key, focused on giving and on the building of solidarity among community-minded runners. These four friends were not in it for the fame. And "thank goodness," said quick-witted Pat O'Brien. "There's no fame or fortune in this gig." But although recognition for their efforts was the furthest thing from their minds, on April 25, 2019, they attended a regal ceremony at Rideau Hall in Ottawa, where Governor General Julie Payette bestowed upon them the Meritorious Service Medal.

Despite the public ceremony, what motivated these men was not an extrinsic reward but their humanitarian effort. Their story provides a clear example of an intrinsic reward—of being motivated by a challenge and a contribution to community and of overcoming the setbacks inherent in organizing any event where weather, participant safety, and countless other headaches are bound to happen.

Extrinsic and Intrinsic Rewards

Does recognition, an extrinsic motivator, help or hinder those of us who are motivated intrinsically by what we do? Noted researchers Edward Deci and Richard Ryan describe intrinsic motivation as "playing and learning in this eager and willing way."[1] The rewards come from the work itself, when our role aligns with our strengths and we find ourselves in the flow of our work. For example, the desire to exceed client expectations is derived from the joy of exceeding client expectations. On the other hand, extrinsic motivation is grounded in the expectation of recognition, status, and money in return for doing hard or repetitive or even dangerous work. And we can find motivation in both types of rewards.

The challenge for leaders is to figure out—based on people's unique attributes and personality as well as the work environment—how to increase the factor of intrinsic motivation to bring out the best in people. Imagine helping create an environment where people's intrinsic needs are met and where we surround them with compelling reasons to do great work.

We ignite what already burns inside them and then we fairly reward and recognize and compensate. Now that's leadership—when we get the blend of intrinsic and external motivators just right with our folks. You may not be able to pull all of those levers to the extent that you would like in working with your team members, but you can pull some of them, and they have an impact because people will feel valued. The first lever we will talk about is social recognition.

Social Recognition

Our four friends were keenly motivated year after year to organize the relay event. You could describe their effort as noble, but most of us can draw great inspiration from the impact our work has on end users, be they clients, patients, or the citizens we serve as public servants. Someone up or down the line benefits from your work. And sometimes leaders need to get creative about understanding everyone's impact up or down the line, direct or indirect, and to really speak to the purpose of people's work in relation to that client, patient, citizen, and so on.

As a consequence of their public recognition at Rideau Hall, the relay organizers came to understand better than most that the power of such recognition has much to do with its public nature and with the multiplier effect of having it known to many people, including a close circle of people who are meaningful to the recipient.

Social recognition has moved on from awarding plaques, years-of-service pins, and gold watches to using the power of recognition—especially from peer to peer—as a motivator. Now technology-assisted, mobile-enabled recognition is the domain of many recognition companies that offer these services to employers large and small. If my colleague provides me with estimable customer service, I can nominate them for recognition via my workstation or mobile app. That recognition can be turned into points that accumulate over time, and the individual's recognition history is available to their team leader for a coaching session or performance review.

But social recognition is not exclusive to employers who deploy their HR teams to devise recognition programs. Enlightened people leaders use low-tech social recognition all the time, which is especially effective with those for whom the social part may be a bit uncomfortable.

Larry Nelson led the Lounsbury Group for many years as the CEO of the storied family- and employee-owned automotive and furniture retailer. Nelson's seemingly boundless generosity and gracious humility are grounded in his leadership style, itself a product of generations of company values. Nelson will tell you, as he told me, that he owes his style to the values of respect and courtesy instilled by his father. Those who knew the teenaged Nelson said he stood out in how he supported and genuinely encouraged others when it was cooler for guys to put each other down. But make no mistake: underneath Nelson's gracious humility beats the heart of a competitor motivated to exceed customer expectations, be successful, and generate a return for shareholders while also being an exemplary corporate citizen.

Nelson's competitive spirit and community-mindedness led him to partner with Bill Whalen, co-owner of Hawk Communications, to co-chair the IAAF Junior World Track and Field Championships in Moncton, New Brunswick, one of the smallest municipalities to ever host a world championship. An event of this scale had never happened in such a small city, and executing it required partnerships for infrastructure funding. The stadium built for the event remains a testament to Nelson and Whalen's achievements, but they would be lightning fast to point out the efforts of many others to pull it off. These leaders are cut from the same social recognition cloth as the Three Mountain Relay founders—a cloth worn by many.

I have the very good fortune of making music with talented co-conspirators and I derive great joy from using that platform to support various causes and community events. We are often the unassuming trio in the corner of the reception or dinner, playing quiet background jazz to provide ambiance. From my double bass chair, I have watched Whalen or Nelson "work the room" *before* the guests show up, putting a different spin on the concept.

The hosts, unassumingly, and with no apparent order in mind, would amble over to servers and hotel staff, the event organizers—and, yes, to the recognition-starved musicians—and in a calm jovial way say things like, "I am sure glad we're here for this function, knowing people of your caliber will be working the event." They then chit chat a bit, maybe have a shrimp, and thank everyone for what they do.

Nelson, a legendary relationship builder, understands the place social recognition holds in a leader's toolbox of motivational devices. He was the leader of a sales organization where extrinsic rewards continue to abound in campaigns and seasonal sales contests, and where bonuses and commissions form an integral part of that world. But he would be the first to acknowledge that recognition in the sales-driven automotive or home furnishings world is not the same as recognition in the hospitality industry, the healthcare sector, or the fast-food business, or at La Bibliothèque Champlain de l'Université de Moncton (my favorite research library, where everyone whispers). The practice of loudly ringing the recognition bell for all to hear (it is an actual bell at one of the Lounsbury car dealerships that peels in celebration when a sale is made) may not work very well elsewhere. Context is crucial to how we use recognition at its best.

Recognition forms a key component of what researchers call perceived organizational support—that is, whether you sense your contribution is valued and whether you believe your employer cares about your well-being. Along with fairness and inclusion, recognition contributes greatly to an employee's sense that they are valued and supported.[2]

Here's the very good news: When your people believe their contribution is valued and their welfare paramount, they will be more hard-working, committed, and innovative.[3] Leaders can readily influence whether people feel valued and cared for. Who doesn't want those in our entourage to be more industrious, engaged, and creative? So how do we as leaders grow that sense in our people that they are valued and respected, and be confident in connecting well-being to clear expectations and high standards?

What Leaders Need to Know about Their People's Psychological Needs

We need to begin with a (ridiculously brief) understanding of the psychological needs people bring to work.[4] We are complex beings from a motivational viewpoint, yet some things we do know:

- People require that their competencies are linked to their strengths, and that growing their competencies will be done through timely feedback, training, and development.

- People need to feel a sense of accomplishment.

- People need autonomy, which speaks to their ability to exercise some degree of control over their work (in some cases both what they do and mostly how they go about it.

- People need relatedness, which speaks to our wish for healthy relationships and positive interactions.[5]

Leaders need to understand that if these needs are frustrated and not resolved, over time people will feel the weight of working with their needs not being met. Their work will be negatively affected and they will become an attitudinal, performance, or flight risk.

Recognition and Rewards: An Example from the Healthcare Sector

Teena Robichaud's email signature line reads "Director of Engagement." She says she loves the work and thrives on the challenge of helping people leaders create an engaged workforce in New Brunswick's largest healthcare authority. She's done it all before in the manufacturing sector, and explains, "Some of the challenges are the same. Whether it's the shop floor or an emergency room or a variety of nonmedical roles throughout huge complexes and medical facilities, we were going to run a credible recognition program with an inviting peer-to-peer recognition component. Our first challenge was simply having people have access to devices to register their recognition nominations in their 'Bravo' recognition program."

She goes on to explain that her team in the healthcare sector focused on three things:

1. Developing a robust peer-to-peer recognition program;

2. Extensive awareness training with managers that clearly linked recognition to engagement; and

3. Enhanced individual and team performance by equipping managers with the training and tools they needed.

Lastly, they "blew up" the corporate service and retirement recognition programs, moving away from the kind of stuffy event few people wanted to attend. Events are now smaller, more intimate, and relaxed. People enjoy them, and managers and senior leaders made a point of attending. This change underscores that employers are continuing to highlight certain milestones but that they are clearly shifting the emphasis of recognition and reward to performance-based outcomes.

When I asked Robichaud for advice on implementing recognition programs, she was quick to stress that executive or senior level commitment to engagement and recognition is essential, noting, "As soon as senior leaders understand the full implications that recognition leading to engagement can have on the effectiveness of their teams and the outcomes—like decreased absenteeism, fewer accidents, and the list goes on—they quickly get on board."

Having sound data is also extremely powerful. Robichaud explained that because the healthcare network's HR department runs system-wide employee engagement surveys, the data are available to the managers and to her team, and most importantly to the managers' managers.

She works tirelessly to educate people leaders about recognition as their most efficient path to strengthening their team's employee engagement scores and ultimately better outcomes. She explains that the notion of the employee experience is not dissimilar to that of the client experience—or in their case, the patient experience. What are the factors that make up how an employee experiences their employment, and how can an understanding of these factors help to best engage and retain them?

Robichaud strongly recommends that all communications be marketing styled—inventive, playful, and clever—not bland like typical corporate communication.

A measurable sustainability plan built into the team's recognition initiatives is also a core requirement, according to the veteran recognition planner. Everything is focused on measurability: results are reported, and the link between recognition participation rates and corresponding bumps in engagement are tracked meticulously.

Robichaud's final point is the importance of accountability. Recognition programs to improve employee engagement outcomes require not only support from the top of the organization but also a flow-through of accountability from senior to mid-level management, tied to performance. Done right, such programs create an ecosystem of recognition that all team members eventually demonstrate; but leaders, both formal and informal, matter immensely. The best leadership tools from social recognition science are crucial too, and Robichaud will gladly show you the proof that a combination of accountability, data, and evidence-based recognition tactics work.

Recognition and Rewards: An Example from the Construction Sector

The construction industry is defined by projects and project management. Businesses in that sector live and die by their labor and by material estimates and project management capabilities. The two recently installed co-owners of a vaunted construction business were as different as night and day in some respects, but eerily similar, too, in how they thought about their business partnership, valued their clients, and treated their people. Top consideration was given to employees' safety and well-being, and emphasis placed on HR and people leadership practices.

One day, as part of an industry trade show panel, the co-owners were answering questions on best practices on the people side of project management. They were asked by an industry journalist what, if anything, they did at the end of each project to acknowledge that the project was winding down. As if they had rehearsed it, the two looked at each other and shrugged uncomfortably, and then one leaned into the microphone and told the room they managed two hundred commercial and industrial projects of varying size and intensity in three provinces, so the end of one project meant that people were already working on other projects.

The journalist, later sought out by one of the two co-owners, introduced the co-owners to a wise project management consultant, who together rejigged the company's end-of-project protocol.

Now as a project winds down, the co-owners conduct several project evaluation and debrief elements. A project is deemed incomplete without an opportunity to allow as many people as possible to learn from the project. Lessons learned sessions now need to be conducted and documented, takeaways brought forward as appropriate, and the deserving recognized.

The co-owners appointed a member of their team, one who enjoyed spearheading social activities—in other words, a social multiplier[6]—as recognition wizard for a while to support the many project managers by training them in ways to recognize both individuals and their teams. In short order, the project managers got the hang of paying close attention, drawing from an impressive list of ideas from Bob Nelson's *1501 Ways to Reward Employees: Low Cost and No Cost Ideas* to recognize employees in fun and playful ways. Workplace teams quite appropriately use humor and good-natured fun as part of activities that figuratively raise others on their shoulders in celebration. (Such humor must always seek to honor and not diminish others and must be in good taste.)

One point of note: Celebrations need to be affirming and respectful of all—to be lighthearted but taken seriously by leaders as an important recognition tool for key individuals, entire departments, and ad hoc groups. People leaders do well to always make the effort to attend such events, even if they're not obligatory. As a leader, your presence alone signals importance and recognition. Even in very decentralized organizations, where local team leaders have enormous influence, people want to see and hear, as well as be recognized by, senior managers, owners, and executives.[7]

Recognition as Integral to a Learning Culture

The construction company's end-of-project protocols also applied to administrative and IT projects, so the process moved the entire company towards being both recognition rich and learning focused.

Facilitating learning through both intrinsic and extrinsic motivation is the work of people leaders. It is not their work to make their people's lives a continuous stream of never-ending tasks. Leaders and their people benefit greatly from beginnings and endings as they weave into their ongoing dialogue mini recognition and celebratory moments to be able to arrive at the realization of a major goal. Here are some recognition odds and ends for your practice:

1. **Recognition grounded in gratitude**: The sheer number of researchers and scholarly work on the subject of gratitude clearly tells us this foundational value has bottom-line implications when practiced by leaders and others in organizations.

    Rasmus Hougaard and Jacqueline Carter, in their 2018 book *The Mind of the Leader*, write about a leadership perspective based on three levels of leadership.[8] They advocate self-leadership, people leadership, and organizational leadership, and the use of mindfulness, selflessness, and compassion to better engage people at their intrinsic motivational level. Hougaard and Carter quote the science showing that gratitude is a contagious productivity and job satisfaction enhancer, and that when leaders practice gratitude (as opposed to simply talking about its importance), it permeates the organization.

    Daniel Coyle, in his 2018 book *The Culture Code*, describes thriving organizations where "the number of thank-you's you hear takes teams over the top." He goes on to say, "It has less to do with thanks than affirming the relationship."[9]

    Brené Brown speaks of the "trust and connection" that small brief moments of gratitude expressed at the start or end of a meeting or gathering can have.

    In their seminal work *The Leadership Challenge*, the high priests of leadership development, James M. Kouzes and Barry Z. Posner, eschew the more recent language and notions of gratitude but speak very convincingly of the substantial business results related to the simple practice of leaders offering a "please" and "thank-you."

    Professor Robert A. Emmons and Michael E. McCullough, in *The Psychology of Gratitude*, outline the advantages of greater health, optimism, and positivity, as well as better responses to stress, from those who practice gratitude.[10] Being thankful potentially opens the door to other positive outcomes for which to be even more grateful!

2. **It is better to give than to receive**: Build a culture of rewarding others and genuinely passing on the credit. At the 2019 annual general meeting and conference of l'Association de la Presse Francophone in Charlottetown, PEI, the progressive, soft-spoken, and always gracious Francis Sonier, volunteer president of the association and the managing editor of *L'Acadie Nouvelle*, a thriving small market newspaper, deflected the praise he was receiving about the paper's success in a topsy-turvy print and digital news media landscape. The self-effacing leader kept responding (as gracious people leaders do) by saying, "I have an amazing team." One of his staff cried out that this was true but that they had an amazing leader! Sonier grinned and blushed.

   Many of you have witnessed, as I have, the opposite of this—or, even more regrettably, have yourself tasted the initiative-crushing experience when a team leader without compunction takes credit for others' ideas. In an exercise I frequently use in leadership development work, participants are asked to complete the following statement: "I lose trust in a leader when they _____." The number of times "take credit for other people's work" comes up is downright alarming. Such despicable behavior needs to be called out.

3. **Recognition engenders progress and improvement**: In Teresa Amabile and Steven Kramer's *The Progress Principle*, the author asks an extremely relevant question when talking about recognition, which is: If you're not recognizing progress or improvement, what exactly are you recognizing? Not to say that effort is not worthy of being encouraged, but recognizing progress and improvement on tasks or projects that people find meaningful is the most powerful type of recognition in a leader's toolkit. If we know what progress and improvement on which elements of our team

members' work is most meaningful to them, why wouldn't we target that specific area as worthy of recognition and celebration?

4. **Learn more about recognition:** Like the Bob Nelson book identified earlier, *The Five Languages of Appreciation in the Workplace* by Gary Chapman and Paul White helps us appreciate the extent to which we differ in how we take in other people's gestures of appreciation. The writers explain that, for some, words of thanks or gratitude are enough, while for others time spent with their team leader or colleague is the greatest of recognition, while still others value small gifts, tokens of people's appreciation, or a thoughtful gesture. Analyzing how our direct reports and others in our entourage respond to different recognition approaches is a great thought experiment.

5. **Read the work of recognition experts:** Workhuman, formerly Globoforce, stands out in a sea of capable recognition software providers, big and small. The research that underpins their work is solid, and Workhuman is highly trusted by researchers and corporate clients alike. The company exemplifies how the industry that services the employer market in recognition has radically pivoted from years-of-service pins to algorithms. In other words, companies are mining data collected in engagement and recognition exchanges with employees and adding that to their collective wisdom of how to get recognition right. O.C. Tanner and Terryberry are other companies worth following for their innovations in employee recognition.

IN CHAPTER 16, we examine the function of human resources as a business partner in the organization, but perhaps more importantly its role of making progress on people-related challenges within a culture defined by its humanity.

Taking Stock of Your Humanity at Work

Teena Robichaud has strong and definite ideas about what reward and recognition should look like. As you answer the following questions about your people leadership practice, take a moment to review Robichaud's thinking and see if your thoughts on reward and recognition have any common ground with hers.

1. What do you celebrate in your workplace? Milestones like years of service and birthdays? Or are celebrations more performance, values, or team based? Do you have the balance right? How might it be different?

2. How would your direct reports respond to the statement, "I usually get timely recognition for excellent work." Notice the word *timely*. Alternatively, consider Marcus Buckingham's statement, "I know I will be recognized for excellent work." Notice the words *know* and *excellent*. If both statements were put on a 5-point Likert scale, from "completely disagree" to "completely agree," how would your direct reports respond?[11] How would you respond to the same statements?

3. Which elements of a leader's role do you find intrinsically motivating?

4. How can you spot when your colleagues are intrinsically motivated?

5. What might you try to up your game in social recognition for your folks?

(16)
How Do I Engage HR to Benefit People, Culture, and Leadership?

MOUNT ALLISON UNIVERSITY has consistently been rated by *Maclean's* magazine as the number one liberal arts college in Canada. Picture in your mind's eye the beautiful setting of the school—nestled in the sleepy yet culturally vibrant town of Sackville, New Brunswick, and a short drive from the well-hiked (and, for Acadians, the historic) Tantramar marshes.

Now consider a different type of prospect: the building of a new arts center, for which the Memorial Library, an edifice of solemn, historical, and nostalgic significance, would be demolished. The plan was highly divisive and was the talk of the town and regional media.

Leading the contentious file was Robert Campbell, Mount Allison's energetic president. Campbell and his wife, Christl Verduyn, hosted more than sixty events a year at their home, and Campbell was always visiting, chairing, attending, cheering, and speaking.

Despite his seemingly endless string of places to be and people to see, Campbell is always focused and in the moment. To engage with him briefly or longer is to witness his quick intellect and genuine curiosity in others, his authenticity and humility. You typically only get to call him "Dr. Campbell" once. "It's Robert," he'll interject quickly.

Campbell gave generously of his time for an interview for this book, during which I made a point of asking him about his commitment to being present and accessible, and the opportunity cost that presents. Did being a visible and accessible "man of the people" and fulfilling the "head of state" capacity of a CEO—especially in the context of the university community—distract him from his all-important work as a senior executive and administrator of a legendary institution?

"That's the job," he quickly replies.

It is my contention, as you know only too well, that to lead successfully, a leader must focus on both task and people. Campbell is a huge fan of using the 2 × 2 matrix to teach and communicate virtually anything. This matrix balances a high regard and concern for people with an equally high regard for task. Mount Allison's strategic plan is set up as a 2 × 2 matrix, with quality academic programming on one axis and sustainability on the other.

But could Campbell, his board of regents, and his management team pull off the controversial demolition of the library to make way for a new arts center, given the decidedly vocal—and some would say influential—group of university community members (both local and from beyond the Maritimes) working diligently to prevent the project from being realized?

In any small university town where alumni abound, locals and sometimes several members of those alums' family work on campus, and the symbiotic town–university relationship is such that virtually every resident is a bona fide member of the university community and is therefore invested in what happens there. Mount Allison was no different, and the approval of the controversial arts center project was dragging on with no resolution in sight. Campbell was hearing from officials like the vice-president of university advancement—the decidedly optimistic and unstoppable Gloria Jollymore—and from folks in university recruitment and other departments, all reminding Campbell of the damaging impact to the "Mount A" brand that the now-protracted standoff between the university and those opposed to the arts center project was having.

An accomplished researcher and author of ten books, Campbell took a holistic view of the issue. First, he explains, in such a situation the stakeholders are many—from students, students' families, and student groups, to workers and worker unions, all levels of government, alumni and university community members, and media and suppliers. The list seems endless. In the context of decision-making within the university community, Campbell reminds us that any stakeholder holds a veto and can slow down, complicate, or derail initiatives undertaken by the university's board of regents and its senior managers. While a smaller school like Mount Allison may be more agile, the smaller scale means there is less margin for error in any project: "A $1 million error is different for a small university with a $45 million annual budget than it is for a university like the University of Toronto with a $1 billion budget."

Moreover, Campbell tells me that the stakeholders function within three different time zones—the past, the present, and the future. Alumni and other groups want to see the past honored, and rightfully so. Students, parents, professors, their unions, and staff are grounded in the present. Campbell and his board, then, are left to shoulder thinking about the future—his "real job," he professes.

He goes on to explain that no group of stakeholders or veto-wielding individual stakeholder or any one time zone should constrain him, his board, or his management team. This is very complex stuff. I ask him where he turns for models or inspiration.

Campbell chuckles and recounts Gloria Jollymore's love for all business, leadership, and management books. He tells me he can't stand them. (The irony of this comment is not lost on either of us as I'm interviewing him for such a book.) Rather, he is drawn to the writings of German political economist Max Weber, citing in particular Weber's *Ethics of Ultimate Ends* and *Ethics of Responsibility*. The essays speak to him of the requirement for setting an agenda with a vision. "People want a leader with a plan, a plan that will improve things," Campbell notes—a leader with the responsibility of being "disciplined about what is possible" when thinking and speaking about the future.

He describes telling his entourage, "We can do anything we want, but we can't do it all," referring to the difficult choices and no-win trade-offs that disciplined leadership involves. And he points to a lack of discipline—our human tendency for overpromising—as the reason why so many university presidents don't enjoy their roles for as long as they might wish. Overpromising and underdelivering has a tendency of catching up with people, killing their credibility and their chances for appointment or for reappointment.

Change does not come easily in a university setting, Campbell observes, given the public funding a university receives, the ongoing trade-offs between creating quality academic programs and sustainability, the many stakeholders with veto power, and the existence of silos—the barriers between organizational units. Campbell is not a fan of silos, given that they inhibit change, choke creativity, and make engaging with others and divergent points of view difficult. He fancies himself a silo destroyer and a grinder.

Though the Montreal-born Campbell was raised on the Canadiens, he speaks joyfully of his admiration for the grinders of his beloved West Ham United Football Club in the English Premier League, and stresses that it's the tireless grinders who keep the shape of the defense and offense by running thoughtfully and endlessly. They do the unpopular and unheralded work that enables others to shine and to secure the sought-after result.

He goes on to speak of his reverence for Harvard political economist Joseph Schumpeter, who inspired Campbell's system of thinking and his belief in the manifest requirement of producing results. "You gotta deliver," he explains.

Cambell delivered. The new $30 million Centre for the Arts, Mount Allison's first new academic building in over thirty years, opened its doors on October 3, 2014. It is named after Purdy Crawford, Mount Allison graduate, chancellor emeritus, and a prominent Canadian in business and philanthropy.

Campbell's strategy, for his team to hold firm to their plan, stay on message, and most of all stay relatively quiet and patient throughout, ultimately led to a solution with the dissenting stakeholders that honored the past while taking action in the present and updating infrastructure for the future.

Presidents, CEOs, and senior executives like Campbell get it. Campbell told me unequivocally that getting the "people thing" right was more important than making money. "With cash, you believe you can always buy yourself out of any organizational or institutional problem. You can't buy your way into getting the people thing right."

Campbell also recognized that no other HR process has more impact than recruiting and selecting the right folks to ensure optimum job-person fit.[1] "If you can't attract talent, you can't bring full value to the organization," Campbell insists. It was the fundamental job-fit decisions for the team he had inherited, and the delicate and at times unpopular HR decisions Campbell had to make, that set him up for success.

I've watched many a leader (and likely you have too) assume responsibility for a team that is new to them, and in time they make the team their own, especially at senior management levels. People leave by choice or otherwise; others join, attracted by the winds of change or expressly recruited by the new CEO. Roles change and structures are adjusted through a series of deliberate acts, some seen as harsh, others timely or long overdue.

Different workplaces respond differently when there is a new sheriff in town. Leaders like Campbell are fortunate to have skilled, seasoned HR talent in place to assist in their initial assessments of folks, crafting and understanding the leaders' options for "moving people around" to better meet their agenda and people requirements against the realities of employment contracts, union contracts, employment law, and a university culture that greatly values time by way of tradition, tenure, and seniority. Campbell had an HR dynamic duo of Ron Sutherland and Katherine Devere (among others on his team) to guide and advise him through the always troubled waters of "adjusting" the team, but most importantly to align his people with what the university needed in a team of professional managers who would support his efforts to propel the university forward.

Mount Allison had a national reputation in HR and labor relations. HR director Ron Sutherland and the then Mount Allison employee union president, Bill Evans, were sought out by Canadian university HR conference organizers to come and tell their story of moving from a more traditional and confrontational contract negotiation to a win–win model of interest-based bargaining contract negotiation.

HR people, amongst ourselves, often speak of people leaders like Campbell (and hopefully like yourself) as leaders who "get it" or at least want to. It's HR code for "This leader understands the potential and competitive advantage people offer any operation, large or small. This leader understands the power of harnessing talent to meet the organization's purpose and delight customers/patients/citizens with its products and services. This leader views and appreciates people as capital assets, not an expenditure—human capital assets that are worthy of investment and stewardship. This leader understands that creating conditions where people are at their best substantially influences how their organization, company, or team will perform."

The Evolution of Human Resources

Everybody wins when people leaders of all stripes understand exactly how human resource departments and HR professionals can add value. People leaders who grasp the bigger picture beyond the critically important transactional administrative HR support (benefit administration, leave tracking, employee record keeping, etc.) and functional process-oriented support (staffing, training, labor relations) enable HR shops to better define their priorities and offerings to support business objectives.

As HR has evolved, so has its impact and the way it adds value. Here's a simple HR framework I've used for planning, or a checklist of sorts I've worked with. It is certainly not exhaustive.

- **Tier 1:** Organizational strategic direction, business priorities, and goals, which feed into #2.

- **Tier 2:** A people strategy to accomplish #1. Includes a people vision for the future; foundational aspirational beliefs about people, the culture, and the workplace; and articulated people principles, methodology, or approach.

- **Tier 3:** An HR plan designed to help the organization deliver on its business priorities and converting the people strategy into a manageable number of concrete, financially resourced, time-bound initiatives that clearly support the organizational strategic direction and people strategy.

- **Tier 4:** A leadership plan that focuses on the sustainable pipeline of leadership talent through recruitment and internal promotion, management development training and retention, and an articulated leadership development strategy driven by senior management (not HR).

- **Tier 5:** An HR client strategy—in other words, how the HR shop can best be designed and structured to meet client needs; where it reports to in the organizational structure; whether it is centralized versus decentralized, etc.

- **Tier 6:** An HR performance dashboard that spells out the requisite measurable indicators that inform the evaluation of the organization's people's performance and the HR unit's performance.

- **Tier 7:** HR systems and processes that lay out all the functional elements of HR we see and experience as employees and team leaders: recruitment and onboarding, compensation, performance management, training, health and safety, employee and labor relations, and increasingly employee services (think of a really broad definition of employee benefits and working conditions) and HR data-gathering and analytics.

Most folks see HR's role as Tier 6, while the greatest impact on an organization may well come from HR being effective in Tiers 2 through 5, based on Tier 1 and then executing well on Tier 6.

The University of Michigan's Dave Ulrich, widely acknowledged as the father of modern HR, has researched and written extensively on HR's need to create value.[2] He argues that HR needs to generate value internally with employees and organizations, and externally with clients and the places they do business—villages, towns, and communities. That's a far cry from HR's purpose in its modest beginnings.

HR was born in the nineteenth century as a humble personnel function that was largely an administrative unit (and in many instances very much an afterthought) and that didn't inform and advise meaningful decision-making in any significant way. But over the years and decades it evolved to manage HR processes (recruitment, training, employee services, etc.) and to become a full business partner, sharing in an organization's business challenges and bringing strategic expertise to assist with their people challenges. Solving difficult people-related problems is at the heart of how HR brings value, and as we have seen, many leaders are ill-equipped for this important work.

These roles are now supported with technology, enabling HR to come to the table with strategic human resource management, where HR aligns an organization's business strategy with the needs of its clients, its people, and its management team.

Dave Ulrich and James Dulebohn chart HR's progress in four waves:

TABLE 16.1

WAVE 1	HR Administration—highly transactional
WAVE 2	HR Practices—learning, internal communications, rewards, staffing, etc.
WAVE 3	HR Strategy—linking HR strategy and priority to the organization's business objectives
WAVE 4	HR Outside In—understanding business context and stakeholders; focused on outcomes in three areas: people, leadership, and culture

Ulrich has chronicled HR's evolution in the first three waves and suggests the need for it to evolve into the fourth wave, where understanding business context, stakeholders, and clients represents the best way for HR to add value. Thus, Ulrich and his many contemporaries suggest that the work of HR is to focus on people, culture, and leadership.[3] For me, that means having the right folks with right skills sitting in the right spots, and then shaping a culture centered on high standards and bringing value to the customer while enabling those same folks to be at their best at work.

Not so very long ago, human resources or human resource management, and certainly personnel management, was never mentioned in the same sentence as leadership. Now HR shops are tasked with assisting senior management teams with their requirements for building an organization's leadership capabilities. The shift isn't that surprising. And now investors look at HR capacity when arriving at valuations of firms. One in three items on the agenda for boards of directors are people-related, such as compensation, executive performance reviews, succession, governance, and so on.[4]

Understanding and Connecting to the Business Context

Veteran HR leader Tina Smith shies away from very little. If part of HR's mandate is to help managers face their tough people challenges and truly understand the environment within which they operate, then employers clearly need more people like Tina. She represents the best of HR's interest to bring people to the profession who are clearly gifted with interpersonal ability and who engender trust very quickly. A razor-sharp wit and intellect help Smith give and take with the best of them, but it is her deep understanding of business context and trends that makes her so effective.

She has had to put her money where her mouth is, and more than once. It's one thing to know the business and the numbers, but it's another to truly understand the implications of the business context and market trends and the very real ways the employer needs to adjust continuously. HR professionals understand that a changing context often means redefined priorities, which results in a redefining of roles and jobs in HR and elsewhere in the company.

Smith knows much about the inner workings and the trends, patterns, and context of US big box store-style retail and commercial hardware, but in her involvement with the region's first Home Depot—when the retailer was expanding into Canada and the HR challenge was launching the employment brand and mass recruitment efforts—it was understanding context that really mattered. Box stores are a world away from the grassroots world of municipal government operations, where she set up and operated a unionized municipal government's first ever HR shop. She would tell you the HR stuff was the easy part. To establish the HR shop, she had to disrupt long-held practices and traditions. It takes a deep understanding of the context—not simply an understanding of the business or the numbers—to pull that off well.

Smith is now in a regional HR role with Wawanesa Mutual Insurance Company, the Winnipeg-based auto, property, and life insurance company founded in 1896. Wawanesa has over $9.5 billion in assets, more than two million policyholders, and five thousand employees. She's applying the same process—and beyond learning the business and the numbers, she's drilling down on context and on understanding how insurance careers currently work, how the sector is faring at recruitment and retention of insurance-specific talent, and how Wawanesa competes for talent in the local communities where they operate that are under her purview. She's getting inside the usual HR metrics to understand her workforce in this specific place at this specific time.

Dave Ulrich urges all HR leaders to understand and follow a variety of trends, including information technology to understand the evolution of virtual work, demographic shifts to better understand the availability of talent, and a host of other global, national, or local labour force patterns within and outside their sector to forecast and plan more effectively.

HR today goes beyond learning the rudiments of knowing the business. The value-added activity of deeply understanding context and trends also extends to a deep understanding of stakeholders.

Emerging HR professionals will be excused if they erroneously point to the employment dynamic as central, and view applicants and candidates as their most important stakeholders. HR's purview is much broader—maybe not university president broad like Robert Campbell, but it is in everyone's interest if HR and the entire organization connects to the bigger business context and the wider swath of external stakeholders.

Emerging HR staffers have also been accused of mistakenly centering on employees as primary stakeholders, when the darlings of stakeholder relationships are clients. HR scholars refer to working from the *outside in,* as opposed to thinking from the *inside out*.[5] Everyone in organizational life would do well to reframe their stakeholder thinking from the outside in, beginning with the end customer and working their way back and around. We would also do well to share, teach, and talk about our respective stakeholders and showcase them to the benefit of everyone in the organization. Connecting not only HR but all noncustomer-facing support functions to the broader business context is advantageous as it enhances organizational focus.

Tina Smith's story showed us that understanding context is huge! So is helping HR get its collective head around the complexity of the stakeholders in its relationship to the business enterprise. I suggest it's everyone's job to understand each other's work and contributions, and the same goes for understanding all our organization's stakeholders, and not just the ones that are logically aligned to our sector of the organization. Whether clients, patients, students, or citizen taxpayers, they are all stakeholders, and HR—as much if not more than most departments—touches the community in part by virtue of the employment relationships that it brokers as well as through other community linkages such as the charitable causes the company supports and the suppliers it buys from.

On Humanness and Partnerships
Cathy Pickard is vice president of human resources for Wawanesa Insurance, and she knows a lot about humiliation in the workplace, but not from her own workplaces.

She has very high standards, her direct reports would tell you, and an unwavering commitment to helping people become successful. More than one manager in Pickard's wake would share that her diligent and usually welcomed coaching helped them be better people leaders. She invested heavily in those who were bright and interested in developing as a leader in order to lead well given their strong technical expertise.

Pickard also brings a desire to be, and to have her team and HR unit be, up to date, progressive, and innovative to add value.

You'd be right in thinking that Pickard's high-profile leading and managing roles in sectors like gaming, the agro-chemical business, and now financial services, and her roles as a community builder in the YMCA movement, as a pioneering fitness instructor, and as a committed board member, would have created ample opportunities for her to learn life's lessons about embarrassment, humility, and humiliation. But the seasoned HR VP learned much more about workplace humiliation watching her sons as they grew up playing hockey, got drafted by National Hockey League teams, and made a living as professional goaltenders at various levels both in North America and Europe.

"Humiliation is baked into that industry," Pickard explains. "The very few people in the world who can earn a living doing that work view that as the price you pay for being an elite athlete, who, let's face it, make considerable sums of money, and as a result elicit very little sympathy except from their friends and family. Those who make it need the mental toughness to get through being humiliated in the selection process. As a rookie, your treatment by your bosses, depending on the organization, is often more humiliation." She questions—as we sit together on an outside terrace during pro hockey's shrinking summer off-season—whether that's the best way to treat humans regardless of their market value or hometown notoriety.

Pickard sees employees as one of many stakeholders or ambassadors—or *partners*, to be more precise. She feels strongly about the notion of partnership, or more specifically being HR business partners with line managers, and she understood long ago what HR researchers like the University of Southern California's John Boudreau have validated: the more time HR expends on strategic partnerships as opposed to day-to-day administration or legislative and regulatory compliance, the better the outcomes.

Embedded HR

In organizations where HR activity is focused on a strategic partnership, there is a consistent pattern of greater strategic HR contribution, greater HR effectiveness, and greater organizational effectiveness.

The more HR leaders and organizational leadership (i.e., all managers) can relate to one another on the stuff that really matters, the better off everyone will be.[6] Fostering such relationships requires several key factors:

- a vision for the kinds of capabilities and skills individuals need to propel the organization forward today and in the future

- a talent plan that meets operational demands
- ideas as to how HR can ignite, sustain, and inspire effective leadership development that transfers and translates seamlessly into the workplace and adds value
- ideas as to how HR can inculcate, radiate, and celebrate an organizational culture that is authentically the expression of what the organization is capable of (more on culture and organizational capability in chapter 17)

Developments like these mean that HR leaders and people leaders will have more face-to-face time with people because administrative matters and functional HR processes will be attended to through automation for the most part, or through really well-honed manual processes. That division of labor leaves us time to talk about (1) how we grow our talent and what our leaders need to be capable of as we tackle new markets or innovations or cost containment, and (2) what we need to do to define and strengthen a culture that values supporting organizational objectives while creating a great employee experience.

By "great employee experience," I mean that employees want to enjoy a personalized relationship with their employer in the person of their team leader (the complete opposite of feeling like a number)—and to doing work they find meaningful in service of better individual, team, and organizational performance. Imagine how powerful HR folks and people leaders can be when their conversations center on collaboratively building the employee experience through a series of micro-employee experiences that happen every single day.

I believe the difference this makes is similar to the difference between employee satisfaction and employee engagement. The former is born of a transactional relationship of exchanging my efforts for pay and rewards (lots to be celebrated here), while the other is about having that same exchange but, in addition, feeling involved and emotionally connected to meaningful work and to my employer.

Researchers have not really figured out whether high-performance HR is the reason some organizations have great performance outcomes while others don't, or whether it is organizations with great performance outcomes who choose to invest in HR that produces positive results.[7] My physician neighbor, who is also a backyard urban poultry farmer, would aptly diagnose the situation as a classic chicken-and-egg quandary. What we are certain of is that an engaged HR shop is linked to effective organizational outcomes.

Research clearly demonstrates that when HR focuses on building, improving, and strengthening everyone's skills, it leads to better organizational outcomes.[8] One of HR's most critical contributions to organizational success is encouraging, brokering, and assuring people's continuous learning.

Cathy Pickard believes in a strategy of being strong business partners with internal clients, focusing on helping them meet their business needs, and tactically using *embedded HR*. As the name suggests, it's where HR intersects with operations—so that HR team members are, whenever possible, physically located with their internal clients—and where business priorities are decidedly HR's priorities. The business relationship is simple if every individual or part is in it for the success of the whole.

Embedded HR is a tactic on a continuum of HR involvement with clients, ranging from centralized to decentralized, and is reflective of how HR wants to partner with its clients.

Partnership, like any other team relationship where people are collectively accountable for a common objective, means sharing information, expectations, and feedback freely and openly, and also pushing back, negotiating boundaries and roles, and having each other's back.

Adding Value with Data

Pickard loves adding value with data—enabling evidence-based human resource management where decisions are well informed by facts. She explains, "You have to take care of the HR basics and do them well. Employees and managers must be able to count on the more administrative, transactional requirements of HR that employees count on. Employees need to trust that vacation calculations, sick leave allotments, and their pension plans and other entitlements are soundly administered. Managers need to count on the data they receive from HR with respect to salary budgets, overtime, and all of the inputs that an effective HR shop generates well that enable decision-makers to base their work on sound data and enable employees to trust that the employer is taking care of their personnel records, their benefits, and their privacy, and that the risk of data breaches are taken seriously. HR has no credibility on larger operational or strategic elements if they cannot get the basics right."

Pickard reminds us that getting the seemingly ordinary HR processes right gives you the credibility and influence to add value in increasingly bigger ways. When an organization trusts that the basics are well handled, the door opens for broader HR thinking—business-focused HR to support others by informing decisions with data and sound interpretation of the numbers, coaching people leaders around the data, and helping bring sound judgment and decision-making to the fore.

HR data proponent Claire Roussel-Sullivan, a former senior HR manager with ExxonMobil-owned Imperial Oil, who has crisscrossed the country in the company's refineries, customer contact centers, and ultimately in its Canadian headquarters, tells a great story in her use of data drawn from human resource information systems (HRIS) with managers. Pre-HRIS, employee data was limited to an information file on each employee available on closed employer computer systems. Roussel-Sullivan recalls discussing HR-related matters with managers—coaxing, nudging, arguing, and arriving at decisions painfully, be they individual employee issues or larger system-wide HR challenges, using the best information available, information that was often anecdotal or largely unsubstantiated. Then everything changed when people leaders gained direct access to aggregated operational HR data in real time.

Roussel-Sullivan chuckles when she remembers sitting with managers, chatting briefly while looking at the numbers—and when they had seemingly just begun, the manager would suddenly stand up, thank her profusely for her insight, and go race-walking down the hall, spreadsheet and evidence-based decision in hand. The engineers loved it; Roussel-Sullivan loved it. Evidence-based HR was a thing. But wait, it gets better. Enter advanced HR analytics, a development that kicked the potential of HR data up several notches.

Whereas HRIS enabled early tracking of descriptive information, through HR analytics the data can be predictive and has even more capability to inform decision-making and choices. Marry that to the power of cloud-based technology and advanced analytics capable of HR predictive analytics and we can imagine the world of HR analytics where data points are algorithmically massaged and where employers see past patterns and trends but then can do sophisticated modeling and what-if scenarios, and so predict the future![9] Well okay, maybe not everything about the future, but HR outcomes can be guesstimated with greater precision and certainty.

Predictive analytics are now assisting organizations by marrying records from people's recent past—let's say turnover information with demographic and engagement data—and employee career management and performance data. Sprinkle in some local and regional and job-specific employment opportunities data and it is possible to generate a scorecard on turnover risk in any one area of the organization. Green means no turnover risk; yellow means be careful, people are itchy; and red means you have serious flight risks on your team.

Researchers have documented that many HR units are wrestling with how to migrate from more operational data that is largely historical and steeped in its record-keeping past to truly embrace the world of predictive analytics.[10] No doubt that will take time, and just as the price point and complexity of smaller employer HR systems have come down substantially and their power has increased exponentially, this will likely happen over time with HR analytics, making it cheaper, more powerful, and user friendly even for small and medium-size enterprises.

An Open Letter from People Leaders to HR

Dear HR,

As your business partners, we people leaders have a few questions in preparation for our ongoing relationship into the future.

As people leaders, we appreciate your ability to support our efforts to continue to build our collective skill set and source the right people, and we remind you it's our biggest expectation. We also urge you to work diligently with us to help meet our business objectives and strengthen our organizational culture with the right programs and processes. Lastly, we need HR to lead the charge on leadership development even when we tell you we're fine.

Given our symbiotic relationship in our shared quest to delight our customers, here are a few questions for us to ponder together:

1. Favorable financial returns, organizational and future financial viability are still the treasure organizations seek, yet we will increasingly measure organizational success in terms of sustainability.[11] Is HR prepared for that shift? What role might HR play in that shift?

2. Value drives our conversations, focuses our client efforts, and defines our purpose. How is HR defining the value it creates? Is HR built and is your strategy defined to deliver value or to serve our more basic transactional needs? What needs to be different, HR?

3. HR, we invite you to work closely with us on our business scorecard that measures, tracks, and reports our progress against business objectives. How can

we be of assistance in keeping external and internal clients front and center as you continuously align and realign your HR strategies, programs, and processes so they are innovative and effective?

4. HR, we're happy to invest, but we need the HR metrics that enable us to understand the returns on our investment in people. We understand that HR metrics, well used, improve decision-making and maximize effectiveness. We also understand that some HR types are not necessarily systems thinkers, and we're happy to help with this type of analysis. How can your business partners assist you in delivering relevant data and analytics? How can you help us raise our game in evidence-based HR?

5. Being effective at how we lead change and getting the culture right to sustain productivity and engagement is a make-or-break proposition for organizations.[12] HR, please ensure your transactions are impeccable and that your tried and true HR processes we count on run smoothly so you can focus most of your time (80 percent?) on helping us lead change well and co-create the culture. (That, plus sourcing and developing top talent, is where we really need you.)

6. HR, please be an influential and trustworthy agitator. People need you to develop your team's capacity to teach us how to better continuously question, nudge, negotiate, coach, and influence us all to be curious and open to experimenting and learning. Help us become more self-aware. Please make us uncomfortable. We want you to find ways to be helpful while standing your ground, negotiating with conviction, and pushing us to improve.

7. People-related problems and decisions are nuanced, sometimes complex, and consequential. We mostly hate the difficult, conflict-riddled, seemingly intractable people situations and would rather avoid them (as you know only too well, HR). Please bring your expertise and your unyielding resolve to swiftly, effectively, and with great humanity help us make progress on our people-related problems. We resolve to call you in as early as possible when appropriate—when we mess it up with our folks—and we apologize for having called you late to the party all those other times.

In closing, dearest HR, we people leaders would like to be your business partner. Please focus on talent, leadership, and our culture. We also need you on matters of teamwork and shaping our workplace.

Great organizational outcomes depend on our long-lasting partnership. Hugs.

PS: We'll even help with all the social stuff you get stuck with. Let's get you out of making employees comfy—let's both get into enabling their learning and building their skills, engaging them, and helping them be productive.

IN THE NEXT section, we embark on a new topic—the building of a culture that nurtures people and offers the organization the opportunity to be sustainable.

Taking Stock of Your Humanity at Work

The evolution of HR into a full business partner is the main focus of this chapter. Do you see any differences between the changes in HR as described in this chapter and your own experience with or role in HR? As you answer the following questions related to your people leadership practice, reflect on the "HR as a business partner" philosophy espoused by Cathy Pickard and how that approach might work in your setting

1. Have you experienced a "new sheriff in town" situation when a new senior executive arrives and over time reshapes their team and other teams to better meet the needs of the organization going forward? What was your takeaway from this process?

2. How can you learn about and help everyone around you better understand your business objectives and the ever-changing business context and trends you operate in?

3. Who are your clients starting from the outside in?

4. How might you articulate your needs differently for your HR partners?

5. How might you help your HR partners better meet business objectives?

6. What is the more nuanced context, patterns, and trends an HR shop in your work world needs to understand? How might you help?

In part six, we look at how leaders can build a workplace culture that also offers an organization the opportunity to be sustainable. The emphasis on building a sustainable culture is inextricably linked with learning. So, why is a learning culture such a big deal? The evidence shows that a learning culture positively and directly impacts clients, staff, and even suppliers. This section highlights specific ideas on how to build a learning culture within your team and underscores the imperative of leading for inclusion, gender equality, and continuous learning for the health of the organization and its people.

PART SIX

Build the Right Culture

(17)
How Do I Align Culture with Team?

THE MIRAMICHI RIVER is a special place. It attracts celebrities, world leaders, and especially fishers to New Brunswick for its world-renowned salmon fishing. The people of the river have had their tales told by none other than Senator David Adams Richards, who hails from the area that was then the separate towns of Chatham and Newcastle. The combined city was renamed to honor its namesake river. Business owner Mike Cormier tells me of the time he spent in communion with the river when he was immersed in a CEO development program at the Wallace McCain Entrepreneurial Institute. His time on the river would turn out to be consequential for himself and the hundred or so employee families his engineering firm touched directly.

Wallace McCain, co-founder of the global McCain french fry and frozen-food empire, was firmly rooted in his home province. He gave a considerable legacy to the University of New Brunswick to strengthen and promote Atlantic Canadian entrepreneurs. Nancy Mathis, who has coached, counseled, and organized learning for

CEOs and their teams for many years, runs the institute's executive development program. She has seen CEOs in all their machinations at the bucolic executive learning facility. Those SME CEOs fortunate enough to be selected for the program come for their own development, but they also bring their organization's challenges to the fore and attempt to make progress on them. These challenges can be tactical, strategic, and in some cases existential, meaning that these business owners are pondering their futures and in some cases the very survival of their enterprises.

Beyond the relevant business training offered by the program, company owners have access to the considerable business acumen and experience of Mathis and other qualified faculty, but just as importantly they seek out each other's coaching and advice, and have the beautiful river to stimulate reflection.

We know leaders benefit immensely from reflection.[1] The places of mental and physical sanctuary discussed in previous chapters have underscored how crucially reflection serves your leadership practice. McGill University's Henry Mintzberg has written extensively on the subject of reflection and observes, "Reflection without action is passive, action without reflection is thoughtless."[2]

For Mike Cormier, the development program was life and business altering. He found the clarity and courage to change the course of his trajectory, which is a testament to the uniqueness of the program's host site—Upper Oxbow Adventures fishing lodge, nestled next to the First Nation community of Red Bank on one of the river's several branches, the Little Southwest Miramichi River.

Like many other business owners and CEOs, Cormier wrestles with the question of legacy and succession, and it was on the banks of the Miramichi that he wrestled with the future of Crandall Engineering—and his own, too. He had already grown the business from a twelve-person firm that he joined out of university to the now hundred-strong workforce in several provinces, and Crandall represents the very best of what small business can be. When founder Bill Crandall had pulled together like-minded people to start a small consulting engineering firm that was highly focused on its clients, I wonder if he thought that what he started would be such a fascinating story these many years later. At the time of the development program, the company's future looked bright with a full pipeline of projects, and it was time for Mike Cormier to think of next steps, which could include selling to a national firm, selling out to partners, or just carrying on.

He shared with me his admiration for arguably the greatest professional American football coach in the history of the game, Bill Belichick, head coach of the multiple-Super Bowl-winning New England Patriots. Belichick is revered (and reviled) within the sport for his systems thinking, for repeatedly surrounding himself with highly skilled managers, and for his attention to detail and meticulous focus and preparation. I have to speculate that Cormier may have invoked his inner Belichick for the master strategist's perspective, because he emerged refocused from his time on the river.

When you think about it, leaders really only have two buttons they can push organizationally: strategy and culture.[3] Business owners, senior managers, and team leaders strive for viability and relevance when shaping strategy. Strategy is defined by goals, and goals require the focus and effort of people to accomplish them. Culture—as expressed through values, beliefs, and assumptions—is manifested in the workplace, and it shapes effort and behavior through powerful norms.

Some researchers argue that cultural change is a direct offshoot of the changes in systems, structures, and processes that leaders bring about in their pursuit of solving business problems. They contend culture is not "fixable" and that it emanates by virtue of the changes you bring about and then is strengthened or weakened by virtue of how those changes are brought into being.[4]

Cormier—who had moved in concert with his partners and an insightful advisory board, and had been bolstered by the wisdom of former Crandall CEOs who acted as elders and sages—knew he had gotten a lot right about the company's business strategy over the years. Cormier now wondered about Crandall's culture and what it would take to get that better aligned if he committed to continuing to build the firm. Reinvigorated by his days on the Miramichi River, he tackled and in time transformed the organizational culture and brought international recognition to the firm.[5] He introduced campaigns like "Rule the Cool," aimed at making the work fun and the workplace more flexible and modern, and at ultimately carrying on with a client-centric legacy.

Bill Crandall and his wife were tragically killed in an accident in 1976, but the company forged on. It was many years later that Cormier joined its ranks, and again many years after that when another equally green engineer from l'Université de Moncton, Cormier's alma mater, joined the firm. Cormier then described to me what transpired as the young engineer presented to one of the firm's clients barely months after having joined the firm. Cormier spoke of the young engineer espousing almost word for word what he, Cormier, had come to understand had mattered most to Bill Crandall over sixty years before. The young engineer spoke of relationships, of clients, and of community. He spoke of those stakeholders wanting to work with like-minded good people with whom they could forge long-term relationships.

Cormier said what the young man was espousing had not been taught to him directly during his short time at the firm. The values that meant so much to Bill Crandall were not articulated to this new engineer per se. But the strength of the culture that was created in the 1950s organically, informally, and unofficially was transmitted to the young engineer. Said Cormier, smiling, "We didn't know we were doing it, and the engineer had no idea either."

In 2018, Crandall Engineering was acquired by Englobe Corp., a Quebec-based firm ten times Crandall's size. Cormier initially stayed on as president of Crandall and was tasked with continuing to grow the company. Cormier has since been appointed co-president of Englobe, and was asked to replicate what he did at Crandall Engineering on a national scale.

So, how does culture emerge and take hold, and what can leaders realistically do to shape it? That is what we explore in this chapter.

Culture or Climate?

Do you know any of the many customers for whom MEC is a destination shopping retailer?

MEC, or Mountain Equipment Co-op, is a proudly Canadian cooperative that in 2019 was once again named the most trusted brand in Canada by the Peter B. Gustavson School of Business at the University of Victoria. The top three brands listed in the school's 2019 index are all member-based organizations—namely MEC, CAA, and Costco—with Home Hardware and Home Depot tied for fourth place. Home Hardware screamed up the index from twenty-second place in 2018.

What is Home Hardware known for? If you shop MEC, what do you think it is known for? Why are people so confident in taking out a membership with CAA? My take is that these companies build trust with the consumer because they understand that a culture that delights clients is rooted in leadership behaviors and that these behaviors must be embedded in strategy and process. The research evidence is very clear. Our best shot at getting the customer experience right and delighting our clients is to focus on leadership behaviors, which in turn create a culture that enables the organization to meet its strategic objectives—in this case, creating trusting relationships with clients.[6]

We throw the word *culture* around quite a bit. I have the pleasure of visiting many workplaces, and you may too. They all have their own vibe, don't they? Is that vibe culture or climate? Let's sort this out.

Edgar Schein is credited with founding the field of organizational culture at the prestigious MIT Sloan School of Management.[7] Schein, who researched and wrote extensively on organizational culture in the early 1980s, has helped define culture and its uses, and has inspired the work of scholars and helped practitioners around the world better understand how to use those theoretical underpinnings to shape their culture, or in some cases fix a broken culture.

Based on my many years of observing behavior in organizations, I would define culture as a series of exchanges and connections that take different forms and follow different conventions, and that occur within a group of people who work and coexist together. People develop certain ways and habits in what they do to get things done. And while we think of an organization as having a culture, a large organization will have micro-cultures, such as within its departments and business units.

If you sit in the lobby of a law firm, or a municipal government office, or a manufacturing facility, your observations and perceptions and the feelings you get from each environment will differ greatly. Cultures differ by virtue of the nature of the enterprise and the people who work there.

Employers knowingly and unknowingly shape, uphold, or attempt to fix elements of their culture every day. The bigger the group, the more complex that work is. Culture is historical, more deeply rooted, and more in the heads and hearts of many than is climate. But both climate and culture research help us better understand the social context of workplaces.

The concept of climate gives us a quantifiable basis upon which to measure an important element of culture.[8] It focuses on a moment in time to identify what people are thinking, feeling, and applying to their roles. Climate feels to me like a snapshot, representative of a certain point in time but limited in its capability to tell the fuller story. Culture, by contrast, is something steeped in the practices and historical ways of any group, team, or company. Culture is often a main factor in answering the question "What is it *really* like to work there?"

Balthazard, Cooke, and Potter's study "Dysfunctional Culture, Dysfunctional Organization" clearly shows that a culture that is constructive and positive has beneficial impacts on people and organizational performance.[9] In direct contrast, operational inefficiencies and ineffectiveness are patently connected to a dysfunctional culture.

The other element connected to culture, be it a functional or dysfunctional one, is leadership. The two factors go "hand in hand," says Harvard's Boris Groysberg, who continues, "For better and worse, culture and leadership are inextricably linked. Founders and influential leaders often set new cultures in motion and imprint values and assumptions that last for decades."[10]

So, let's explore some of the elements of thriving cultures where (hint hint) learning and teaching are central to their DNA.

The Expression of Values

Let's say you're about to have a job interview and are waiting (nervously) in the lobby. As you look around, you see artifacts of what the company celebrates, formally recognizes, and trumpets for inspiration.

There will likely be the requisite business awards or signals of peer recognition within the public sector. The public way an organization manifests its sense of social responsibility speaks to what matters to it or may reveal what is of no importance. Some companies and their people go beyond the perfunctory requirements to be good corporate citizens and choose to be truly engaged in the community in a meaningful way. That says a lot. Where and how an organization fulfils its intentions to the planet, its community, and its stakeholders speaks to its values. Are its financial donations accompanied by the most treasured of the charitable ask: time as a volunteer? For example, when Assumption Mutual Life decided to become a B Corp, it solidified and communicated loudly how it wanted to be measured and evaluated beyond traditional financial ratios.

Volunteerism and countless other small yet extraordinarily meaningful gestures seek to benefit the ecosystem within which the business operates. Opportunities are brokered for people to contribute to community life, as they bring the knowledge that comes from working in such thoughtful and reasonably well-resourced organizations.

Have you seen values posted on employers' walls? Are they on yours? Posting such statements is like driving a stake in the ground and saying, "These are the things we believe in." We spoke of some of these values in chapter 3 on ethics. What truly matters is not whether the values are framed in a lobby for all to see, but whether those values, practices, and traditions positively influence everyday behavior and are "the way things really work around here." Failing to live up to explicit or implicit values will drive people out the door. Incongruity between appearance and reality will be quickly revealed to new hires.

That incongruity or disconnect is a rupture of the psychological contract between the employee and their organization, no matter how big or how small, as defined by the concept's pioneer, Denise Rousseau, in her book *Psychological Contracts in Organizations: Understanding Written and Unwritten Agreements*.[11]

We all have an understanding of the unwritten—or psychological—contract or agreement with our employer, and in the creation stage of this contract, early in the employment relationship, breaches of it sting considerably and can leave their mark over the course of the employment relationship.[12] This is significant because the psychological contract also connects directly to an employee's sense of engagement with their work.[13]

Have you experienced an employment situation where your psychological contract with your employer had broken down? Where your understanding of how things worked—what you believed to be certain shared beliefs or agreed-to obligations—was violated in a way that had an impact on or consequences for how you thought about the employment relationship?

A commonplace example of a shared belief is the expectation throughout a workplace that it will close ahead of a federal or provincial holiday. The company may not have a written policy that it will close early—for Christmas holidays, for example—but is has done so in the past and an expectation is set with the employees. Should the company decide against closing early in one instance, there will be a perceived breach of the expectation by employees, even though the company is under no obligation to let its staff have an extra day or two off.

A breach of a much more serious nature in the psychological contract occurs when it comes to matters of values—especially trust, honesty, and integrity. Workers who are conscientious will not look the other way, and a company risks losing good people if it loses its ethical compass.

Microcosm: Culture and Team

Culture is based in collective learning that shapes how we speak and relate to each other and, as a result, how engaged and productive we are. If a group has been together for only a brief time, its members might not have learned much about each other, but the unwritten rules that underpin ways of working will soon begin to emerge. The leader must be cognizant of these rules and ensure their alignment with the organization's values and attributes.

For example, imagine a team has a certain rhythm or loose process to how it does morning check-ins, exchanging pleasantries and then taking no more than ten minutes to review the status of projects and what needs to be accomplished in the day ahead. The team's process has evolved in such a way that it is considered inappropriate to have a side conversation with another team member while someone is addressing the group. It has become a collective belief that undivided attention is the order of the day, and that to speak at the same time as someone who has the floor is disrespectful to the speaker and the others. This rule may never have been overtly spelled out, but the team simply works that way. The expectation is set for each new team member, through either osmosis or gentle but direct intervention.

This example might be somewhat simplistic, but you get the idea. Ratchet up the stakes and we can see how it's in a leader's interest to quickly observe, learn, and internalize the manifestations of team culture.

The largest impact any leader exerts is within their own team, and that impact matters to the organization at large.[14] But that impact can expand if the leader is in a position of greater organizational influence and is developing strategy and policies—notably, human resource policies that frame and provide a type of container for culture.[15]

Our best outcomes emerge when managers, team leaders, and others who directly supervise or coordinate the work of employees assume their leadership role as a cultural ambassador and transformer. Such leaders, through their engagement, positivity, and alignment, influence others enormously and have a substantial impact on the health of an organization's climate.

Senior leaders may have a more substantial influence on culture organization-wide, but the truth is that we have the most impact on those who are nearest to us—our teams.

Macrocosm: Culture and Organization

Culture within larger organizations can vary greatly from one unit or department to the next. Culture is uneven, and diverse workgroups will have their own particular way of experiencing the larger culture.

Ideally, employees represent the employer not only by virtue of their skills but by the way they fit with and belong to the culture. When this happens, the culture is congruent with who they are. One peek at the description in MEC's "Working Here" employment tab on its website tells us about the company's culture. The slogans "Show up," "Make it happen," and "Carry the fire" speak to the company's commitment to help people be active and healthy and to nurture promising futures.[16]

Communicating culture is critical, as it can stand as a differentiator between businesses. MEC has tied its purpose, brand, and culture to getting people outdoors, and living up to its considerable values means attracting good hires and making customers happy.

Organizations that can rightly boast of their culture are transparent and focused on allowing team members to be heard. Think of Hilton, where friendliness in the hotel business defines not only the company's marketing brand but its employment brand. Mars, the family-owned chocolate bar enterprise, widely communicates its Five Workplace Principles: Quality, Responsibility, Mutuality, Efficiency, and Freedom. Adecco, the global temporary and permanent staffing and related workplace services provider, rated by Great Place to Work® as the fifth most attractive company in the world to work for in 2018,[17] has a culture focused on being extraordinary and doing more for its colleagues and clients.

EY, the global accounting giant with over 250,000 employees, speaks via its website of a culture composed of "unicorn makers and bot builders, change agents and cyber gurus, trust builders, blockchain professionals, performance improvers and problem-solvers. Data scientists and growth hackers. Risk managers and confidence builders. Software developers and business consultants to solve the toughest problems on the planet." The site goes on to describe a culture of inclusiveness, innovation, and flexibility.[18] Admittedly, this is employment branding intended to attract—nay seduce—talent and mesmerize clients. But if you've been with EY's folks and on the company's premises as I have, you've seen that EY's employment branding is rooted in the reality of a business widely recognized as progressive.

But this points to the contrast among three key perspectives: how organizations portray themselves, through their employment branding work, as exceptional workplaces that promote a healthy culture; how their leaders see the organization from their vantage point; and ultimately how the bulk of employees experience the actual workplace, which I view as a daily manifestation of both culture and climate.

Organizations that pass the data-driven, employee-engagement-driven test of becoming an employer of choice are often those that value and commit to alignment and integrity in how they (1) characterize their people's employment experience, (2) have a data-driven accurate picture that informs the leaders, and (3) measure employee experience to confirm that the organization's intentions are carried out. I've certainly witnessed the misalignment between an employer's advertisement of itself and the actual employee experience. How would you rate your own organization on that type of alignment?

I am convinced that a leader's most significant impact is on the handful of people they lead every day—their team. Each team has its own ways of working, and it is the imperative of the leader to connect the team's way of working to the cultural drivers of the larger organization. When the leader is inspired by the ethos of the organization and the kind of workplace it wants to shape, they can influence the level of engagement of those on the team. Leaders who are aligned across an organization determine how successful (or not) the organization will be in establishing the culture it wants. Team leaders gobble up the best parts of a company's culture and then replicate them within their unit. If the focus of the business is customers, then it is the leader's role to bring that element to life in their team's culture, through concerted attention on improving the customer's experience.

The question, dear reader, then becomes whether your leadership actions are aligned to the culture your employer is trying to create.

IN THE NEXT and final chapter, we discuss learning and why it is important for the health of the organization and its people. As a leader, learning is a profound aspect of your role.

> **Taking Stock of Your Humanity at Work**
>
> Through Mike Cormier's story, we saw how culture has staying power in a company—that when it is right, it is communicated organically across an organization and, like an oral tradition, handed down from generation to generation. As you answer the following questions about your people leadership practice, reflect on Cormier's revelations about how workplace culture spreads deliberately and unwittingly.
>
> 1. Would you describe relationships, clients, and community as critical parts of your organization's ecosystem? Would you say that you go to work every day with nice like-minded people and work with them to build a healthy culture?

2. As a leader, to what degree would you suggest your team is an advocate for the company's brand—most specifically, its employment brand? To what degree are *you* an advocate for that brand?

3. Do you agree with the evidence that "operational inefficiencies and ineffectiveness are patently connected to a dysfunctional culture"? Are you prepared to discuss this topic with your team?

4. Do your organization's values impact the way people work?

5. Have you or your team experienced a breach in company values? How did you or other leaders explain or make sense of this event and explain it to others?

6. How well are you connected and aligned with other team leaders?

7. As a team leader, what do you do consciously every day to bring your organization's values to life?

(18)
How Do I Build a Learning Culture?

AFTER HEARING ABOUT how some of the very best workplaces in the world define their cultures, you must now be wondering which magical combination of culture elements is most likely to succeed. My thinking about culture runs along two distinct continuums, as highlighted in the 2020 essay collection *On Building a Great Culture*: (1) people interactions (think of cultures that value autonomy and independence on one end versus those who value collaboration and teams on the other) and (2) response to change (think of flexibility on one end and stability on the other).[1]

At a deeper level of analysis, the Society for Human Resource Management suggests that workplace cultures vary based on several factors:

- values
- degree of hierarchy
- degree of urgency

- a focus on people versus task

- which functions within the organization are deemed more or less important

- the extent to which subculture or micro cultures exist under the larger tent of the broader organizational culture[2]

The makeup of any one culture is as unique as the singular composition of any one set of individuals who are brought together based on a common goal or shared skill set. That said, researchers have given us rich insight since we've been studying how we comport ourselves within teams, groups, and organizations.

Your team's culture is unique to its members and the various processes that guide its work. Its culture represents its collective learning over time—a result of trying assumptions and finding solutions—and its shared experience. Understanding your team's culture is the first step in being able to work with it or strengthen it. In the same way that we focus on strengths when we work with people, when we want to shift, fix, or tweak a culture, organizational strategist and author Jon Katzenbach suggests that "leaders should take care to honor their culture's strengths, focusing on changing just a few critical behaviors rather than attempting a wholesale transformation."[3]

The breadth and depth of organizational culture and all of its components is too broad for full consideration here, but there is one element that I would like to focus on—learning.

Teams can call theirs a customer culture, an employee culture, or a unicorn culture, but let's agree on this: if the underpinnings of the culture you create within your group or team infect your entire organization with learning by virtue of your role as a senior leader, you're on the right track. Scientists call this an organizational learning culture (OLC),[4] but we'll use "learning culture" for short.

You'd be forgiven if you thought of a learning culture or learning organization as one that places a priority on training and development, or one that emphasizes learning, or one in which everyone believes they have a training role. It's these things indeed, but much more. First, a bit of clarity.

A learning organization or a learning culture is one that provides people with the opportunity to learn and so develop a learning mindset. In *The Fifth Discipline: The Art and Practice of the Learning Organization*, Peter Senge introduced us to the learning organization and its core disciplines, including

- personal mastery, the steady quest to explain and better understand our vision and where to place our attention and energy;
- mental models, or the suppositions and generalizations we make; and
- building a shared vision through team learning, with a focus on dialogue and systems thinking that links it all together.[5]

Learning is baked into everything. You wouldn't dream of completing any activity that required a modicum use of human, financial, and material resources without a plan that was tested as it went through its stages. You would conduct a rigorous assessment at the end to identify what went right and what went wrong, so you could learn and do it differently the next time. Why is a learning culture such a big deal? The evidence shows that a learning culture positively and directly impacts clients, staff, and even suppliers.[6] Numerous studies link a learning culture to increased financial performance as a result of its direct impact on employee productivity, and there is evidence that a learning culture leads to job satisfaction that reduces employee turnover.[7]

In their book *An Everyone Culture: Becoming a Deliberately Developmental Organization*, Harvard developmental psychologist Robert Keegan and Lisa Laskow Lahey, the associate director of the Change Leadership Group at the Harvard Graduate School of Education, present us with organizations that use their culture as a distinct strategy and where leaders spend as much of their time working on culture to strengthen both the business and their people. They put it this way: "These companies develop their cultures as principal investments in their own business success [and] they refuse to separate the people who make up the business from the business itself.... [The] culture is rooted in the unshakable belief that business can be an ideal context for people's growth, evolution, and flourishing, and that such personal development may be the secret weapon for business success in the future."[8]

Here's what teams, groups, and entire organizations that have a learning culture do differently, according to a study co-authored by David Garvin, Amy Edmondson, and Francesca Gino.[9]

1. They use data-driven problem-solving grounded in repeatable processes, thus lowering the frequency of the need to make pure judgment calls or guesses.

2. They use selective experiments. Trying to sort your way between two equally appropriate options? Test drive one of them with pilot projects or trial runs, or put your idea on probation as we do with new employees. (Isn't "putting new hires on probation" awful terminology?)

3. They seize upon mistakes as teachable moments. Assigning blame is offside. The objective is to use rigorous evaluation and debriefing to establish lessons learned and move towards course correction. That said, repeating mistakes—i.e., not learning and correcting—is still not a good idea and can have dire consequences. Learning organizations are not soft; in fact, they can be extremely rigorous, and while learning is paramount, so is performance.

4. Colleagues turn to colleagues to learn.*

5. Teaching and learning from others is expected and looked forward to by both teachers and learners.*

6. The environment is safe and inclusive, and reflection is valued and central to learning.

7. Key learning processes are mapped out.

8. Leaders bolster, champion, and facilitate learning, and they understand that their support is not enough (see points 1 through 7 above).

9. People are accountable for their continuous learning, which is often tracked and accompanied by timely coaching tied to performance management programs. A learning culture is not an attitude; it's mapping out and executing learning plans with teeth.

10. Leaders are on the hook to provide an environment and tools necessary for continuous learning.

* Points 4 and 5 above are key.

Learning and Leadership Practice

Karin Aurell, who was assistant principal flute in the Norrköping Symphony Orchestra on Sweden's Baltic coast before relocating to Canada in 2001, leans into the concert hall seat in front of her, seemingly playing along with every note of a clarinet quartet's recital performance. She's taught and coached top talent, performed throughout Europe with distinguished conductors, and recorded with symphony orchestras and ensembles and as a solo performer.

On this Sunday afternoon, she is leaning into the performance of a quartet of adult hobbyist musicians, many rekindling their love of their childhood school instrument. Following the concert, I ask her about her trance-like state while her weekend charges—in this case a collection of four clarinetists—proudly presented a chamber music rendition for family and friends.

"I'm invested!" she tells me enthusiastically. I press a bit, underscoring that I would understand her edge-of-the-seat posture with high-potential students on the cusp of professional careers in nerve-wracking and life-altering auditions, but that this was a handful of inspired hobbyists playing "She'll Be Coming Around the Mountain" for family and friends. She smiles and replies, "When you're invested in people's learning you're invested!" Bravissimo, Karin!

Have you worked in a setting where people were noticeably invested in others' learning? In yours? Learning cultures make it easy for people not only to invest in their own learning but to be invested in the learning of others. Creating a learning culture within your company, team, or department makes learning central to achieving results and can define your workplace culture, too.

I hope you've had the opportunity to work with a supervisor whose intent and actions were to help you be successful. But I really hope you've had the chance to work with someone who *helped you get better at what you do* and be successful. Two of the most successful European football managers in history, Pep Guardiola and José Mourinho, are legendary figures in world football, both having led top clubs to success at the highest levels. Play for them and it is widely acknowledged you will be successful and win. From 2016 to 2019, they were both managers of highly regarded UK teams—Guardiola with Manchester City and Mourinho with Manchester United football clubs. What was widely reported and known in the industry is that if you went to Manchester and played for José, you'd likely be successful and win, and if you played for Pep, you'd be successful, you'd win, and you would emerge a better skilled footballer. To be led by Mourinho ensured you would give everything you had and you'd be on a successful team, but you would not grow as a footballer. Your abilities would have been put to good use but not developed. In contrast, Guardiola got the best from players by teaching continuously and promising his charges they will learn constantly and become better at their craft, all while playing for a successful club. Which coach would you rather play for? Which coach would you rather work with?

Leading for learning is not an HR training thing or a fad; rather, leaders who practice it bake learning into the way they do everything. It comes to define a considerable part of their leadership practice. This certainly reframes those evaluation sheets you are used to filling out after a training event. Learning organizations transfer that automatic reflex of training evaluation after a training day to meetings, projects, initiatives, etc. We learn at every turn.

My wish is that your organization has the kind of folks who will move a learning culture forward. We know that you have the most impact on the people who are immediately around you, and that's why the science is clear: training and developing people who will one day lead a team is the most substantive investment an organization can make. Turning team leaders into learners and teachers enables a learning culture that is a straight line to organizational effectiveness, productivity, and performance. As I have previously stated, business owners, executives, deputy ministers and directors, and university administrators and deans have the potential to impact organizational culture more than anyone else within the organization.[10]

In my view, no emphasis on culture would be complete without addressing the themes that follow here. Some of these are specific assumptions and beliefs that I wish most workplace cultures would operate from and entrench, as I believe them to be the ones that enable organizations to truly meet their purpose in the full sense of having impact for their owners, communities, and stakeholders—in short, all participants in their ecosystem.

A learning culture positions any organization for improvement, progress, and change. In fact, a learning organization is your best shot at anchoring meaningful change that then becomes accepted practice. A fundamental piece of a leader's work with regard to any useful change initiative, big or small, is moving the new process into the "this is how things are done around here" category—i.e., culture. No change, then no improvement and no progress.

All the work you have done in this book leading up to this point puts you on the path to lead consistent with a learning culture's practices. Our best workplace science is clearly pointing at the team lead and/or manager as the linchpin in organizational performance and success. Gallup got it right with its publication *It's the Manager: The Quality of Managers and Team Leaders Is the Single Biggest Factor in Your Organization's Success.* Some have cheekily suggested it should instead be titled, "It's the Manager, Stupid!" harkening back to the famous "It's the economy, stupid!" slogan for Bill Clinton's 1992 presidential campaign. Their implication is that this statement should be fairly obvious. The leader makes the difference!

That said, anyone can take on the challenges I've outlined below, regardless of whether their employer or organization outwardly holds these things to be of value. You can make a difference in your daily orbit, and the impact of these practices is such that they can quickly go from something you do with your team to something your entire organization does and becomes known for. Never underestimate the impact one leader can have on a group of people and what impact that group can then have on other groups. We have already established how infectious we are.

Leading for Gender Equality and the Advancement of Women

I believe in gender balance, and that when it is prioritized, the decisions made in business, public office, and educational institutions will generate better outcomes. Tomas Chamorro-Premuzic, in his book *Why Do So Many Incompetent Men Become Leaders? (And How to Fix It)*, suggests (with impressive data to back up his perspectives) that electing and promoting fewer incompetent men will go a long way towards improving social order and increasing business competency.[11]

Avoiding stereotypes and bias is a central focus whenever we work to create diverse and inclusive workplaces. In *What Works: Gender Equality by Design*, Iris Bohnet states that we need to "debias how we do things," and provides a compelling way to do just that when she notes, "Contact with other social groups can change stereotypical beliefs and help people collaborate across groups."[12] If you want to undermine the stereotypical negative images of women in leadership roles, part of the answer is to just do it—promote deserving women and other underrepresented groups, and enable others to have their stereotypes soften as they interact.

Our local community in Moncton, New Brunswick, has had the pleasure of hearing Dr. Manju Varma's voice on many issues as a very engaged citizen. Her insights on inclusion and diversity warrant our attention. Varma has a practical suggestion for leaders based on her organizational experience, which she shared with me in conversation, and that is to leave their team or department in better shape than it was before. More inclusive; stronger. She then goes on to ask what our workplaces might look like in time if each one of us (1) took on the challenge of agitating in an appropriate way, but agitating nonetheless for the very next recruitment exercise to be an opportunity to diversify the team; and (2) became vocal about the need for inclusion and took specific action vis-á-vis recruitment and promotion within our team environments to make that happen. What would your workplace look like if you tried this?

The data around women on boards of directors are very compelling. A 2018 study found that having more women on companies' boards of directors had a positive association with overall financial performance, and the correlation between women CEOs and company performance, especially sales performance, has also been positive.[13] So, how do we pursue this goal with our frontline teams, our management teams, and our ownership groups? What can we do as people leaders within workplaces to contribute in a meaningful way to the promotion of women?

Global accounting giant EY does it with its "Women. Fast forward." platform, which integrates the development, promotion, and ascension of women leaders in all areas of its global practice, establishing firm timelines, specific actions, and accountability at all levels for what the company considers to be a business issue essential to the sustainability of the enterprise.

Atlantic Canadian law practice Cox & Palmer established regular programming for its women lawyers to talk to each other in a dedicated forum about building their practices and navigating the traditions of the practice of law within a century-old firm, and about realizing much-needed change. Achieving this delicate balance between tradition and change is what CEO George Cooper sees as the quintessential challenge. Cooper stresses the responsibility that leaders have throughout their firm for stewarding into the future something that was built, shaped, and cared for by generations of clients, partners, associates, and staff who came before them.

The notion of stewardship is spoken about more in some leadership cultures than in others. Some organizations, like political parties and their grassroots structures, understand the importance of their elders and the role of stewardship. Robert Goguen, whom you met in earlier chapters, related to me how critical the political elder is in shaping a party's future by holding experience and tradition in great reverence while eying constant renewal to remain relevant. Wisely balancing past, present, and future is the work of leaders. (Mount Allison's Robert Campbell stickhandling of the past, present, and future time zones of his stakeholders is an excellent example.) Pushing for the advancement of women in the law while recognizing a responsibility to the past is the stewardship challenge that George Cooper has taken on.

The underrepresentation of women in decision-making roles is not a women's issue; it's a societal one, and it's one that men must take up vigorously. Our workplaces are a perfect starting point. One of my projects is helping others create the kind of workplace where *everyone* feels safe; but in the context of this idea, women in particular—whether you, or your daughter, niece, aunt, or mom—would be honored, celebrated, and feel very much at home in such a workplace.

I have seen progress as organizations that have turned a blind eye to sexist conduct and toxicity have diligently made their workplaces inhospitable to overt misogyny, harassment, and bullying. Other employers are working to advance women's careers within historically male-dominated sectors by collaborating with professional non-profits—for example, the Canadian Association of Women in Construction (CAWIC)[14] in the construction sector. The Canadian accounting profession, through its certification and training body the Chartered Professional Accountants of Canada (CPA), advocates for the benefits of forward-thinking CPAs as business partners and promotes its Women's Leadership Ambassadors' Group—a collection of CPA members in a host of sectors and industries upholding the value of women leaders.

Moncton's first woman mayor, Dawn Arnold, places role modeling to young women and girls high among her priorities, and believes she needs to showcase opportunity for women leaders in public service and elsewhere. But she also believes she needs to showcase hard work and perseverance. Before civic duty called, Arnold was a veteran community organizer who year after year, with collaborator Suzanne Cyr and the rest of her volunteer board and minuscule staff, raised the hundreds of thousands of dollars required to build useful partnerships and founded the Frye Festival, honoring literary scholar Northrop Frye, the Moncton-educated literary giant. It is Canada's only thriving bilingual (French and English) literary festival, and one that went from an afterthought on the national scene to one of the most sought-after by book lovers and by best-selling authors, their agents, and publishers. Most notably, Arnold and Cyr ensured the festival moved beyond the usual public venues for author readings and into schools and imaginative locations like large open foyers in office buildings, municipal council chambers, and bars. Cyr was honored by the prestigious Académie française for her work in promoting the French language.[15] The two women have helped make reading cool for kids in a province with a historically troublesome level of literacy.

There are companies that through their community work lead programs to empower young women and girls, while others quietly support organizations like the United Nations' Girl Up, the global initiative to empower young women leaders who defend gender equality.

Megan Rapinoe, celebrated captain of the US Women's World Cup soccer team, has become increasingly known for her thoughtful activism and eloquence on this matter and for speaking of our collective responsibility to create "spaces to be exactly who you are and whatever you want to be."[16] Brings us back to our conversation on psychological safety in chapter 12, doesn't it?

Leading so Leaders Learn Continuously

It fell to Marilyn Luscombe—in a highly collaborative effort consistent with her organization's values, and with the support of a committed senior executive team and a host of capable teams throughout the organization—to usher into a community college system of nine thousand students and six campuses a new era of governance and accountability. The modernization of New Brunswick Community College (NBCC) meant a deeper connection to stakeholders and a separation from government administrative practices. That transition has gone well for some colleges across Canada, and not so well for others. The enormity of the cultural change is staggering. Leaving the safe bosom of government has its challenges from a funding perspective. As with any other organizational transformation, there is an enormous knowledge gap that needs to be filled. It is often left to the middle managers and team leaders, shaped by the previous culture, to define and implement the new culture. The question is: Do they know how? But by all accounts, Luscombe and her teams supported and created a culture shift, and data are telling the story. Forward-thinking vice president of human resources and student services Suzanne Desrosiers reveled in the challenge of being the founding VP HR and embraced the chance to reshape the culture with the help of a strong and progressive CEO, an enlightened college leadership team, and now Luscombe's successor, Mary Butler, who was also an important part of the college's transformation from the jump.

One of the key components in transitioning the culture was the creation of the NBCC Management Academy, whose role was to train a succession of cohorts to lead and manage in NBCC's environment. This was a way to build leadership and management horsepower in a focused and structured manner completely in tune with the organization's needs. As Butler explained, "The Academy's role is to develop and enhance management skills for current and aspiring managers, and to establish a culture of effective leadership, including the collective engagement and motivation of employees."

Notice how NBCC wisely and quite deliberately integrates management skill building into their stated purpose of establishing an effective leadership culture. The Academy wields a two-part focus: first on management basics and then on more nuanced leadership challenges, such as the realities of leading and managing in a geographically dispersed, recently non-governmental, flatter organization with funky new reporting relationships where your team is virtual and organizational structures are shifting to meet student needs.

The college leads in many other ways as well, diversity among them. NBCC has made inclusion its business, and its work partnerships with First Nations is in keeping with the pioneering work done at St. Thomas University in Fredericton, New Brunswick. The college strives to honor the land upon which any NBCC gathering is taking place, but land recognition is only a small part of the college's diversity mission. Inclusion was designed into NBCC's branding. The inclusion of the color blue in the college's logo specifically refers to the importance of watercourses and their significance for First Nations people and, as Butler explained, "reminds everyone that in the case of NBCC's six campus regions, major watercourses reflect the college's journey and the flow of ideas, motion, and transformation."

Desrosiers and Butler enthusiastically embrace the challenge of evolving the NBCC culture in a very meaningful and intentional way. They have chosen leadership development as one of the key mechanisms, and their commitment to diversity and an outcome based, open, and inclusive culture is something to behold. Their investment in leadership learning to bring that about is world class.

Leading for Innovation and Change

We've already tied the presence of a learning culture to several indicators of organizational performance. There is also strong evidence that a learning culture contributes to innovation and to being competitive in the marketplace, which ultimately lead to better economic and financial results[17]—or, for an educator like Annick Arsenault Carter, to better student outcomes.

Carter is a committed and experienced middle school teacher who is highly sought after by francophone educational jurisdictions as far flung as France, Louisiana, and Quebec, as educators seek out this Atlantic Canadian Acadian francophone to talk about the idea of the "flipped classroom." It's something she has become known for, such is her passion for the approach. In this conception, the teacher is no longer the focal point for the transmission of information, becoming instead a facilitator of knowledge by stimulating the student's curiosity.

Carter is the daughter of an academic turned highly sought-after workplace trainer and interpersonal communication sage. (Hmm: I wonder if there's a connection.) Equally as compelling for me is that she works in a francophone education system that rewards and values innovation.

There are others who've come before her within the New Brunswick educational system and who are equally deserving of public accolades for innovation. Sophie Lacroix, a Department of Education staffer, understood that in this part of the world education goes well beyond schooling—it is a cultural imperative for the language and way of life. This is because New Brunswick has constitutional duality in education, meaning that citizens have the right to schooling in either French or in English, and the province therefore has two separate and distinct school systems. The francophone system has a mandate that is designed to be broader in scope as it is also focused on preserving the French language and enabling it to flourish. Successive provincial governments, minority rights groups, and experts in education recognized that the vibrancy and survival of a language in a minority setting depends on school curriculum but also on public policy. Legislation needs to enable the school to work in concert with other arts and cultural groups to provide the best possible chance for students to not only study in French but to be able to choose from arts and cultural offerings that complement the work being done in the schools. New Brunswick's approach puts the schools at the table with the myriad actors playing their part in a coordinated strategy. Lacroix (along with hundreds of others, she would quickly add) played a key role in enshrining a sweeping reform of culture and language policy for francophone students. Educational jurisdictions across Canada and in Europe, Asia, Africa, and South America have wanted to hear her message. She and her team have now turned to creating educational partnerships in French in places such as Tunisia, which joins other jurisdictions using New Brunswick curricula in English in Bangladesh, Brazil, and China.

While these examples come from the world of education, I want to stress that education is not any more apt than business to have a learning culture. Regardless of the industry, it's all about leadership driving learning, which drives innovation.

Without wanting to get into what I understand is a long-standing and contentious debate over whether continuous improvement is innovation or not, one thing is clear: like innovation and creativity, continuous improvement depends upon learning cultures as a staging ground or foundational support mechanism. The absence of a learning culture is often the cause of continuous improvement initiatives being one-offs—grounded in short-term thinking and ultimately abandoned because they don't produce big results or the next shiny new thing.

We understand that everything a culture does it does through its processes. And bringing a continuous improvement mindset—with its valuable structured problem-solving approaches that get beyond symptoms and enable us to really impact root causes—is at the heart of innovation and is the nucleus of great teams.[18]

Gardiner MacDougall's accolades as a Canadian university hockey coach just keep piling up: winningest University of New Brunswick coach, winningest Atlantic conference coach, winner of multiple national men's hockey championships and multiple national coach-of-the-year awards, and builder of B.E.S.T.—Better Every Single Time—a continuous improvement program he tells me aims to produce better athletes and better people. A widely read devotee of personal and organizational leadership and motivation, MacDougall draws inspiration from those worlds for his coaching practice. While we should not attempt to incorporate every lesson from the world of sports into our workplace leadership practices (many don't work), MacDougall's approach rings true. Imagine the organizational impact of making such an improvement theme a way of life when, through sound leadership practices, it becomes central to how everyone works.

I suggest we take one more thing from this coach's very successful playbook. I've watched leaders refuse to end planning meetings until an inspiring tagline (like MacDougall's B.E.S.T.)—crafted by the entire gang and encapsulating their focus for the next month, quarter, or year—was agreed upon. Such taglines are intended to remind the team of their commitment to a specific ideal throughout the upcoming period, and as a senior banker related to me, "This tagline will be everywhere for a while, and it's a daily reminder to shake a leg and meet our commitments to each other and to ourselves and recapture the energy of that day."

Taking Stock of Your Humanity at Work

Leading to instill and sustain a learning culture creates the foundation upon which many important organizational practices and initiatives are dependent. A learning culture enables a continued emphasis on team leader learning; creates favorable conditions for change, innovation, and improvement; and empowers diversity and gender balance. As you answer the following questions about your people-leadership practice, reflect on Karin Aurell's "I'm invested in their learning" statement and how that perspective shapes your thinking.

1. Do you think your organization has a learning culture? Are there pockets/teams where such a culture is more evident? If so, why?

2. How would you rate your organization on a scale of 1 to 5 at providing the necessary tools and support for learning?

3. Are you yourself an active learner? Do you support a learning environment for your team?

4. Which of the following suggestions, inspired by the 2019 work of Amy Edmondson and her colleagues, might you adopt to foster a learning culture?
    - Ask more open-ended unbiased questions that sincerely and inquisitively delve into something.
    - Find ways to share information horizontally throughout the organization.
    - Try tactics and approaches that are untested and unproven.
    - Talk a lot about mistakes and what we've learned.
    - Seek robust feedback on everything.
    - Actively take on other people's point of view to see what it feels like.
    - Learn and practice observing without judging.[19]

5. Which element of a learning organization gives you the best chance of anchoring meaningful change?

6. Does your company champion inclusivity and gender equality? How?

7. If you were to work for the advancement of women in leadership roles, what might you do?

8. How could learning be a competitive advantage in your world?

9. What snappy tagline or catchphrase might you attach to your leadership practice or to a campaign or theme you espouse as part of how you lead?

Afterword

CHILD POVERTY, HOMELESSNESS, and other challenging social issues are the talk of elections, committed civic leaders, and well-intentioned individuals, but business owner, philanthropist, and not-for-profit leader Ken MacLeod thought it could also be the talk of business people like him and others in his community who seek to effect change.

The trip to Venezuela that Ken MacLeod, "ad man" David Hawkins, and musical educator and professional symphony violinist David Adams made from Atlantic Canada to Caracas, Venezuela, in 2009 was meant only to be a fact-finding trip. The trio were to witness firsthand the work of El Sistema, the UNESCO-recognized program effecting social change for at-risk children through classical music.[1] El Sistema was founded in Venezuela, where it flourished and became a model for other similar programs thriving around the world. The Atlantic Canadian contingent was curious about the program's success and voluntarily traveled to Venezuela to investigate it up close, in anticipation of shepherding such a program to Canada in their role as a youth orchestra board of directors.

The three Canadians knew they were in for an eye-opening experience, and they got what they bargained for and more when they were led into what MacLeod described as a "shell of a neighborhood, buildings in rubble that looked like they had been bombed out." Picking their way to makeshift classrooms, they "found room after room filled with children, music, and joy!" Every day after school, and in some programs on weekends, children met for three hours with inspired teaching artists, to spend hours learning to play music with others. The point is that music is best played not by yourself, not with a teacher followed by solitary practice, but with your friends and your peers, the very people with whom the development of your social skills can be integral to breaking the cycle of poverty.

MacLeod, when pressed for the lessons that have enabled him, as a leader, to make an impact for the betterment of our communities, boils his success down to building and nurturing relationships, and being action-oriented—driving for results.

MacLeod explains, "Leaders don't wait: the decision to do in one year what we thought we could do in three is what leadership is about." MacLeod and a thoughtful and right-minded board of directors of the youth orchestra chose to take on and shepherd setting up what has turned out to be Canada's largest El Sistema–inspired program.

Results don't always come sooner than expected as they did for MacLeod's group, nor do they necessarily happen quickly when you take an approach that balances relationships and results.

Leaders achieve sustained results through a bias for action, but building relationships is a deliberate, intentional process that takes time and calls for certain personal qualities. Each of us comes to the work of leadership with our own inherent "glass half full or half empty" perspective, but the most effective leaders are those who can adopt a realistically optimistic leadership stance and find their own authentic voice through which to communicate it. We mustn't underestimate the demands of a leadership journey that starts from within and requires us to develop lifelong self-awareness about our core values and our personal bottom line.

While voice, values, and self-awareness are invaluable to a leadership practice, so are the daily habits and systems that enable you to get things done. And remember, when you can connect tasks to a purpose that is recognized as meaningful, you will awaken and inspire others and create the conditions for success in yourself and in your team.

When you give yourself the mandate to strengthen the culture of your team, regardless of your role, performance and morale will inevitably improve. When you commit to conveying clear expectations, asking questions fueled by curiosity, and providing ongoing feedback and recognition, you will see accountability and engagement increase. And when you consciously work to create psychological safety, and learn how to raise and lower the temperature of a group's energy, you'll know your leadership practice is evolving.

Leading for innovation, learning, and gender balance are longer-term outcomes and are measured as such. Lots of our work as leaders only bears fruit over time. Yet it is the daily work experiences we have and those we create for others, the things we choose to pay attention to as leaders each day, that make the biggest difference and shape our impact.

As a people leader, you have the power to create better experiences for yourself and for your teams, clients, and community through your humanity. As you juggle the many demands of the day, I suggest you give yourself permission to close your door from time to time and think about what "humanity at work" might look like in your organization, and how best to support your people to achieve better results and build better relationships.

Acknowledgments

IT LOOKS LIKE we have a couple of things in common—namely, we made it to the end of the book, and we both read book acknowledgments.

First, to those who graciously agreed to let me tell their stories, my humble thanks. Your generosity and openness provided rich examples to help readers better understand my ideas. Thank you for enabling others to learn from your rich anecdotes and enlightening experiences.

A number of composite characters in the book were based on and inspired by real-life clients and client organizations, and I thank you for providing me with your lessons. Many of the stories and examples were first "workshopped" in my training work with partner organizations like LearnSphere Canada, UNB's College of Extended Learning, and l'Université de Moncton's Formation Continue, as well as with clients, trainees, and conference audiences, so I wish to acknowledge those who put up with the early iterations. Your feedback was most helpful.

Dr. Tammy Carroll (TLC), your critical thinking, hard questions, and encouragement allowed this project to go forward. I am eternally grateful. A-plus.

ACKNOWLEDGMENTS

As you've surmised, dear reader, I am a music student since forever. I'm surrounded by wonderful musical friends and acquaintances. I'm fortunate to have some close and generous musical allies with whom I share lessons and rehearsals, home studios, and stages. To my musical allies, know that you all inspire me and provide the counterweight needed for this project to happen. *Practice!*

I will be putting publisher Maggie Langrick and the entire team at LifeTree up for a "pain and suffering commendation" for breaking in this first-time author. This virtual team cooks and I am so thankful you were there. Maggie, you're the unapologetic optimist everyone needs in their life. To have your oversight was a gift. I am so grateful to editorial director Sarah Brohman for her perspective, to line and copy editor Tara Tovell for her eye for detail, and to publishing coordinator Jesmine Cham for keeping the train on the tracks.

I now understand why editors are often referred to as long-suffering. The description refers to how long the editor's suffering may last well after the author and editor have completed a book together. Don Loney, with the sensibility of a saint, you guided this endeavor. I am forever grateful for your friendship, musicality, and your daily practice of thinking about the book, not to mention the gargantuan task of editing my writing. Your humanity shaped this work immensely. It touched me even more. *Merci*.

Carrying on the long-suffering theme, my colleague and dear friend Claire LeBlanc, you've been there these so many years, and with exemplary dedication moving us along, getting it done well, and smiling through it all. Thanks George and Sophie: I know your eyes, ears, and more are often drawn into our work. *Merci infiniment*. Pierre Babineau, trusty social marketer and web wizard, *merci beaucoup!*

This project was buoyed by my CBC Radio One colleagues. The decade plus of weekly interviews propelled the germ of this work forward, thanks to insightful questions posed by some of the smartest people I know during, before, and after our weekly columns. Thank you Karin Reid-LeBlanc, Mary-Pat Schutta, Vanessa Blanch, Jonna Brewer, Terry Seguin, Matt Rainnie, Denis Robichaud, Dave

MacDonald, Rhonda Whittaker, Denise Gauvin, Mitch Cormier, Hans Colburn, and a host of other hosts across Canada.

I've been mesmerized by the imaginative do-gooding team of clever marketers and ingenious community builders at BrainWorks Razor: Kathryn Basham, Brad Leblanc, and Rita-Anne Malenfant. So fortunate to have you all aboard, along with publicist extraordinaire Debby de Groot from MDG and Associates.

Special thanks to Françoise Roy, Raymond Hebert, and David Hawkins, who started down this path with me long before a word was ever written. Your friendship, confidence, and encouragement inspire me and enabled this publication.

A word of thanks to colleagues and dear friends—knowingly or unwittingly, you all contributed: Don Arsenault, Jane Atkinson, Zev Bagel, Bernie Belliveau, Mark Black, Laurie Bourque, Alyson Bryant, Jessica Doria-Brown, Norma Dubé, Cathleen Fillmore, Monique Gallie, Jennifer Houle, Maxime Labbé, Martin Latulippe, Annette LeBlanc, Joanne LeBlanc, Michael R. LeBlanc, Cluny Macpherson, John Oxner, Mario Patenaude, Warren Redman, Don Richard, Maurice Richard, Mark J. Surrette, and Carolyn Watson. I am forever grateful.

Endnotes

CHAPTER 2

1 Peter L. Molloy, "A Review of the Managerial Grid Model of Leadership and Its Role as a Model of Leadership Culture" (1998), api.semanticscholar.org/CorpusID:158251318.

CHAPTER 3

1 Spying cases in the news: In Canada, the fascinating and perplexing 2019 case of Colonel Mark Norman, charged with breach of trust by a public officer. This very high-profile case that received extensive media coverage was eventually dismissed. Former Royal Canadian Navy intelligence officer Jeffrey Delisle was convicted in Halifax, Nova Scotia, in 2012 of having sold secrets to Russia. In the US, American government worker Edward Snowden released classified information to the media in 2013. At the time of writing, he is living in exile in Russia.
2 "Sleep on it": Kathleen's mom, as a French-speaking Acadian, would have said the much more profound and instructional *La nuit porte conseil*—the night provides counsel or wisdom.
3 James M. Kouzes and Barry Z. Posner, *The Leadership Challenge: How to Make Extraordinary Things Happen in Organizations*, 6th ed. (New York: John Wiley & Sons, 2017), 54.
4 Adam Grant, *Give and Take: A Revolutionary Approach to Success* (New York: Penguin, 2013), 21.

5 Participants are asked to complete the following questions and then in turn survey three to five other participants to determine the most common responses:
   1. I am most likely to trust a leader if...
   2. I feel like a leader understands me when...
   3. A leader most inspires confidence when...
   4. I am attracted to a leader who...
   5. The personal attribute I most admire in a leader is...
   6. I get worried when a leader...
   7. I lack confidence when a leader...
   8. I feel that a leader does not understand me when...
   9. A leader loses credibility when...
   10. The personal attribute I find least appealing in a leader is...
   11. I feel most engaged when a leader...
   12. I feel strong loyalty to a leader when...

6 I first became aware of the notion of a leader's disproportionate impact through the work of Tony Schwartz, author and CEO of the Energy Project and contributor to the *Harvard Business Review*. His quote, "Leaders, by virtue of their authority, exert a disproportionate impact on the mood of those they supervise," was about emotional contagion, but the idea of a leader's *disproportionate impact* has merit in ways well beyond people's moods.

7 Michelle McQuaid, "Are You An Ethical Leader?" *Psychology Today*, May 21, 2015, psychologytoday.com/nz/blog/functioning-flourishing/201505/are-you-ethical-leader. Mayer was commenting on his research paper "Who Displays Ethical Leadership, and Why Does It Matter? An Examination of Antecedents and Consequences of Ethical Leadership," published in *The Academy of Management Journal* 55, no. 1 (2012).

8 Chris MacDonald, "Jim Pattison Ethical Leadership Education and Research Program," Ted Rogers Leadership Centre, Ryerson University, accessed January 2, 2020, ryerson.ca/tedrogersschool/trlc/our-programs.

9 Canadian Broadcasting Corporation, "Google Employees around the World Walk Out to Protest Sexism, Inequality," November 1, 2018, cbc.ca/news/technology/google-employee-walkout-1.4887064.

10 Referring to Wynton Marsalis as an exceptional musician does not adequately recognize the greatness of the man and his contribution to society. He is a nine-time Grammy Award–winning jazz and classical trumpeter, band leader, and the first ever Pulitzer Prize–winning jazz composer. But it is his work as an educator and his lifelong leadership and dedication to the musical art form of jazz that has garnered him a Peabody Award, the uppermost award for journalism, several honorary degrees, awards too numerous to mention including for distinguished leadership, as well as France's highest honor, Chevalier de la Légion d'Honneur.

11 Respondents who were all middle managers in a public safety environment or individuals who were being groomed for such positions in 2017 and 2018 were asked to react to the statements by responding to a standard Likert scale in an online anonymous questionnaire: 1-Strongly Disagree, 2-Disagree, 3-Neither Agree nor Disagree, 4-Agree, 5-Strongly Agree; N=43.

CHAPTER 4

1. Distinguished professor Barbara Fredrickson, principal investigator at the University of North Carolina at Chapel Hill's Positive Emotions and Psychophysiology Laboratory, identified ten forms of positivity: joy, gratitude, serenity, interest, hope, pride, amusement, inspiration, awe, and love. See Barbara Fredrickson, *Positivity: Top-Notch Research Reveals the Upward Spiral that Will Change Your Life* (New York: Random House, 2009), 37.
2. Fredrickson, *Positivity*, 18-19.
3. Martin E.P. Seligman, director of the Penn Positive Psychology Center, Zellerbach Family Professor of Psychology in the Penn Department of Psychology, and director of the Penn Master of Applied Positive Psychology program (MAPP), is widely recognized as the father of Positive Psychology, with 250 scholarly articles and twenty books to his credit. He is most noted for his work in learned helplessness.
4. Fredrickson, *Positivity*, 21.
5. Kim Cameron, *Positive Leadership: Strategies for Extraordinary Performance* (San Francisco: Berrett-Koehler, 2012), xi.
6. Cameron, *Positive Leadership*, 2-3.
7. Adapted from Courtney E. Ackerman, "Positive Leadership: 30 Must-Have Traits and Skills," April 7, 2019, positivepsychology.com/positive-leadership.
8. Ackerman, "Positive Leadership."
9. Stephen Pinker, *Enlightenment Now: The Case for Reason, Science, Humanism, and Progress* (New York: Viking, 2012).
10. Tony Schwartz, "Emotional Contagion Can Take Down Your Whole Team," hbr.org/2012/07/emotional-contagion-can-ta.html. Sigal Barsade, "The Ripple Effect: Emotional Contagion and Its Influence on Group Behaviour," *Administrative Science Quarterly* 47, no. 4 (1977): 644-675.
11. Dan Moshavi, F. William Brown, and Nancy G. Dodd, "Leader Self-Awareness and Its Relationship to Subordinate Attitudes and Performance," *Leadership & Organization Development Journal* 24, no. 7 (2003): 407-418, doi.org/10.1108/01437730310498622.
12. Amanuel G. Tekleab et al., "Are We On the Same Page? Effects of Self-Awareness of Empowering and Transformational Leadership," *Journal of Leadership and Organizational Studies* 14, no. 3 (2008): 185-201, doi.org/10.1177/1071791907311069.
13. Daniel Goleman, *The Emotionally Intelligent Leader* (Cambridge, MA: Harvard Business Review Press, 2019), 10.
14. Goleman, *The Emotionally Intelligent Leader*, 60.
15. Warren Bennis, *On Becoming a Leader*, 4th ed. (New York: Basic Books, 2009).
16. Daniel Pink, *When: Scientific Secrets of Perfect Timing* (New York: Riverhead Books, 2018).
17. Kim Cameron, *Practicing Positive Leadership: Tools and Techniques That Create Extraordinary Results* (Oakland: Berrett-Koeler, 2013), 55.
18. Cameron, *Practicing Positive Leadership*, 55.
19. Cameron, *Practicing Positive Leadership*, 54.
20. Martin E.P. Seligman, *Learned Optimism: How to Change Your Mind and Your Life* (New York: Vintage, 2006).

21 Heidi Grant Halverson, *The 9 Things Successful People Do Differently* (Cambridge, MA: Harvard Business Review Press, 2011).
22 Seligman, *Learned Optimism*.

CHAPTER 5

1 Amy Jen Su and Muriel Maignan Wilkins, *Own the Room: Discover Your Signature Voice to Master Your Leadership Presence* (Cambridge, MA: Harvard Business Review Press, 2013).
2 Amy Jen Su, "You Don't Just Need One Leadership Voice — You Need Many," *Harvard Business Review,* January 10, 2018, hbr.org/2018/01/you-dont-just-need-one-leadership-voice-you-need-many.
3 Theatre of Leadership. "Success in the Spotlight, Redefining Excellence in Leadership and Communication," theatreofleadership.com.
4 Chris Anderson, *TED Talks: The Official TED Guide to Public Speaking* (Toronto: Collins, 2016), 201.
5 Mona Weiss, Michaela Kolbe, Gudela Grote, Donat R. Spahn, and Bastian Grande, "We Can Do It! Inclusive Leader Language Promotes Voice Behavior in Multi-professional Teams," *The Leadership Quarterly* 29, no. 3 (2018), doi.org/10.1016/j.leaqua.2017.09.002.
6 Linn Van Dyne, Dishan Kamdar, and Jeffrey Joireman, "In-role Perceptions Buffer the Negative Impact of Low LMX on Helping and Enhance the Positive Impact of High LMX on Voice," *Journal of Applied Psychology* 93, no. 6 (2008), doi.org/10.1037/0021-9010.93.6.1195.
7 Amy C. Edmondson, *The Fearless Organization: Creating Psychological Safety in the Workplace for Learning, Innovation, and Growth* (New York: John Wiley & Sons, 2019).
8 Susan Cain, *Quiet: The Power of Introverts in a World that Can't Stop Talking* (New York: Broadway Books, 2012). Cain's subsequent book is aimed at children and teens. Susan Cain, Gregory Mone, Erica Moroz, *Quiet Power: The Secret Strengths of Introverts* (New York: Dial Books, 2016). Cain's TED Talk is one of the most viewed in TED's history: ted.com/talks/susan_cain_the_power_of_introverts?language=en.
9 Quiet Revolution, quietrev.com.

CHAPTER 6

1 The exodus from many coastal communities worsens when not only do college- and university-aged residents move away for school, but in time, their parents, wanting to be closer to their grandkids, sell their homes in soft or depressed markets when they retire and move to more populated centers, deepening the outward migration from rural areas.
2 www.heritage.nf.ca/articles/economy/moratorium-impacts.php.
3 Amy Wrzesniewski et al., "Jobs, Careers, and Callings: People's Relations to Their Work," *Journal of Research in Personality* 31 (1997): 21–33.
4 For example, Simon Sinek, *Start with Why* (New York: Portfolio Penguin, 2009) and David Ulrich and Wendy Ulrich, *The Why of Work: How Great Leaders Build Abundant Organizations that Win* (New York: McGraw Hill, 2010).
5 Marshall Goldsmith and Mark Reiter, *Triggers: Creating Behavior that Lasts: Becoming the Person You Want to Be* (New York: Crown Business, 2015). The "how to find

meaning" question is part of Goldsmith's six engaging questions he proposes we ask ourselves daily: 1. Did I do my best to set clear goals today? 2. Did I do my best to make progress on my goals today? 3. Did I do my best to find meaning today? 4. Did I do my best to be happy today? 5. Did I do my best to build positive relationships today? 6. Did I do my best to be fully engaged? Marshall states, "Active self-questioning can trigger a new way of interacting with our world."

6 Ronald A. Heifetz and Marty Linsky, *Leadership on the Line: Staying Alive Through the Dangers of Leading* (Cambridge, MA: Harvard Business Review Press, 2002), 208-209.

7 Kim Cameron, *Practicing Positive Leadership: Tools and Techniques That Create Extraordinary Results* (Oakland: Berrett-Koeler, 2013).

8 Petri Böckermana and Pekka Ilmakunnas, "Interaction of Working Conditions, Job Satisfaction, and Sickness Absences: Evidence from a Representative Sample of Employees," *Social Science & Medicine* 67, no. 4 (2008): 520-528, doi.org/10.1016/j.socscimed.2008.04.008.

9 D. van Dierendonck, P. Le Blanc, and W. van Breukelen, "Supervisory Behavior, Reciprocity and Subordinate Absenteeism," *Leadership & Organization Development Journal* 23, no. 2 (2002): 84-92, doi.org/10.1108/01437730210419215.

10 Cameron, *Practicing Positive Leadership*, 94: "...workers who could see the effects of their work on others, who were aware of the contributions they made to the welfare of people, had a significantly higher sense of meaningfulness." Ron Friedman, *The Best Place to Work: The Art and Science of Creating an Extraordinary Workplace* (New York: Perigee, 2014), 167: "We tend to view our work as more meaningful when we can see beyond our day-to-day activities and identify a long-term benefit, ideally one that helps others.... We also feel better when our goals center on benefiting others instead of ourselves." Teresa Amabile and Steven Kramer, *The Progress Principle: Using Small Wins to Ignite Joy, Engagement, and Creativity at Work* (Cambridge, MA: Harvard Business Review Press, 2011), 95: "What matters is whether you *perceive* your work as contributing value to something or someone who matters (even your team, yourself, or your family). It can simply be making a useful and high-quality product for your customer or providing a genuine service for your community."

11 Canada has long had so-called "have" and "have not" provinces. The determining factor is the state of the provincial economy. "Have not" provinces receive more federal monies than "have" provinces through a complex "equalization" scheme that attempts to level the playing field for Canadians and the provinces in which they reside.

12 Atlantic Canada Opportunities Agency (ACOA)'s end goal is economic development through direct investing, convening, relationship building, promoting federal programs and pathfinding, capacity building, policy, and advocacy. ACOA seeks to help grow SMEs, strengthen innovation, contribute to a skilled workforce, and help economic sectors be competitive. Under McGuire's presidency, its focus is on ten Champion Files (priority areas) such as Indigenous Economic Development, advanced manufacturing, and immigration. Multiple staffers have commented to me directly how McGuire's laser focus and bias for action on the ten Champion Files has invigorated the agency, refocused its efforts, and given new meaning to the agency's work.

13 Harry M. Jansen, Jr., *From Values to Action: The Four Principles of Value-Based Leadership* (San Francisco: Jossey-Bass, 2011).
14 Amabile and Kramer, *The Progress Principle*.
15 Adapted from Jeffrey Hull, *Flex: The Art and Science of Leadership in a Changing World* (New York: Tarcher Perigee, 2019), 24.

CHAPTER 7

1 Henry Mintzberg, *Simply Managing: What Managers Do—and Can Do Better* (San Francisco: Berrett-Koehler, 2013), 17.
2 The Eisenhower matrix is a 2 x 2 priority setting and time management philosophy and approach pioneered by US President Dwight D. Eisenhower. Stephen R. Covey popularized the approach in his 1989 seminal book *The 7 Habits of Highly Effective People*. Contemporary personal effectiveness sage and author of *Atomic Habits*, James Clear, has written extensively on the Eisenhower matrix, and apps are widely available based on the Eisenhower matrix.
3 David Allen, "Getting in Control and Creating Space," TEDx Talk video, November 28, 2014, in Amsterdam, Netherlands, youtube.com/watch?v=k0SFxKaqOm4.
4 Ronald A. Heifetz and Marty Linsky, *Leadership on the Line: Staying Alive Through the Dangers of Leading* (Cambridge, MA: Harvard Business Review Press, 2002), 127.
5 Marshall Goldsmith and Mark Reiter, *Triggers: Creating Behavior that Lasts: Becoming the Person You Want to Be* (New York: Crown Business, 2015), 18.
6 Daniel J. Levitin, *The Organized Mind: Thinking Straight in the Age of the Information Overload* (Toronto: Allen Lane, 2014).
7 Morton T. Hansen, *Great at Work: How Top Performers Do Less, Work Better, and Achieve More* (New York: Simon & Schuster, 2018).
8 Mintzberg, *Simply Managing*, 39.
9 Robert Steven Kaplan, *What You Really Need to Lead: The Power of Thinking and Acting Like an Owner* (Cambridge, MA: Harvard Business Review Press, 2015).
10 Larry Bossidy and Ram Charam, *Execution: The Discipline of Getting Things Done* (New York: Crown Business, 2002), 69.
11 Kaplan, *What You Really Need to Lead*, 89.
12 Hansen, *Great at Work*.
13 Paul H. Hersey et al., *Management of Organizational Behavior: Leading Human Resources*, 10th ed. (New York: Pearson, 2012).
14 Deborah Grayson Riegel, "8 Ways Leaders Delegate Successfully," *Harvard Business Review*, August 2019, hbr.org/2019/08/8-ways-leaders-delegate-successfully.
15 Mintzberg, *Simply Managing*.
16 One of the most validated measures of workplace bullying is the Negative Acts Questionnaire, Revised, © (Einarsen & Hoel, 2001; Einarsen et al., 2009), for which Carroll and Hoel (2007) identified five dimensions: (1) overt physical intimidation and aggression (e.g., "being shouted at"); (2) excess of supervision (e.g., "excessive monitoring of your work"); (3) social isolation (e.g., being humiliated or ridiculed in connection with your work); (4) impossible job demand (e.g., "being exposed to an unmanageable workload"); and (5) job isolation (e.g., "someone withholding information which affects your performance").

17 Kaplan, *What You Really Need to Lead*.
18 Thomas L. Brown, *Delegating Work* (Cambridge, MA Harvard Business Press, 2008).
19 Linda A. Hill and Kent Lineback, *Being the Boss: The Three Imperatives for Becoming a Great Leader* (Cambridge, MA: Harvard Business Review Press, 2011).

CHAPTER 8

1 2017 Aon Hewitt (now Kincentric), Employer of Choice Platinum Award for Small and Medium-Sized Business.
2 Laurence J. Peter, *The Peter Principle: Why Things Always Go Wrong* (New York: HarperBusiness, 2011).
3 Daniel J. Levitin, *The Organized Mind: Thinking Straight in the Age of the Information Overload* (Toronto: Allen Lane, 2014), 209.
4 Ron Friedman, *The Best Place to Work: The Art and Science of Creating an Extraordinary Workplace* (New York: Perigee, 2014), 44.
5 Levitin, *The Organized Mind*, 16.
6 Levitin, *The Organized Mind*, 96.
7 Levitin, *The Organized Mind*, 97.
8 Kostadin Kushlev and Elizabeth W. Dunn, "Checking email less frequently reduces stress," *Computers in Human Behavior* 43 (2015): 220-228.
9 Francesco Cirillo, *The Pomodoro Technique* (San Francisco: Creative Commons, 2006).
10 Cal Newport, *Deep Work: Rules for Focused Success in a Distracted World* (New York: Grand Central Publishing, 2016).
11 Marshall Goldsmith and Mark Reiter, *Triggers: Creating Behavior that Lasts—Becoming the Person You Want to Be* (New York Crown Business, 2015).
12 Morton T. Hansen, *Great at Work: How Top Performers Do Less, Work Better, and Achieve More* (New York: Simon & Schuster, 2018).
13 Marcus Buckingham and Ashley Goodall, *Nine Lies about Work: A Freethinking Leader's Guide to the Real World* (Cambridge, MA: Harvard Business Review Press, 2019).
14 Adapted from Peter Bregman, *18 Minutes: Find Your Focus, Master Distraction, and Get the Right Things Done* (New York: Business Plus, 2011).
15 Barbara Fredrickson, *Positivity: Top-Notch Research Reveals the Upward Spiral that Will Change Your Life* (New York: Random House, 2009).
16 Newport, *Deep Work*.
17 Philip Toshio Sudo, *Zen Guitar* (New York: Fireside, 1998), 121.

CHAPTER 9

1 Daniel Pink, *When: Scientific Secrets of Perfect Timing* (New York: Riverhead Books, 2018), 95.
2 Carol A. Walker, *Saving Your Rookie Managers from Themselves* (Cambridge, MA: Harvard Business Review Press, 2011), 77-90.
3 G.T. Doran, "There's a S.M.A.R.T. Way to Write Management's Goals and Objectives," *Management Review* 70, no. 11 (1981).
4 Kim Cameron, *Practicing Positive Leadership: Tools and Techniques That Create Extraordinary Results* (Oakland: Berrett-Koeler, 2013).

5   Jim Collins, *Good to Great: Why Some Companies Make the Leap and Others Don't* (New York: Harper Business, 2001).
6   Peter Drucker, *Managing for Results* (New York: Harper Row, 1964).
7   John Doerr, *Measure What Matters: How Google, Bono, and the Gates Foundation Rock the World with OKRs* (New York: Portfolio, 2018).
8   Marcus Buckingham and Ashley Goodall, *Nine Lies about Work: A Freethinking Leader's Guide to the Real World* (Cambridge, MA: Harvard Business Review Press, 2019).
9   Jeffrey Hall, *Flex: The Art and Science of Leadership in a Changing World* (New York: Tarcher Perigee, 2019).
10 Buckingham and Goodall, *Nine Lies about Work*.
11 Storytelling and leadership research articles, books, courses, and articles abound. I am drawn to the work of Paul Smith, *Lead with a Story: A Guide to Crafting Business Narratives that Captivate, Convince, and Inspire* (New York: Amacom, 2012); Stephen Denning, *The Leader's Guide to Storytelling: Mastering the Art and Discipline of Business Narrative* (San Francisco: Jossey-Bass, 2011); and Murray Nossel, *Powered by Storytelling: Excavate, Craft, and Present Stories to Transform Business Communication* (New York: McGraw-Hill, 2018).
12 Hendrie Weisinger and J.P. Pawliw-Fry, *Performing Under Pressure: The Science of Doing Your Best When It Matters Most* (New York: Crown Business, 2015).
13 Jon Katzenbach and Douglas K. Smith, "The Discipline of Teams," *Harvard Business Review* (July-August 2005).
14 Daniel Goleman, *What Makes a Leader* (Cambridge, MA: Harvard Business Review Press, 2017), 1-21.
15 W. Chan Kim and Renée Mauborgne, "Fair Process: Managing in the Knowledge Economy," *Harvard Business Review* (January 2003): 111-121.
16 Rotary International, "Guiding Principles," my.rotary.org/en/guiding-principles.
17 Jean-François Manzoni and Jean-Louis Barsoux, "The Set-Up-to-Fail Syndrome," *Harvard Business Review* (March-April 1998): 51-74.
18 Alex Ferguson and Michael Moritz, *Leading: Learning from Life and My Years at Manchester United* (New York: Hachette, 2015), 377.
19 Angela Duckworth, *Grit: The Power of Passion and Perseverance* (New York: Scribner, 2016).

CHAPTER 10
1   Frederick Anseel et al., "How Are We Doing after 30 Years? A Meta-Analytic Review of the Antecedents and Outcomes of Feedback-Seeking Behaviour," *Journal of Management* 41, no. 1 (January 2015): 318-348, doi.org/10.1177/0149206313484521.
2   Elad N. Sherf and Elizabeth W. Morrison, "I Do Not Need Feedback! Or Do I? Self-Efficacy, Perspective Taking, and Feedback Seeking," *Journal of Applied Psychology*, (June 2019), dx.doi.org/10.1037/apl0000432.
3   Douglas Stone and Sheila Heen, *Thanks for the Feedback* (New York: Penguin, 2015).
4   Douglas Stone and Jenn David-Lang, "Stop Sabotaging Feedback," *Educational Leadership* 74, no. 8 (May 2017): 47-50.
5   Sheila Heen and Douglas Stone, "Find the Coaching in Criticism," *Harvard Business Review* (January-February 2014), hbr.org/2014/01/find-the-coaching-in-criticism.

6 Brené Brown, *Dare to Lead: Daring Greatly and Rising Strong at Work* (New York: Random House, 2018), 20.
7 Bill George, "Leadership Skills Start With Self-Awareness," February 28, 2011, billgeorge.org/page/leadership-skills-start-with-self-awareness.
8 Daniel Goleman, *Working with Emotional Intelligence* (New York: Bantam, 1998).
9 Seigyoung Auh, Bulent Menguc, Pimar Imer, and Aypar Uslu, "Frontline Employee Feedback-Seeking Behaviour: How Is It Formed and When Does It Matter?" *Journal of Service Research* 22, no. 1 (2018): 44–59.
10 Jae Uk Chun, Donseop Lee, and John J. Sosik, "Leader Negative Feedback-seeking and Leader Effectiveness in Leader-Subordinate Relationships: The Paradoxical Role of Subordinate Expertise," *The Leadership Quarterly* 29, no. 4 (2018): 501–512.
11 Lisa A. Streelman and Leah Wolfield, "The Manager as Coach: The Role of Feedback Orientation," *The Journal of Business and Psychology* 33, no. 1 (February 2018): 41–53.
12 Manuel London and James W. Smither, "Feedback Orientation, Feedback Culture, and the Longitudinal Performance Management Process," *Human Resource Review* 12, no. 1 (2002): 81–100.
13 Streelman and Wolfield, "The Manager as Coach."
14 Mpomelelo Longweni and Japie Kroon, "Managers' Listening Skills, Feedback Skills and Ability to Deal With Interference: A Subordinate Perspective," *Acta Commercii* 18, no. 1 (2018), dx.doi.org/10.4102/ac.v18i1.533.
15 Joyce Lo and Zhu Li, "The Profundity of the Character 'Listen' in Chinese." *The Epoch Times*, May 21, 2017, theepochtimes.com/the-profundity-of-the-character-listen-in-chinese_2230261.html.
16 Jim Clifton and Jim Harter, *It's the Manager: Gallup Finds that the Quality of Managers and Team Leaders Is the Single Biggest Factor in Your Organization's Long-Term Success* (New York: Gallup Press, 2019), 79.

CHAPTER 11

1 Jim Clifton and Jim Harter, *It's the Manager: Gallup Finds that the Quality of Managers and Team Leaders Is the Single Biggest Factor in Your Organization's Long-Term Success* (New York: Gallup Press, 2019), 79.
2 Clifton and Harter, *It's the Manager*, 79.
3 Edgar Schein, *Humble Inquiry: The Gentle Art of Asking Instead of Telling* (San Francisco: Berrett-Koehler, 2013).
4 Daniel Goleman, *Working with Emotional Intelligence* (New York: Bantam, 1998).
5 Marcus Buckingham and Ashley Goodall, *Nine Lies about Work: A Freethinking Leader's Guide to the Real World* (Cambridge, MA: Harvard Business Review Press, 2019).
6 Bob Nelson, *1501 Ways to Reward Employees: Low Cost and No Cost Ideas*, 3rd ed. (New York: Workman, 2012).
7 Jack Zenger and Joseph Folkman, "The Ideal Praise-to-Criticism Ratio," *Harvard Business Review* (March 2013).
8 Tom Rath, *Are You Fully Charged? The 3 Keys to Energizing Your Work and Life* (San Francisco: Silicon Guild, 2015), 80.
9 Ken Blanchard, "Catch People Doing Something Right," How We Lead (blog), December 24, 2014, howwelead.org/2014/12/24/catch-people-doing-something-right.

10 Rath, *Are You Fully Charged?*, 81.
11 Carlton J. Fong, Erika A. Patall, Ariana C. Vasquez, and Sandra Stautberg, "A Meta-Analysis of Negative Feedback on Intrinsic Motivation," *Educational Psychology Review* 32, no. 1 (2019): 121–162.
12 Daniel Coyle, *The Culture Code: The Secrets of Highly Successful Groups* (New York: Bantam, 2018).
13 Fong, Patall, Vasquez and Stautberg, "A Meta-Analysis of Negative Feedback on Intrinsic Motivation."
14 Rita Dunn et al., "A Meta-Analytic Validation of the Dunn and Dunn Model of Learning-Style Preferences," *The Journal of Educational Research* 88, no. 6 (1995): 353–62, doi.org/10.1080/00220671.1995.9941181.
15 Peter Honey and Alan Mumford, "Honey and Mumford," University of Leicester Doctoral College, www2.le.ac.uk/departments/doctoralcollege/training/eresources/teaching/theories/honey-mumford.
16 Angela Duckworth, *Grit: The Power of Passion and Perseverance* (New York: Scribner, 2016), 123.
17 REM, "Shiny Happy People," from *Out of Time*, Warner Bros., March 1991.
18 Coyle, *The Culture Code*, 55.
19 Kim Scott, *Radical Candor: Be A Kick-Ass Boss without Losing Your Humanity* (New York: St. Martin's Press, 2017).

CHAPTER 12

1 Ronald A. Heifetz and Marty Linsky, *Leadership on the Line: Staying Alive Through the Dangers of Leading* (Cambridge, MA: Harvard Business Review Press, 2002), 107.
2 World Health Organization, "Mental Health," October 2, 2019, who.int/features/factfiles/mental_health/en/.
3 Amy C. Edmondson, *The Fearless Organization: Creating Psychological Safety in the Workplace for Learning, Innovation, and Growth* (New York: John Wiley & Sons, 2019), 15.
4 Heifetz and Linsky, *Leadership on the Line*, 107.
5 Chris Weller, "So You Want Psychological Safety—To Do What?" Your Brain at Work (blog), January 29, 2019, neuroleadership.com/your-brain-at-work/psychological-safety-to-do-what.
6 Amy C. Edmondson, *Teaming: How Organizations Learn, Innovate, and Compete in the Knowledge Economy* (San Francisco: Jossey-Bass, 2011).
7 G. Graen, J.C. Canedo, and M. Grace, "Team Coaching Can Enhance Psychological Safety and Drive Organizational Effectiveness," *Organizational Dynamics* (March 2019).
8 Amy C. Edmondson, "Psychological Safety, Trust, and Learning in Organizations: A Group-Level Lens," in *Trust and Distrust in Organization: Dilemmas and Approaches*, ed. Roderick M. Kramer and Karen S. Cook (New York: Russell Sage, 2004), 239–271.
9 J.R. Detert and E.R. Burris, "Leadership Behaviour and Employee Voice: Is the Door Really Open?" *Academy of Management Journal* 50, no. 4 (2007).

CHAPTER 13

1. Saul Scheidlinger, "The Lewin, Lippitt and White Study of Leadership and 'Social Climates' Revisited," *International Journal of Group Psychotherapy* (1994): 123–127, doi.org/10.1080/00207284.1994.11490737.
2. Jan Schilling, "From Ineffectiveness to Destruction: A Qualitative Study on the Meaning of Negative Leadership," *Leadership* 5, no. 1 (2009), doi.org/10.1177/1742715008098312
3. Victor Lipman, "Under-Management Is the Flip Side of Micromanagement—and It's a Problem Too," *Harvard Business Review* (November 2018).
4. Helge Hoel, Lars Glasø, Jørn Hetland, Cary L. Cooper, and Ståle Einarsen, "Leadership Styles as Predictors of Self-reported and Observed Workplace Bullying," *British Journal of Management* 21, no. 2 (May 2010), doi.org/10.1111/j.1467-8551.2009.00664.x. These are the top researchers on bullying, and I worked with Hoel.
5. Niko Canner and Ethan Berstein, "Why Is Micromanagement So Infectious?," *Harvard Business Review* (August 2016), hbr.org/2016/08/why-is-micromanagement-so-infectious.
6. Richard D. White, "The Micromanagement Disease: Symptoms, Diagnosis, and Cure," *Public Personnel Management* 39, no. 1 (Spring 2010): 71–76, homepages.se.edu/cvonbergen/files/2012/12/The-Micromanagement-Disease_Symptoms-Diagnosis-and-Cure.pdf.
7. Chip Heath and Dan Heath, *Decisive: How to Make Better Choices in Life and Work* (Toronto: Random House Canada, 2013).
8. Mahzarin R. Banaji and Anthony G. Greenwald, *Blindspot: Hidden Biases of Good People* (New York: Bantam, 2016).
9. Tomas Chamorro-Premuzic, *Why Do So Many Incompetent Men Become Leaders? (And How to Fix It)*, (Cambridge, MA: Harvard Business Review Press, 2019).
10. Adrian Wojnarowski, "Rockets Coach Mike D'Antoni," *The Woj Pod*, ESPN Radio, July 15, 2019, espn.com/espnradio/podcast/archive/_/id/26974840.
11. Steve Alper, Dean Tjosvold, and Kenneth S. Law, "Conflict Management, Efficacy, and Performance in Organizational Teams," *Personnel Psychology* 53, no. 3 (September 2000): 625–642, doi.org/10.1111/j.1744-6570.2000.tb00216.x.
12. Warrren Bennis, *On Becoming a Leader*, 4th ed. (New York: Basic Books, 2009).

CHAPTER 14

1. Ronald A. Heifetz and Marty Linsky, *Leadership on the Line: Staying Alive Through the Dangers of Leading* (Cambridge, MA: Harvard Business Review Press, 2002), 134–139.
2. International Thunderbird Class Association, thunderbirdsailing.org.
3. Randy Pennington, "Viewpoint: Employee Discipline for the New Workplace," *Society for Human Resource Management*, September 18, 2019, shrm.org/resourcesandtools/hr-topics/employee-relations/pages/viewpoint-employee-discipline-for-the-new-workplace.aspx.
4. Montana Consulting Group. Turnaround Interview, montanahr.com/turnaround-interviewr.

CHAPTER 15

1. Edward L. Deci and Richard M. Ryan, "The What and Why of Goal Pursuits: Human Needs and the Self-Determination of Behavior," *Psychological Inquiry* 11, no. 4 (2000): 227-268.
2. S.J. Wayne, L.M. Shore, W.H. Bommer, and L.E. Tetrick, "The Role of Fair Treatment and Rewards in Perceptions of Organizational Support and Leader-Member Exchange," *Journal of Applied Psychology* 87, no. 3 (2002): 590-598, dx.doi.org/10.1037/0021-9010.87.3.590.
3. Robert Eisenberger, Peter Fasolo, and Valerie Davis-LaMastro, "Perceived Organizational Support and Employee Diligence, Commitment and Innovation," *Journal of Applied Psychology* 75, no. 1 (February 1990): 51-59.
4. Richard M. Ryan and Edward L. Deci, "Self-Determination Theory and the Facilitation of Intrinsic Motivation, Social Development, and Well-Being," *American Psychologist* 55, no. 1 (January 2000): 68-78.
5. Caroline Aubé, Vincent Rousseau, and Estelle Morin, "Perceived Organizational Support and Organizational Commitment: The Moderating Effect of *Locus* of Control and Work Autonomy," *Journal of Managerial Psychology* 22, no. 5 (2007): 479-495, doi.org/10.1108/02683940710757209.
6. Liz Wiseman, *Multipliers: How the Best Leaders Make Everyone Smarter* (New York: Harper Business, 2017).
7. Wayne, Shore, Bommer, and Tetrick, "The Role of Fair Treatment and Reward."
8. Rasmus Hougaard and Jacqueline Carter, *The Mind of the Leader: How to Lead Yourself, Your People and Your Organization for Extraordinary Results* (Cambridge, MA: Harvard Business Review Press, 2018).
9. Daniel Coyle, *The Culture Code: The Secrets of Highly Successful Groups* (New York: Bantam, 2018), 78-79.
10. Robert A. Emmons and Michael E. McCullough, *The Psychology of Gratitude* (New York: Oxford University Press, 2004).
11. "I know I will be recognized for excellent work" is question #6 taken from the eight engagement questions in the 2019 book *Nine Lies about Work* by Buckingham and Goodall. The book expands upon the pioneering work done by the Gallup organization and builds on the science that resulted in the famous Gallup Q12, in which twelve questions zeroed in on the best-known engagers at that time. Since then, researchers like Buckingham have evolved the engagement science by refining the questions. The word *know* is the critical word in that statement, and the knowledge that *excellent* work will result in recognition is the stuff of high-performing teams. In yet another extremely useful iteration of the initial engagement science, the recognition question is one of four questions that zero in on an employee's individual experience of work, whereas the other four questions speak to a person's team experience.

CHAPTER 16

1. John Story, ed. *Leadership in Organizations, Current Issues and Trends*, 2nd ed. (New York: Routledge, 2011).
2. Dave Ulrich has published over two hundred articles and book chapters and over twenty-five books. He edited the journal *Human Resource Management* from 1990

to 1999; served on the editorial board of four journals, the board of directors for Herman Miller, and the board of trustees at Southern Virginia University; and is a fellow in the National Academy of Human Resources, michiganross.umich.edu/faculty-research/faculty/dave-ulrich.

3 Dave Ulrich and James H. Dulebohn, "Are We There Yet? What's Next for HR?" *Human Resource Management Review* 25, No. 2 (June 2015), 188-204, doi.org/10.1016/j.hrmr.2015.01.004.

4 Alexander Alonso, James N. Kurtessis, and Shonna D. Waters, "Enough Already! HR Is Rising (with I-O)," *Industrial and Organizational Psychology* 10, no. 1 (2017), doi.org/10.1017/iop.2016.101.

5 Alonso, Kurtessis, and Waters, "Enough Already! HR Is Rising (with I-O)."

6 John W. Boudreau and Edward E. Lawlor, "How HR Spends Its Time: Is It Time for a Change?," Center for Effective Organizations, February 2012.

7 Patrick M. Wright, Timothy M. Gardner, Lisa M. Moynihan, and Mathew R. Allen, "The Relationship between HR Practices and Firm Performance: Examining Causal Order," *Personnel Psychology* 58, no. 58 (May 2005), 409-446, doi.org/10.1111/j.1744-6570.2005.00487.x.

8 Kaifeng Jiang, David P. Lepak, Jia Hu, and Judith C. Baer, "How Does Human Resource Management Influence Organizational Outcomes? A Meta-Analytic Investigation of Mediating Mechanisms," *Academy of Management Journal* 55, no. 6 (December 2012), 1264-1294, dx.doi.org/10.5465/amj.2011.0088.

9 Martin R. Edwards and Kristen Edwards, *Predictive HR Analytics, Mastering the HR Metric* (Philadelphia: Kogan Page, 2016).

10 John Boudreau and Wayne Cascio, "Human Capital Analytics: Why Are We Not There?" *Journal of Organizational Effectiveness: People and Performance* 4, no. 2 (2017): 119-126, doi.org/10.1108/JOEPP-03-2017-0021.

11 John W. Boudreau and Peter M. Ramstad, "Talentship, Talent Segmentation, and Sustainability: A New HR Decision Science Paradigm for a New Strategy Definition." *Human Resource Management* 44, no. 2 (Summer 2005): 129-136, doi.org/10.1002/hrm.20054.

12 Alonso, Kurtessis, and Waters, "Enough Already! HR Is Rising (With I-O)."

CHAPTER 17

1 Iain Densten and Judy Gray, "Leadership Development and Reflection: What Is the Connection?," *International Journal of Educational Management* 15, no. 3 (2001): 119-124, doi.org/10.1108/09513540110384466.

2 Henry Mintzberg, *Simply Managing: What Managers Do—And Can Do Better* (San Francisco: Berrett Koehler, 2013), 110.

3 Boris Groysberg et al., "The Leader's Guide to Corporate Culture," in *On Building a Great Culture* (Cambridge, MA: Harvard Business Review Press, 2020), 1-32.

4 Jay W. Lorsch and Emily Gandi, "Culture Is Not the Culprit," in *On Building a Great Culture* (Cambridge, MA: Harvard Business Review Press, 2020), 137.

5 Crandall Engineering was recognized in 2016 and 2017 as one of the "Best Firms To Work For" in North America by the Zweig Group, who, through employee surveys, annually recognizes top architectural, engineering, and construction firms throughout North America on the basis of workplace practices, benefits, and retention.

6 Joseph A. Schmidt and Dionne M. Pohler, "Making Stronger Causal Inferences: Accounting for Selection Bias in Associations Between High Performance Work Systems, Leadership, and Employee and Customer Satisfaction," *Journal of Applied Psychology* 103, no. 9 (2018): 1001-1018, doi.org/10.1037/apl0000315.

7 "Edgar H. Schein," MIT Sloan School of Management, mitsloan.mit.edu/faculty/directory/edgar-h-schein.

8 B. Schneider, V. González-Romá, C. Ostroff, and M.A. West, "Organizational Climate and Culture: Reflections on the History of the Constructs in the Journal of Applied Psychology," *Journal of Applied Psychology* 102, no. 3 (2017): 468-482, ncbi.nlm.nih.gov/pubmed/28125256.

9 P. Balthazard, R. Cooke, and R. Potter, "Dysfunctional Culture, Dysfunctional Organization: Capturing the Behavioral Norms That Form Organizational Culture and Drive Performance," *Journal of Managerial Psychology* 21, no. 8 (2006): 709-732, doi.org/10.1108/02683940610713253.

10 Groysberg et al., "The Leader's Guide to Corporate Culture," 1.

11 Denise M. Rousseau, *Psychological Contracts in Organizations: Understanding Written and Unwritten Agreements* (Thousand Oaks, CA: Sage Publications, 1995), 9.

12 Denise M. Rousseau, Samantha D. Hansen, and Maria Tomprou, "A Dynamic Phase Model of Psychological Contract Processes," *Journal of Organizational Behavior* 39, no. 9 (2018): 1081-1098, doi.org/10.1002/job.2284.

13 Bruce A. Rayton and Zeynep Y. Yalabik, "Work Engagement, Psychological Contract Breach and Job Satisfaction," *The International Journal of Human Resource Management* 25, no. 17 (2014): 2382-2400, doi.org/10.1080/09585192.2013.876440.

14 Jim Clifton and Jim Harter, *It's the Manager: Gallup Finds that the Quality of Managers and Team Leaders Is the Single Biggest Factor in Your Organization's Long-Term Success* (New York: Gallup Press, 2019).

15 Susana Perez Lopez, "The Influence of Leadership on Learning. The Mediating Role of the Organizational Context," *Revista Innovar* 22, no. 45 (2012): 141-154. go.galegroup.com/ps/anonymous?id=GALE%7CA439035506&sid=googleScholar&v=2.1&it=r&linkaccess=abs&issn=01215051&p=IFME&sw=w.

16 Mountain Equipment Co-Op, "Inside MEC," mec.ca/en/explore/inside.

17 Great Place to Work® Each Year. "Great Place to Work® undertakes the world's largest global study of workplace cultures across industries and geographies. Last year alone, our survey represented the voices of roughly 12 million employees. Annually, these survey results and other cultural aspects of our study are reflected in a series of '100 Best' lists published around the world, including the *Globe & Mail* list of 100 Best Workplaces (Canada) and *Fortune*'s list of 100 Best Companies to Work For (USA). Heralded by researchers at the London School of Economics, Harvard Business Review and other international authorities, this ongoing study is unsurpassed in its rigor, credibility, and capacity to predict business performance."

18 EY, "What It's Like to Work Here," ey.com/en_gl/careers/what-its-like-to-work-here.

CHAPTER 18

1. Boris Groysberg et al., "The Leader's Guide to Corporate Culture," in *On Building a Great Culture* (Cambridge, MA: Harvard Business Review Press, 2020), 1-32.
2. Society for Human Resource Management, "Understanding and Developing Organizational Culture," shrm.org/resourcesandtools/tools-and-samples/toolkits/pages/understandinganddevelopingorganizationalculture.aspx.
3. Jon R. Katzenbach et al., "Cultural Change that Sticks," in *On Building a Great Culture* (Cambridge, MA: Harvard Business Review Press, 2020), 95.
4. Egan, Yang, and Bartlett, "The Effects of Organizational Learning Culture and Job Satisfaction on Motivation to Transfer Learning and Turnover Intention," *Human Resource Development Quarterly* 15, no. 3 (2004): 279-301, doi.org/10.1002/hrdq.1104.
5. Peter Senge, *The Fifth Discipline: The Art and Practice of the Learning Organization*, 2nd ed. (New York: Doubleday, 2006).
6. Miha Škerlavaj, Mojca Indihar Štemberger, Rok Škrinjar, and Vlado Dimovski, "Organizational Learning Culture—the Missing Link Between Business Process Change and Organizational Performance," *International Journal of Production Economics* 106, no. 2 (April 2007): 346-367, doi.org/10.1016/j.ijpe.2006.07.009.
7. Egan, Yang, and Bartlett, "The Effects of Organizational Learning Culture and Job Satisfaction."
8. Robert Keagan and Lisa Laskow Lahey, *An Everyone Culture: Becoming a Deliberately Developmental Organization* (Cambridge, MA: Harvard Business Review Press, 2016), 55.
9. Adapted from David A. Garvin, Amy C. Edmondson, and Francesca Gino, "Is Yours a Learning Organization?" *Harvard Business Review* 86, no. 6 (2008): 109-116, 134, hbr.org/2008/03/is-yours-a-learning-organization.
10. Karen E. Watkins and Khalil M. Dirani, "A Meta-Analysis of the Dimensions of a Learning Organization Questionnaire: Looking across Cultures, Ranks, and Industries," *Advances in Developing Human Resources* 15, no. 2 (2013): 148-162, doi.org/10.1177/1523422313475991.
11. Tomas Chamorro-Premuzic, *Why Do So Many Incompetent Men Become Leaders? (And How to Fix It)*, (Cambridge, MA: Harvard Business Review Press, 2019), 10.
12. Iris Bohnet, *What Works: Gender Equality by Design* (Cambridge, MA: Belknap, 2016), 16.
13. Jenny M. Hoobler, Courtney R. Masterson, Stella M. Nkomo, and Eric J. Michel, "The Business Case for Women Leaders: Meta-Analysis, Research Critique, and Path Forward," *Journal of Management* 44, no. 6 (2018): 2473-2499, doi.org/10.1177/0149206316628643.
14. CAWIC (Canadian Association of Women in Construction), cawic.ca.
15. Suzanne Cyr, the co-imaginer and co-everything of the Frye brain trust, earned honors (though she would tell you the honors belong to the entire festival) from the prestigious Académie française for her promotion of the French language and French literature. Sylvie Moreau, "Suzanne Cyr honorée par l'Académie française," *Acadie Nouvelle*, July 23, 2012, acadienouvelle.com/arts-et-spectacles/2012/07/23/suzanne-cyr-honoree-par-l-academie-francaise.

16 Jo Currie, host, "*The Big Interview-With Megan Rapinoe,*" BBC Radio 5 Live Football Daily, podcast audio, December 24, 2019, bbc.co.uk/programmes/p07yvdq8.
17 S. Pérez López, J. Manuel Montes Peón, and C. José Vazquez Ordás, "Organizational Learning as a Determining Factor in Business Performance," *The Learning Organization* 12, no. 3 (2005): 227-245, doi.org/10.1108/09696470510592494.
18 Robert E. Hamm, Jr., *Continuous Process Improvement in Organizations Large and Small: A Guide for Leaders* (New York: Momentum Press, 2016).
19 Amy C. Edmondson, Tiziana Casciaro, and Sujin Jang, "Cross-Silo Leadership," *Harvard Business Review* 97, no. 3 (May-June 2019): 130-139.

AFTERWORD

1 El Sistema-inspired programs provide what the *International Journal of Applied Psychoanalytic Studies* describes as "free classical music education that promotes human opportunity and development for impoverished children."

Recommended Reading

Buckingham, Marcus, and Ashley Goodall, *Nine Lies about Work: A Freethinking Leader's Guide to the Real World.* Cambridge, MA: Harvard Business Review Press, 2019.

Clifton, Jim, and Jim Harter, *It's the Manager: Gallup Finds that the Quality of Managers and Team Leaders Is the Single Biggest Factor in Your Organization's Long-Term Success.* New York: Gallup Press, 2019.

Coyle, Daniel, *The Culture Code: The Secrets of Highly Successful Groups.* New York: Bantam, 2018.

Delegating Work: Match Skills with Tasks, Develop Your People, Overcome Barriers. Cambridge, MA: Harvard Business Review Press, 2014.

Dweck, Carol S., *Mindset: The New Psychology of Success.* New York: Ballantine Books, 2016.

Epstein, David, *Range: Why Generalists Triumph in a Specialized World.* New York: Riverhead, 2019.

Fisher, Roger, and William Ury, *Getting to Yes: Negotiating Agreement Without Giving In,* 3rd ed. New York: Penguin, 2011.

Frede, Monica, and Keri Ohlrich, *The Way of the HR Warrior: Leading the CHARGE to Transform Your Career and Organization.* Vancouver, BC: LifeTree Media, 2018.

Friedman, Stewart D., *Leading the Life You Want: Skills for Integrating Work and Life*. Cambridge, MA: Harvard Business Review Press, 2014.

Grant, Heidi, *Reinforcements: How to Get People to Help You*. Cambridge, MA: Harvard Business Review Press, 2018.

Hicks, Donna, *Leading with Dignity: How to Create a Culture that Brings Out the Best in People*. New Haven, CT: Yale University Press, 2018.

Hougaard, Rasmus, and Jacqueline Carter, *The Mind of the Leader: How to Lead Yourself, Your People and Your Organization for Extraordinary Results*. Cambridge, MA: Harvard Business Review Press, 2018.

Laloux, Frederic, *Reinventing Organizations: A Guide to Creating Organizations Inspired by the Next Stage of Human Consciousness*. Brussels, Belgium: Nelson Parker, 2014.

Lencioni, Patrick, *The Advantage: Why Organizational Health Trumps Everything Else in Business*. San Francisco: Jossey-Bass, 2012.

Little, Brian R. *Me, Myself, and Us: The Science of Personality and the Part of Well-Being*. Toronto: HarperCollins, 2014.

Mitchell, Barbara, and Cornelia Gamlem, *The Conflict Resolution Phrase Book*. Wayne, NJ: Career Press, 2017.

Newport, Cal, *Digital Minimalism: Choosing a Focused Life in a Noisy World*, New York: Portfolio/Penguin, 2019.

Novak, David, and Christa Bourg, *O Great One!: A Little Story About the Awesome Power of Recognition*. New York: Portfolio/Penguin, 2016.

Pantalon, Michael V., *Instant Influence: How To Get Anyone to Do Anything—Fast*. New York: Little, Brown and Company, 2011.

Rosenberg, Marshall B., *Nonviolent Communication: A Language of Life*, 3rd ed. Encinitas, CA: PuddleDancer Press, 2015.

Schein, Edgar, and Peter Schein, *Humble Leadership: The Power of Relationships, Openness, and Trust*. Oakland, CA: Berrett-Koehler, 2018.

Scott, Kim, *Radical Candor: Be A Kick-Ass Boss without Losing Your Humanity*. New York: St. Martin's Press, 2017.

Stookey, Crane Wood, *Keep Your People in the Boat: Workforce Engagement Lessons from the Sea*. Halifax, NS: Alia Press, 2012.

Swora, Carolyn, *Rules of Engagement: Building a Workplace Culture to Thrive in an Uncertain World*. Burlington, ON: BrightFlame, 2017.

Index

Tables indicated by page numbers in italics

absenteeism, 73, 77-78
accessibility, 169, 217
accomplishment, sense of, 99, 208
active listening, 134-36, 136-37
Adams, David, 273
Adecco, 250-51
Ali (temperature example), 197-98
alignment, and goals, 116-17
Allain, Diane, 147
Allain, Mario, 104-5
Allen, David: *Getting Things Done*, 85-86
Alongside Inc., 167-68
Amabile, Teresa, 81, 213, 283n10
Amirault, Peter, 169
analytics, predictive, 232
André (positive force example), 41-43, 43-44, 45, 46
approachability, 169, 217
Arnold, Dawn, 264
Assumption Mutual Life Insurance Co., 95-96, 107, 247
assumptions, 185

Atlantic Canada Opportunities Agency (ACOA), 79-80, 283n12
attention, paying, 190-91
Aurell, Karin, 258-59
authenticity, 62, 132, 151
autonomy, 208
awareness. *See* self-awareness

Balthazard, P., 246
Barra, Mary, 130-31
B Corp, 107, 247
Belichick, Bill, 243
Bell Canada, 106
Bennett, Richard, 203-4, 205
Bennis, Warren, 50
bias, 181
Blake, Robert, 20
Blanchard, Ken, 89, 150
Blindspot (Banaji and Greenwald), 181
boards of directors, 165
Bohnet, Iris, 261
Bonnie (unsolicited feedback example), 132-33
Boudreau, John, 228
Boudreau, Yves, 167-68
boundaries, 169

Broad, Eli, 89
Brown, Brené, 130, 212
Bryden, Lea, 47-48
Buckingham, Marcus, 104, 215; *Nine Lies about Work* (with Goodall), 104, 118, 290n11
bullying, workplace, 91, 175, 183, 284n16
busyness, 84, 117, 176
Butler, Mary, 265, 266

CAA, 245
Cain, Susan, 64
Caisse populaire acadienne ltée (Les Caisses), 16-17, 18, 22-23
Caissie, Norm, 9-10
calendars, for planning, 101-2
Cameron, Kim, 45-46, 283n10
Campbell, Robert, 216-21, 263
Canada, 166, 279n1, 283n11
Canadian Association of Women in Construction (CAWIC), 263
candor, 154-56, 168
Capital Health District (Nova Scotia), 47-48
Carnegie, Dale: *How to Win Friends and Influence People*, 61
Carroll, Tammy, 49, 65, 177, 183-84
Carter, Annick Arsenault, 267
Carter, Jacqueline, 212
CBC radio hosts, 98
Chamorro-Premuzic, Tomas, 261
Chapman, Gary: *The Five Languages of Appreciation in the Workplace* (with White), 214
Chartered Professional Accountants of Canada (CPA), 263-64
choices: in decision-making, 180-82; in leadership voice, 62-63
Clear, James, 284n2
climate, 246. *See also* culture
coaching: definition, 137; for teams, 170-71. *See also* feedback; mentorship
cod fishery, 72-73

commitments, 29-30, 30-32, 35
communication: active listening, 134-36, 136-37; candor, 154-56, 168; for culture, 250; for delegation, 91-92; difficult conversations, 150-52, 165-66, 185; for priorities, 88, 104; teaching skills for, 19-20. *See also* feedback
community, commitment to, 29
competencies, recognition of, 207
competitiveness, 48, 266-68
conflict, 20, 177, 182-85
connection, human, 75, 78-79
construction sector, 210-11, 263
continuous improvement, 213-14, 268-69
contract, psychological, 248-49
control, self-, 51-53
conversations, difficult, 150-52, 165-66, 185
Cooke, R., 246
Cooper, George, 262-63
Cormier, Mike, 241, 242-44
Costco, 245
Covey, Stephen R., 284n2
Cox & Palmer, 262-63
Coyle, Daniel, 152-53, 154, 212
Crandall Engineering, 242-44, 291n5
creativity, 45
credit, sharing, 213
criticism, 149-50. *See also* feedback
cultural appropriateness, 136-37
culture: communication of, 250; comparison to climate, 246; Cormier and Crandell Engineering example, 241-44; customer experience and, 245; definition, 245-46; functional vs dysfunctional cultures, 246; at Imperial Manufacturing Group, 11, 13; leadership and, 246-47, 255; nature of, 243, 254-55; in organizations, 250-52; psychological contract and, 248-49; in teams, 249-50; values and, 247-49. *See also* learning culture

customer experience, 245
Cyr, Suzanne, 264, 293n15

daily leadership, 9-11, 12-14
daily rituals, 106
Dallaire, John, 203-4, 205
D'Antoni, Mike, 182
dashboards, 102-3
data, adding value with, 102-3, 155, 230-32, 257
Deci, Edward, 204
decision-making, 180-82, 231, 232
deep work, 86, 101
delegation: benefits of, 86-87, 88; communication for, 91-92; concerns with, 89; DCSD cycle of, 89, 90; growth from, 91; problem-solving and, 93; questions to consider before, 90-91; self-awareness and, 92; skill matching for, 93; tools for, 93. *See also* prioritization
d'Entremont, Katherine, 191-92
Desrosiers, Suzanne, 265, 266
Devere, Katherine, 221
Dieppe (NB), 101-2
difficult conversations, 150-52, 165-66, 185
discipline, progressive, 194-95
distractions, management of, 87-88
diversity and inclusion, 59, 63, 136-37, 262, 266. *See also* gender equality
Donohue, Jack, 153
Duckworth, Angela, 153-54
Dulebohn, James, 223-24

Edmondson, Amy, 164, 257
education sector, 267-68
Eisenhower matrix, 84, 284n2
El Sistema, 273-74, 294n1
email batching, 99-100
embedded human resources, 230
Emmons, Robert A., 212-13
emotions: decision-making and, 181; emotional intelligence, 49
employees: absenteeism, 73, 77-78; engagement, 229; insights from new hires, 86; recruitment, 11, 29; satisfaction, 229, 256; turnover, 10, 11-12, 232, 256. *See also* culture; expectations; feedback; human resources; learning culture; meaningful work; recognition and rewards
energy levels, reading, 197
Englobe Corp., 244
EQ-i 2.0, 184
equalization program, 283n11
ethics. *See* values and ethics
Evans, Bill, 221
expectations: co-creating objectives, 124-26; connecting goals to real work, 118-20; fairness and, 121-22; goals and alignment, 116-17; realistic goals, 122-24; retreats for goal setting, 120-21; self-awareness and, 121; Thomas's example, 113-16, 119, 122, 123-24
experiments, selective, 257
extrinsic motivation, 204. *See also* motivation
EY, 251, 262

fairness, 121-22
fear, 176
feedback: ability to receive, 130-31; active listening, 134-36; benefits of, 131-32; candor, 154-56; clarity, 146; as context specific, 148-49; detailedness, 147; as dialogue, 147; difficult conversations, 150-52; emphasizing the rewards of, 134; environment for, 133-34; excuses for avoiding, 144-45; importance of, 129-30, 141-44; learning from, 153-54; mentorship, 137-39, 144; negative feedback and motivation, 152-53; permission for, 146; praise-to-criticism ratio, 149-50; self-awareness from, 132; sharing vs imposing, 147; tips for, 146-48;

unsolicited feedback, 132–33; weekly feedback, 145–46. *See also* coaching
Ferguson, Alex, 122–23
First Nations, 266
fish processing plant, 71–73, 73–74, 76–78
flipped classroom, 267
focus, 100–101
Folkman, Joseph, 149, 150
francophone education system (NB), 267–68
Fredrickson, Barbara, 44, 281n1
fresh starts, 114
Friedman, Ron, 98, 283n10
Frye Festival, 264

Gagnon, Rachelle, 95–97, 103, 107
Gallup, 135, 144; *It's the Manager*, 142, 260–61
Garvin, David, 257
Gaudet, Marie Andrée, 50
Gauvin, Simon, 100
gender equality, 261–64
George, Bill, 132
Gibson, Richard, 148
gig economy, 12
Gino, Francesca, 257
Girl Up, 264
Globoforce. *See* Workhuman
goals: alignment and, 116–17; co-creating objectives, 124–26; connecting to real work, 118–20, 124; fairness and, 121–22; in mentorship, 138; perfection and, 124; realistic goals, 122–24; retreat tactic for setting, 120–21; self-awareness and, 121; stretch goals, 123
Goguen, Robert, 33, 135–36, 263
Goldsmith, Marshall, 87, 282n5
Goleman, Daniel, 49, 145
Goodall, Ashley: *Nine Lines about Work* (with Buckingham), 118, 290n11
Google, 35
Grant, Adam, 29

gratitude, 139, 212–13
Great Place to Work, 292n17
grit, 123
growth, personal, 91
Groysberg, Boris, 246–47
Guardiola, Pep, 259

habits. *See* leadership habits
Harvard Pilgrim Healthcare, 105
Hawkins, David, 273
health and safety, 163–64
healthcare sector, 47–48, 105, 208–10
Hebert, Ray, 120
Heen, Sheila, 130, 131, 150
Heifetz, Ron, 75, 93, 163
Hill, Linda: "Prep-Do-Review" delegation approach, 93
Hilton, 250
hockey, 227–28
Home Depot, 225, 245
Home Hardware, 245
honesty, 28, 30. *See also* values and ethics
Hougaard, Rasmus, 212
human connection, 75, 78–79
humanity, definition, 2. *See also* people leadership
humanness, 227–28
human resource information systems (HRIS), 231–32
human resources (HR): business context and, 225–27; Campbell and Mount Allison University example, 216–21; data, adding value with, 230–32; embedded HR, 230; evolution of, 223–24, 224; framework for, 222–23; humanness and, 227–28; leaders who "get it," 221; open letter to, 233–35; organizational outcomes and, 228–30; outside in, 226–27; partnership and, 228, 230
humiliation, 227–28
humility, 92, 169, 205–6

IAAF Junior World Track and Field
  Championships, 206
Imperial Manufacturing Group (IMG),
  9-11, 12-14
improvement, continuous, 213-14,
  268-69
inclusion and diversity, 59, 63, 136-37,
  262, 266. *See also* gender equality
Indigenous peoples, 266
innovation, 45, 266-68
Insights, 184
integrity, 28, 30. *See also* values and
  ethics
internet use, 101
interventions: boundaries and, 169;
  conflict management, 182-85;
  decision-making, 180-82;
  excuses for avoiding, 175-77;
  knee-jerk reactions, 179-80;
  laissez-faire leadership and, 174-
  75; learning moments, 191-92;
  micromanagement, 178-79; moving
  beyond conflict, 185-86; passive
  leadership, consequences of, 175;
  paying close attention, 190-91;
  progressive discipline, 194-95;
  psychological safety and, 162-63,
  165-66; question combo, 193-94;
  team coaching, 170-71; temperature,
  control of, 163, 166, 196-98;
  Turnaround Interview, 195-96;
  "watch and wait" (WAW) approach,
  174. *See also* psychological safety
intrinsic motivation, 204.
  See also motivation
introverts, 63-65

"job-career-calling" concept, 74-75
Jollymore, Gloria, 218
joy, 45

Kathleen (values example), 25-27, 32,
  33-34, 38
Katzenbach, Jon, 255
Keegan, Robert, 256-57

knee-jerk reactions, 179-80
Kouzes, James M., 28, 212
Kramer, Steven, 81, 213, 283n10

L'Acadie Nouvelle (newspaper), 213
Lacroix, Sophie, 267-68
Lahey, Lisa Laskow, 256-57
laissez-faire leadership, 174-75
law of the vital few (Pareto's Law),
  85, 102
leadership: daily leadership, 9-11,
  12-14; fishbowl of, 31, 52-53;
  humanity in, 2; identifying aspiring
  leaders, 21; laissez-faire leadership,
  174-75; situational leadership,
  21-22; tone-setting leadership, 55,
  122. *See also* delegation; feedback;
  interventions; leadership habits;
  leadership voice; people leadership;
  positive leadership; prioritization
leadership habits: calendars, 101-2;
  daily dashboards, 102-3; daily
  rituals, 106; email batching,
  99-100; focus techniques, 100-101;
  Gagnon's example, 95-97, 103, 107;
  multitasking, 98-99; priorities,
  focus and communication on, 104;
  saying no, 103-4; time tracking, 102;
  well-being, 104-6
leadership voice: acknowledging people,
  61; award ceremony example, 58-60,
  60-61; choices expressed by, 62-63;
  inclusivity and, 63; introverts, giving
  voice to, 63-65; making your voice
  heard, 65-66; speaking technique,
  61-62
learning culture: benefits of, 256-57;
  definition, 255-56; elements
  of, 257-58; gender equality and,
  261-64; innovation and continuous
  improvement, 266-69; leadership,
  learning by, 265-66; leadership
  for, 258-61; New Brunswick
  Community College example, 265-
  66; psychological safety and, 168;

recognition and, 211-14; teachable moments, 34-35, 191-92, 257
LeBlanc, Robert, 203-4, 205
Levitin, Daniel, 97, 98-99
Lewin, Kurt, 174-75
Linsky, Marty, 163
listening, active, 134-36, 136-37
loyalty, 34
Luscombe, Marilyn, 265

MacDonald, Chris, 34
MacDougall, Gardiner, 268-69
MacLeod, Ken, 273-74
Madeleine (prioritization and delegation example), 83, 84-85, 86, 88, 89
Malley, Archie, 162
Malley, Kayla, 162
Malley, Maudie, 162
Malley, Myles, 162
Malley, Terry and Kathy, 80-81, 161-62, 165-66
managerial impotence, 176-77
Manchester City Football Club, 259
Manchester United Football Club, 259
mantra, personal ethical, 35-36, 37-38
Mars (company), 250
Marsalis, Wynton, 35, 280n10
Mathis, Nancy, 241-42
Mayer, David, 32-33
McBride, Christian, 40-41, 43, 45, 46
McCain, Wallace, 241
McCullough, Michael E., 212-13
McGuire, Francis, 79, 283n12
McKinnon, Maura, 9, 10-11, 12-14
meaningful work: Atlantic Canada Opportunities Agency example, 79-80; finding meaning in work, 79-81; fish processing plant example, 71-73, 73-74, 76-78; human connection and, 75, 78-79; self-motivation and, 74-75
MEC (Mountain Equipment Co-op), 245, 250

meetings, 100, 115-16
mental health, 106, 164. *See also* psychological safety; Three Mountain Relay; well-being
mental models, 256
mentorship, 137-39, 144. *See also* coaching
Merrithew, Lisa, 154-56
Meyers-Briggs Type Indicator (MBTI), 49, 184, 185
micromanagement, 115, 178-79
Mikhael, Henri, 186
Milton, Doug, 86
mindbugs, 181
mindfulness, 105
Mintzberg, Henry, 84, 242
Miramichi River, 241
mistakes, as teachable moments, 257
Moncton (NB), 206, 264
Montana HR, 195
moral code. *See* values and ethics
motivation: intrinsic vs extrinsic, 204; meaningful work and, 74-75; negative feedback and, 152-53; positive energy and, 53-54
Mountain Equipment Co-op (MEC), 245, 250
Mount Allison University, 216-21, 263
Mourinho, José, 259
Mouton, Jane, 20
multitasking, 98-99

Negative Acts Questionnaire, 284n16
Nelson, Bob, 146; *1501 Ways to Reward Employees*, 211
Nelson, Larry, 205-7
New Brunswick, 191-92, 208-10, 267-68
New Brunswick Community College (NBCC), 265-66
Newfoundland and Labrador, 72-73
new hires, insights from, 86
Newport, Cal, 101
no, saying, 103-4
notebook assignment, 86

Nova Scotia: Capital Health District, 47-48

objectives. *See* goals
O'Brien, Patrick, 203-4, 205
observation, 190-91
O.C. Tanner, 214
On Building a Great Culture (book), 254
optimism, realistic, 54-56, 181
organizational learning culture (OLC). *See* learning culture
outside in, 226-27
overconfidence, 181

Pareto's Law (law of the vital few), 85, 102
partnership, 228, 230
passive leadership, 175
Patton, Bruce, 150
paying attention, 190-91
paying it forward, 29
people leadership: introduction, 1-4; balancing people and results, 16-24; culture, 241-53; daily leadership, 9-15; definition, 2-3; expectations and goals, 113-28; human resources (HR), 216-36; interventions, 174-88, 189-99; journey of, 274-75; leadership habits, 95-108; leadership voice, 58-67; learning culture, 254-71; meaningful work, 71-82; positive leadership, 40-57; prioritization and delegation, 83-94; providing feedback, 141-57; psychological safety, 161-73; receiving feedback, 129-40; recognition and rewards, 203-15; values and ethics, 25-39. *See also specific topics*
perceived organizational support, 207
perceptions, 185
perfection, 124
perseverance, 123, 264
personal mastery, 256
personal values. *See* values and ethics

Pickard, Cathy, 227-28, 230-31
Pink, Dan, 114
Pinker, Stephen, 47
Poirier, Norbert, 190
Pomodoro technique, 100
positive leadership: André (mining example), 41-43, 43-44, 45, 46; as choice, 43-44; keys to, 46-47; McBride (jazz example), 40-41, 43, 45, 46; positive energy, 53-54; realistic optimism, 54-56; science of positivity, 44-46; self-awareness and, 47-50; self-control and, 51-53
Posner, Barry Z., 28, 212
Potter, R., 246
praise-to-criticism ratio, 149-50. *See also* feedback
predictive analytics, 232
"Prep-Do-Review" delegation approach, 93
prioritization: Allen on, 85-86; communication for, 88, 104; Eisenhower matrix, 84, 284n2; insights from new employees and, 86; Madeleine's example, 83, 84-85, 86; managing distractions, 87-88; number of priorities, 88; Pareto's Law, 85, 102; scheduling priorities, 101; separating urgent from important, 84-85. *See also* delegation; leadership habits
problem-solving, 45, 93, 151, 257
progress, 213-14
progressive discipline, 194-95
psychological contract, 248-49
psychological needs, 207-8
psychological safety: Alongside Inc. example, 167-68; definition, 164-65; elements of, 168-69; inclusivity and, 264; interventions and, 162-63; Malley's example, 161-62, 165-66; speaking up and, 171; suggestions for nurturing, 169-70; tough questions and, 165-66; trust and, 171

question combo, 193-94

radio hosts, 98
Raine, George, 195
Rapinoe, Megan, 264
Rath, Tom, 149-50
realistic optimism, 54-56, 181
recognition and rewards: construction example, 210-11; extrinsic and intrinsic motivation, 204; gratitude, 212-13; healthcare example, 208-10; leadership in, 211; learning culture and, 211-14; learning from the experts, 214; perceived organizational support and, 207; for progress and improvement, 213-14; psychological needs and, 207-8; recognition programs, 205; sharing credit, 213; social recognition, 205-7; Three Mountain Relay example, 203-4, 205; for values and ethics, 35
recruitment, 11, 29. *See also* human resources
reflection, 242. *See also* self-awareness
relatedness, 208
relationship skills, 19-20
respect, 151-52, 168
results, balanced with people: communication and relationship skills, 19-20; identifying aspiring leaders and, 21; situational leadership and, 21-22; Thériault (Les Caisses) example, 16-18, 22-23
rewards. *See* recognition and rewards
Richards, David Adams, 241
rituals, daily, 106
Robichaud, Teena, 13, 208-10
role modeling, 35, 264
Rousseau, Denise, 248
Roussel-Sullivan, Claire, 231-32
rural communities, 11, 18, 72-73, 282n1
Ryan (micromanagement example), 178-79
Ryan, Richard, 204

safety and health, 163-64
Savoie, Martine, 101-2
Schein, Edgar, 144, 245
Schumpeter, Joseph, 219
Schwartz, Tony, 280n6
Scott, Kim: *Radical Candor*, 156
Scott, Susan: *Fierce Conversations*, 150
Sculley, John, 19
Self-Aware Leader program, 49
self-awareness: being a positive force and, 47-49; benefits of, 3, 242; conflict prevention and, 184; definition and development of, 49-50; delegation and, 92; goals and, 121; leadership and, 50, 132; receiving feedback and, 132
self-control, 51-53
self-motivation. *See* motivation
Seligman, Martin E.P., 281n3
Senge, Peter, 256
shutdown rituals, 106
situational leadership, 21-22
skills, matched to job, 93
Smith, Tina, 225-27
social recognition, 205-7
Society for Human Resource Management, 254-55
soft skills, 19-20
Sonier, Francis, 213
speaking technique, 61-62
speaking up, 171
sprints, 114
spying, 279n1. *See also* Kathleen (values example)
stewardship, 263
Stone, Douglas, 130, 131, 150
storytelling, 120, 286n11
strategy, 243
St. Thomas University, 266
Sutherland, Ron, 221
Swissair Flight 111 accident, 17-18
Symes, Mark, 102-3

taglines, 269
teachable moments, 34-35, 191-92, 257

teams: culture and, 249-50; team building, 185; team coaching, 170-71
temperamental behavior, 51-52
temperature, control of, 163, 166, 196-98
tension, 182. *See also* conflict
Terryberry, 131, 214
Thériault, Camille, 16, 17-18, 22-23
Thomas (expectations example), 113-16, 119, 122, 123-24
Thomas-Kilmann Instrument, 185
Three Mountain Relay, 203-4, 205
time tracking, 102
tit-for-tat baby steps, 186
tone-setting leadership, 55, 122
tough questions, 165-66. *See also* difficult conversations
trust, 171, 213
Turnaround Interview, 195-96
turnover, employee, 10, 11-12, 232, 256
2 × 2 matrix, 217

Ulrich, Dave, 223-24, 226, 290n2
unconscious bias, 181
UNI Financial Cooperative, 23. *See also* Caisse populaire acadienne ltée
United Nations: Girl Up initiative, 264
United States of America, 161, 166, 279n1

value, creating, 85
values and ethics: in challenging situations, 29-30; common ethical challenges, 36-37; culture and, 247-49; ethical leadership, 32-34; Kathleen's example, 25-27, 32, 33-34, 38; keeping your word, 30-32; loyalty, 34; as personal bottom line, 28-29; personal ethical mantra, 35-36, 37-38; recruitment and, 29; teachable moments, 34-35
Van Gundy, Jeff, 55
Varma, Manju, 262
vision, shared, 256

voice. *See* leadership voice
volunteerism, 29, 96, 165, 247

Wallace McCain Entrepreneurial Institute, 241-42
"watch and wait" (WAW), 174
Watts, Charlie, 106
Wawanesa Mutual Insurance Company, 225-26, 227
Weber, Max, 218-19
well-being, 104-6
Whalen, Bill, 206
White, Paul: *The Five Languages of Appreciation in the Workplace* (with Chapman), 214
women, advancement of, 261-64
Workhuman, 214
World Health Organization, 164

Zenger, Jack, 149, 150

About the Author

PIERRE BATTAH IS a long-time workplace columnist and blogger for CBC Radio One, a past TEDx presenter, and a member of the Canadian Association of Professional Speakers. Previously, he occupied senior management roles with the Atlantic Lottery Corporation, Assumption Mutual Life, and KBRS, and taught management at Mount Allison University. He has delivered hundreds of workshops and keynote addresses across Canada and the United States, and provided counsel to tens of thousands of managers, management teams, and educational institutions.

Fluently bilingual in French and English, Pierre holds an MBA from l'Université de Moncton and a bachelor's degree in business from the University of New Brunswick; is a certified management consultant (CMC) and a certified Human Resources Professional (CHRP); and has been awarded his CSP™ (Certified Speaking Professional) designation by the National Speakers Association (US). He was recognized as the 2016 HR Professional of the Year by his peers at the Human Resources Association of New Brunswick. Pierre lives in Moncton, New Brunswick.